AF684547

HEALTH INSURANCE: CURRENT ISSUES AND BACKGROUND

HEALTH INSURANCE: CURRENT ISSUES AND BACKGROUND

WILLIAM S. STEVENS (EDITOR)

Nova Science Publishers, Inc.
New York

Senior Editors: Susan Boriotti and Donna Dennis
Coordinating Editor: Tatiana Shohov
Office Manager: Annette Hellinger
Graphics: Wanda Serrano
Editorial Production: Marius Andronie, Vladimir Klestov, Matthew Kozlowski, Tom Moceri, Anthony T. Sovik and Maya Columbus
Circulation: Ave Maria Gonzalez, Vera Popovich, Raymond Davis, Melissa Diaz, Magdalena Nuñez, Marlene Nuñez and Jeannie Pappas
Communications and Acquisitions: Serge P. Shohov
Marketing: Cathy DeGregory

Library of Congress Cataloging-in-Publication Data

Health insurance: current issues and background / [edited by] William S. Stevens.
p. cm.
Includes bibliographical references and index.
ISBN: 1-59033-687-9 (hardcover)
1. Medical policy—United States. 2. Insurance, Health—United States.
[DNLM: 1. Insurance, Health—economics—United States. 2. Insurance, Health—statistics & numerical data—United States. 3. Health Care Costs—United States. 4. Health Services Accessibility--economics—United States. 5. Insurance Coverage—statistics & numerical data—United States. 6. Medically Uninsured—statistics & numerical data—United States. W275 AA1 H424 2003] I. Stevens, William S.

RA395.A3H4243 2003
368.38'2'00973—dc21 2003013771

Copyright © 2003 by Nova Science Publishers, Inc.
400 Oser Ave, Suite 1600
Hauppauge, New York 11788-3619
Tele. 631-231-7269 Fax 631-231-8175
e-mail: Novascience@earthlink.net
Web Site: http://www.novapublishers.com

All rights reserved. No part of this book may be reproduced, stored in a retrieval system or transmitted in any form or by any means: electronic, electrostatic, magnetic, tape, mechanical photocopying, recording or otherwise without permission from the publishers.

The publisher has taken reasonable care in the preparation of this book, but makes no expressed or implied warranty of any kind and assumes no responsibility for any errors or omissions. No liability is assumed for incidental or consequential damages in connection with or arising out of information contained in this book.

This publication is designed to provide accurate and authoritative information with regard to the subject matter covered herein. It is sold with the clear understanding that the publisher is not engaged in rendering legal or any other professional services. If legal or any other expert assistance is required, the services of a competent person should be sought. FROM A DECLARATION OF PARTICIPANTS JOINTLY ADOPTED BY A COMMITTEE OF THE AMERICAN BAR ASSOCIATION AND A COMMITTEE OF PUBLISHERS.

Printed in the United States of America

Contents

PREFACE

The health insurance issues and background covered in this new book encompass the latest and most controversial problems and events in an area of crucial interest to everyone. The latest statistics indicate more than 45 million people are currently uninsured; a number which is consistently increasing. This dire situation forms part of a sociological crisis in America where a large segment of the population will be subject to severe health problems while the wealthy enjoy first rate medical care and longevity.

Based on data from a 1995 national survey of physicians, chapter 1 compares the frequency of diagnostic services and therapeutic services during office visits to physicians who participated in health maintenance organizations (HMOs) and those who did not. It also describes the methods employed by managed care organizations (MCOs) to reduce unnecessary use of health care services, and summarizes the findings of previous research on the effect of managed care on health care utilization and outcomes. Results of the analysis of physician office visits in 1995 are then displayed in a series of tables that show the percentage of visits during which specific classes of services were performed by physicians who participated in each of four kinds of health insurance arrangements. Statistical analysis of the results indicates that while physician participation in an HMO had a significant positive effect on the proportion of visits during which these services were performed, the patient's health status had the largest impact among all variables studied on the likelihood of receiving a diagnostic or therapeutic service during an office visit.

The Health Insurance Portability and Accountability Act of 1996 (HIPAA, P.L. 104-191, 42 USC §1320d) mandates significant changes in the health insurance industry, and includes as a small part of the overall insurance reforms, requirements for the standardization of electronically transmitted health insurance financial claims and administrative transactions. These HIPAA requirements are intended to reduce administrative costs and paperwork, improve the efficiency of the health care system, detect fraud and abuse, and facilitate access to medical information. HIPAA requires Congress to enact federal privacy protections by August 1999 to protect health information transmitted electronically. While several privacy proposals were considered during the 105th Congress, no agreement was reached on how to protect health information. The implementation of the unique health identifier for individuals required under HIPAA was particularly controversial. In response, Congress enacted a provision which prohibits federally appropriated funds from being used to adopt a final standard providing for a unique health identifier for an individual until legislation is enacted specifically approving the standard. Chapter two discusses these developments.

A central issue in debates about health care reform in the United States has been what to do about the increasing number of the Nation's citizens who are without health insurance. Estimates of the number who are uninsured have been cited to quantify the dimensions of the problem, but the estimates, coming from different sources, have significant differences numbering in the millions. These differences have raised concern over why they occur and which number(s) should be used. Chapter 3 explains the differences in the more commonly referred to estimates of the uninsured.

Chapter 4 discusses the current legislation in tax benefits for health insurance. The 108th Congress is likely to consider a number of new or expanded tax benefits for health insurance. Proposals may include the creation of a refundable tax credit for all workers, the expansion and permanent extension of medical savings accounts, and the creation of tax credits for small employers.

An issue of continuing concern to Congress is the number of Americans who lack health insurance coverage. In 2001, an estimated 41.2 million Americans were uninsured for the entire year, 99% of whom were under age 65. The number of non-elderly uninsured rose each year from 1987 to 1998 and then declined in both 1999 and 2000, before increasing again in 2001. Much of this expansion has been due to sustained increases in health care costs, which in turn drive up health insurance premiums.

In response to the increase in the uninsured population, policymakers at the state and federal levels of government have been searching for effective, affordable, and politically feasible ways to expand access to adequate health insurance coverage. While a variety of proposed solutions have been analyzed and debated, recent Congresses have shown an emerging bipartisan interest in tax-based approaches. In the 107th Congress, for example, numerous bills to create tax deductions or credits for the purchase of health insurance by those not covered under employer-provided or public health insurance were introduced. Proposals to create tax subsidies for the expansion of health insurance coverage are beginning to surface in the 108th Congress.

Chapter 5 summarizes what is known about the factors shaping the cost-effectiveness of tax subsidies for expanding health insurance coverage. It opens with an explanation of the economic justification for government intervention in the market for health insurance. It then moves on to examine key considerations in designing tax subsidies for expanding health insurance coverage and concludes with a review of the principal findings of recent studies assessing the cost-effectiveness of a variety of proposed tax subsidies, many of which resemble proposals that have attracted attention in recent Congresses.

The Federal Employees Health Benefits Program (FEHBP) provides health insurance coverage for 8.6 million individuals, including 2.2 million federal and postal employees, 1.9 million federal annuitants, and 4.5 million dependents of employees and annuitants. In FY2001, the program cost over $21 billion, of which enrollee premium payments and the U.S. Postal Service financed about $10.3 billion.

Chapter 6 provides an overview of the background and operations of the FEHBP. Although the FEHBP is an employer-sponsored program for federal employees and annuitants, it is often cited as a model design for provision of health insurance for other populations, including Medicare beneficiaries. The first section of this chapter discusses the origins and purpose of the program; the second section describes FEHBP's multiple plan design and enrollee choice. The sections that follow address benefit coverage and cost-sharing; the covered population; payments to participating plans; premium costs and increases over time; program financing and budget costs; administration; grievance and appeals procedures; and the relationship of FEHBP to state insurance laws. The final section discusses the relationship of FEHBP to Medicare, compares covered benefits and enrollee out-of-pocket costs, and addresses the rules and issues pertaining to coverage and costs for individuals eligible for both programs.

The events of September 11, 2001, the economic aftermath and the relocation of American-based firms abroad are separating persons from employment and reducing access to health insurance. In response, Congress has considered a wide array of provisions intended to stimulate the economy and promote job growth, addressing such areas as trade practices, tax policy, labor, state fiscal relief and health care. Part of this debate has been about whether, and how, to continue (or restore) health insurance for displaced workers and their families.

The proposals offered in the House and Senate reflect concerns among some Members of Congress that existing law may not provide a sufficient safety net for the unique economic situation the U.S. is currently facing. This concern is likely due to three contributing factors: health insurance is costly; continuation coverage for those who had employer-based coverage, also known as COBRA coverage has limited reach; and coverage under programs designed to help lower income individuals, such as Medicaid and the State Children's Health Insurance Program (SCHIP), are not available to all displaced workers.

On August 6, 2002, the President signed the Andean Trade Preference Act (P.L. 107-210), a bill which contains, among other things, provisions aimed at assisting workers who have lost jobs and are receiving Trade Adjustment Assistance (TAA) with the purchase of health insurance. The law provides a refundable and advanceable tax credit of up to 65% of a TAA recipient's health insurance premiums and authorizes grant programs intended to encourage states to establish or expand programs for the uninsured.

Chapter 7 discusses enacted legislation as well as other proposed bills to show the scope of options considered by Congress. It also discusses some of the issues raised by the legislation, including timeliness, affordability, populations impacted, gaps in coverage, and state participation.

Most Americans with private group health insurance are covered through an employer. That coverage is generally provided to active employees and their families. A change in an individual's work or family status can result in loss of coverage. In 1985, Congress enacted legislation to provide temporary access to health insurance for qualified individuals who lose coverage due to such changes. Under Title X of the Consolidated Omnibus Budget Reconciliation Act of 1985 (COBRA, P.L. 99-272), an employer with 20 or more employees must provide those employees and their families the option of continuing their coverage under the employer's group health insurance plan in the case of certain events. The coverage can last up to 36 months, depending on the nature of the triggering event. The employer is not required to pay for this coverage; instead, the beneficiary can be required to pay up to 102% of the premium. Employers who fail to provide the continued health insurance option are subject to tax and other penalties.

In 1987, the Internal Revenue Service issued proposed regulations providing guidance for employers on COBRA. The regulations were finalized in February 1999 and January 2001.

Some believe that COBRA went too far in requiring employers to provide continuation coverage. They argue that it resulted in extra costs for employers (in the form of increased premiums for employers' group health insurance policies) as well as added administrative burdens. In contrast, others believe that COBRA should be expanded to include new eligibility categories and longer coverage periods, so that more workers and their families have a source of group health insurance coverage during periods of job or family transitions. They argue that the financial and administrative burdens on employers have been exaggerated.

The Trade Act of 2002 provided a tax credit for the purchase of health insurance (including COBRA coverage) for workers displaced by trade. Provisions in the House-passed economic stimulus legislation would have allowed states to use block grant funds to assist with the purchase of insurance coverage (including COBRA) for workers displaced by the terrorist attacks of September 11, 2001. Other legislation would have subsidized COBRA premiums for workers who lost health coverage as a result of the terrorist attacks, extended COBRA benefits to retirees whose former employer eliminates or substantially reduces their retiree health insurance, and provided tax credits for individuals for the costs of COBRA premiums. These bills were not enacted. Chapter 8 provides background information on COBRA, on the COBRA population, and on legislation affecting COBRA.

The number of people without health insurance continues to be a key public policy concern. Numerous sources of data, both public and private, gather information on the uninsured but they produce estimates that vary widely. This chapter discusses estimates of the number of uninsured using data from four federally administered surveys: the March Supplement to the Current Population Survey (CPS), the Survey of Income and Program Participation (SIPP), the National Health Interview Survey (NHIS), and the Medical Expenditure Panel Survey (MEPS).

In 1998 (the most recent year for which data are available from all four surveys), estimated of the number of uninsured for the full year ranged from 21.2 million using SIPP data to 43.6 million using data from the March CPS, a difference of more than 22 million individuals. Estimates of the number of uninsured at a point in time as well as the number who were ever uninsured during the year also vary among MEPS, NHIS, and SIPP (the March CPS does not support these estimates). The number of uninsured at a point in time in 1998 ranged from 39.2 million from SIPP to 42.3 million from MEPS. Estimates of the number who were *ever* uninsured during 1998 ranged from 50.0 million from NHIS to 60.3 million from MEPS.

To date, no clear consensus has emerged that explains why these differences exist in the survey estimates of the uninsured. However, researchers have offered a number of explanations that may account for some of the variation. These include:

- the surveys ask different questions and use different methodologies to determine who is insured;
- compared to administrative data, the surveys report estimates of the percent enrolled in Medicaid that indicate an under-reporting of Medicaid coverage by survey respondents, which would affect uninsured estimates;
- the surveys differ in the amount of time for which they ask individuals to remember their health insurance status. Individuals who are asked to report their status for a period of time might not accurately report changes in their health insurance status over that period; and
- the surveys are designed in ways that permit different types of analyses, but may limit comparability of the results. For example, while the SIPP and MEPS allow

researchers to track the same individuals over a period of years, this is not possible using the CPS or NHIS. Therefore, the varying designs of the surveys permit different types of analyses of health insurance status, but the comparability of the estimates may be limited.

Chapter 9 outlines the major advantages and limitations of four federally administered surveys - the March Supplemental to the Current Population Survey, the Survey of Income and Program Participation, the National Health Interview Survey, and the Medical Expenditure Panel Survey - in providing estimates of the uninsured population. It begins by describing the characteristics of each of these four surveys. Estimates of the uninsured from these datasets are then presented, followed by a discussion of possible reasons for the variation among the estimates. Finally, it discusses potential areas in which each data source might be useful to respond to questions of interest to policymakers outlining proposals to reduce the number of uninsured.

The proportion of children without health insurance varies among states both because of differences in states economies and in state policies with respect to the Medicaid program and other publicly funded health insurance plans. Both the economic climate in a state - its rate of unemployment and growth in household incomes, for example - and the industrial structure of its economy influence the prevalence of private health insurance among families and children. States also differ with respect to the eligibility rules for their Medicaid programs and their State Children's Health Insurance (SCHIP) programs and in the degree to which they have established other public insurance programs for children who are not covered by private health insurance and are not eligible for Medicaid or SCHIP. An estimated 9.2 million children under age 18 were without health insurance in 2000, representing 12 percent of all children in the United States. The proportion of children without health insurance varies significantly from state to state. Chapter 10 discusses these issues.

In 1991, an estimated 35.4 million people were without any form of health insurance coverage. The uninsured were often young and poor, but many of them did have some tie to the labor force, frequently in small firms. By contrast, only 1 percent of the elderly (age 65 and over) were uninsured. Most people with health insurance had employment based coverage, while others were covered under government sponsored plans such as Medicare and Medicaid or nongroup privately purchased health insurance. The rising cost of health care (national health expenditures totaled $808 billion in 1992) and the availability of adequate health insurance coverage continue to be issues of national concern. Chapter 11 examines characteristics of both the insured and the uninsured populations.

An estimated 14.6 percent of the U.S. population lacked health insurance coverage in 2001, up from 14.2 percent in 2000. When examined by state, estimates of the percent uninsured ranged from a low of 7.5 percent in Iowa to a high of 23.5 percent in Texas. Generally, states in the Midwest have lower rates of uninsured, while states in the Southwestern and Southern portions of the nation have higher shares of their populations without coverage. Chapter 12 examines characteristics of both the insured and the uninsured populations by each individual state.

I. BACKGROUND

Chapter 1

HEALTH INSURANCE AND MEDICAL CARE: PHYSICIAN SERVICES UNDER MANAGED CARE

Patrick Purcell

INTRODUCTION

The financing and delivery of health care services in the U.S. have undergone significant changes in recent years. In response to rapidly rising health care costs, insurers, physicians, and employers have formed a variety of managed care organizations (MCOs) in an effort to achieve greater efficiency. Much has been written about the potential savings in national health expenditures that may be realized from the transition to managed care, but less is known about how this transition may affect the specific medical services that patients receive. Studies that focus on the *patient's* insurance would be likely to find differences in treatments between patients of comparable health status in prepaid and fee-for-service (FFS) plans only if physicians differentiated their treatment decisions based on the kind of health insurance by which the patient was covered. This chapter adds to the literature on medical services under managed care by analyzing data from a recent national survey of physicians. It compares the frequency with which several classes of medical services were performed during physician office visits classified according to the kind of insurance plans that the physician accepted.

This chapter makes several findings:

- In 1995, 84% of all office visits to primacy care physicians by people under age 65 with employer-group or other private health insurance were made to physicians who participated in both managed and non-managed health insurance plans.
- Diagnostic and screening services were performed more frequently during visits both to pure FFS and pure HMO physician offices than during visits to physicians who accepted multiple kinds of insurance.
- Both male and female patients were more likely to receive diagnostic or screening services in a visit to an HMO-only physician office than during a visit to a physician

office that participated in a PPO, but the difference from the overall average was greater for men than for woman.

- Therapeutic and preventive services were performed more frequently during office visits of HMO-only physicians than during visits to physicians who accepted multiple kinds of insurance. For people who had no chronic medical conditions, the likelihood of receiving therapeutic or preventive services did not vary significantly according to the type of insurance accepted by the physician.
- Men were much more likely to receive therapeutic or preventive services in and HMO-only office setting than in physician offices that accepted other kinds of insurance. Women were equally likely to receive these services in HMO-only or fee-for-service-only office settings.

Managed care comes in many forms, but all managed care organizations (MCOs) share two basic goals. The most fundamental reasons for managing the delivery of health care are to *control costs* while providing *necessary and appropriate medical services*. The number and variety of MCOs reflect the multitude of approaches to achieving these objectives.[1] Although much has been written about the potential savings in national health expenditures that may be realized from the transition to managed care, less is known about how this transition may affect the specific medical services that patients receive. If medical care services differ between managed care and non-managed care or among the different kinds of MCOs, the reasons could be related to the physicians' treatment practices, characteristics of the patients being treated, or both. This information can be useful both to users of health care services and to policy-makers who must decide priorities in selecting and managing the methods of financing and delivering health care for millions of beneficiaries in public programs such as Medicare and Medicaid.

This chapter uses data from a national survey of physicians to compare the frequency with which several kinds of medical services were performed during office visits in 1995 to physicians who participated in various kinds of MCOs and visits to physicians who did not participate in managed care. The results presented here are based on physician office visits by people under age 65 who were covered by employer-group or other private health insurance.[2] We have focused on privately insured, non-elderly patients because it is among this segment of the population that the transition to managed care has been occurring for the longest period of time, and because the analysis is not complicated by issues of eligibility, enrollment, financing and regulation that pertain specifically to the Medicare and Medicaid programs. Nevertheless, the experience of patients and physicians in the delivery of office-based medical care under privately-financed MCOs may hold important lessons that can be used to make the transition to managed care in the Medicare and Medicaid programs more efficient and equitable for all interested parties.

[1] For a description of the ways in which health care providers and insurers have formed MCOs see CRS Report 97-913, *Managed Health Care: A Primer,* by Jason S. Lee.

[2] Some of these individuals also may have been covered by Medicare or Medicaid, but the office visits included in this report all were covered by a private health insurance plan.

Managing Health Care Use and Costs

Arrangements for managing the financing and delivery of health care have become more common in recent years, in part because the cost of health care rose faster than the prices of most other goods and services from the 1960s through the mid-1990s. Managed care seeks to make the provision of health care services more efficient by using no more than the resources necessary to deliver care, while meeting the community's prevailing standards of quality. The challenge faced by any MCO, therefore, is one of controlling the *cost* of health care while maintaining the *quality* of care. MCOs attempt to control costs by eliminating unnecessary or inappropriate services. To do this they can:

- create a *financial relationship* with the health care provider that encourages efficient use resources.[3]
- substitute *less expensive care* (for instance, office-based care) for more expensive care (such as inpatient hospital care), and
- *reduce the demand for health care services* by promoting good health practices among those who are enrolled in the managed care plan.

The Financial Relationship with the Health Care Provider

The two most common types of payment for medical care are "fee-for-service" (FFS) and prepayment, which is also called "capitation." As its name implies, in a FFS reimbursement arrangement the health care provider bills the patient for each individual services provided. If the patient is insured, the insurer will usually pay some or all of the bill, generally, after the patient has paid the first few hundred dollars of medical bills incurred during a calendar year, which is called a *deductible amount.* Insurance that pays expenses as they are incurred for each office visit, hospital stay, or other episode of care is called *indemnity insurance*.

Some indemnity insurers have negotiated special low reimbursement rates with providers of health care. In exchange for these lower rates, the insurer designates the health care professional as a "preferred provider." Patients who visit an insurer's preferred providers are usually rewarded with a lower copayment (the share of the total bill that is the patient's responsibility) than if they visit providers who are not members of this network. Preferred provider organizations, or "PPOs," are considered to be MCOs because they use financial incentives to include health care providers to deliver services efficiently. The financial incentives used by PPOs can include amounts added to or withheld from the FFS reimbursement paid to the provider. Inefficient providers may be dropped from the PPO, creating another incentive for the provider to eliminate unnecessary services.

Under the FFS method of reimbursing health care providers, each additional test, procedure, or office visit increases the provider's revenue, creating a financial incentive for health care professionals to provide more services. This incentive exists even in a PPO, although it may be tempered by the possibility that the provider could be dropped from the PPO. Another type of MCO, the health maintenance organization, or HMO, reduce the

---

[3] See also CRS Report 97-482, *Managed Health Care: The Use of Financial Incentives* by Jason S. Lee and Beth C. Fuchs.

financial incentive to provide additional care either by employing the physician directly on a salary basis of by "prepaying" the physician a fixed amount per month for each of the HMOs' members in exchange for providing all (or most) of the health care services that they require. In the so-called "staff-model" HMO, the physicians are employed directly, and their medical practice patterns can by monitored and rewarded or sanctioned, just like the performance of an employee in any other kind of firm. In "group-model" HMOs and in another kind of HMOs called an "independent practice association" (IPA), the HMO contracts with physician groups or independent physician practices to provide health care services to the HMO's members, usually in exchange for a monthly "capitation payment."[4] If the total cost of care provided to the members of the HMO is less than the sum of these capitation payments, the physician group keeps the difference as profit. If costs exceed the sum of the capitation payments, the physicians suffer a financial loss.[5]

Substituting Less Expensive Care for More Expensive Care

MCOs also are able to reduce costs by employing primary care physicians as "gatekeepers" to regulate patients' access to more expensive specialists, and by providing as much care as possible in physician offices, clinics, and hospital outpatient departments rather than in an inpatient hospital setting. Lower rates of hospitalization and shorter stays in hospitals associated with MCOs - specifically with HMOs - have been shown to be an important source of savings in MCOs compared with traditional indemnity insurers.[6]

Reducing the Demand for Care

By promoting good health practices that emphasize early intervention and preventive medicine, such as immunizations, screening for specific conditions, and regular check-ups, MCOs may lower the total cost of health care by catching incipient illness when they can be treated which the greatest effectiveness and at the least expense. In such cases, more frequent use of health care services in the near-term may result in reduced need for medical services in the long-term.[7]

---

[4] Even HMOs that pay most primary-care physicians on a capitation basis will often reimburse specialists FFS. Members of an HMO may sometimes see non-participating physicians who are reimbursed on a FFS basis if the HMO offers a "point-of-service" (POS) option.

[5] In 1996, 74% of HMO contracts with primary-care physicians provided for prepaid, capitated reimbursement, according to Hoechst-Marion-Roussel's *HMO-PPO Digest.*

[6] To date, reductions in health care costs resulting from managed care have been attributed mainly to reductions in the number and length of inpatient hospital stays. See, for example, KPMG Peat Marwick. *The Impact of Managed care on U.S. Markets.* Washington DC, 1996 and, Richardson, James C. Decline in Hospital Utilization and Cost Inflation Under Managed Care in California. *Journal of the American Medical Association,* v. 276, no. 13, October 2, 1996.

[7] Early diagnosis and treatment of illness may be desirable for their public health benefits, but they may not result in savings to national health expenditures. A person who detects a medical condition at age 70, for example, and has it treated successfully, possibly preventing premature death, may eventually suffer another illness or series of illness requiring medical treatment and additional expenditures.

PREVIOUS RESEARCH ON AMBULATORY UNDER MANAGED CARE

Access to Care

Numerous studies published in recent years have examined issues of access to care, intensity of service utilization, and quality of care in managed and non-managed health insurance plans. A review of the literature evaluating managed care plan performance between 1980 and 1993 found that, compared to indemnity insurance plans, HMOs had "the same or more physician office visits per enrollee, less use of expensive procedures and tests, greater use of preventive services, [and] mixed results on outcomes."[8] A more recent literature review by the same authors found that "there was no overall pattern to physician use or expenditure results" in 10 studies published between 1993 and 1997.[9] Another recent study found that as the average number of inpatient hospital days among patients in HMOs has been declining, the frequency of physician office visits has been rising.[10] Data from the 1994 Health Interview Survey analyzed by CRS show that the frequency at which people in HMOs visited physician offices did not differ substantively from the rate for people in traditional indemnity insurance plans. These data show that 15.0% of privately insured people under age 65 in HMOs had made at least one office visit in any given 2-week period in 1994, compared to 14.1% of people covered by indemnity insurance plans that paid providers on a FFS basis.[11]

One reason that the frequency of physician visits differ only slightly between people enrolled in HMOs and those with FFS insurance is that average health status, as measured by the percentage of people who have chronic health problems differs very little between these two groups. In the 1994 National Health Interview Survey, 37% of people enrolled in indemnity insurance plans and 37% of those in HMOs reported that they had a medical condition of any kind. Among those covered by indemnity plans, 30.7% reported one or more *chronic* medical conditions, versus 29.9% of those in HMOs.[12] The frequency of office visits was similar between the HMO and FFS enrollees even among those who reported having a medical condition.[13] Of the people who reported having an acute or chronic medical

---

[8] Miller, R.H. and H.S. Luft. "Managed Care Plan Performance Since 1980." *Journal of the American Medical Association,* v. 271, no. 19, May 18, 1994.

[9] Miller R.H. and H.S. Luft. "Does Managed Care Lead to Better or Worse Quality of Care?" *Health Affairs,* v. 16, no. 5, September/October 1997.

[10] Wholey, D. et al. HMO Market Structure and Performance: 1985-1995. *Health Affairs,* v. 16, no. 6, November/ December 1997.

[11] Although small, this difference is statistically significant at the 95% confidence level, based on a two-tailed t-test.

[12] The extent, if any, to which HMOs experience favorable selection in terms of the health status of their enrollees remains an open question. Data from the 1994 National Health Interview Survey indicate little difference in the health status of people enrolled in HMOs compared to those in indemnity insurance plans. Taylor and colleagues (1995), reporting on an analysis of data from the 1987 National Medical Expenditure Survey, also found "very little evidence that individuals enrolled in HMOs were healthier than those in FFS plans." Likewise, Fama and colleagues (1995) found little observable difference in the health status of people in HMOs and those in other insurance plans. Hellinger (1995), however, in a review of the literature on the subject reported that a majority of studies found that HMOs and other plans with closed provider networks experienced favorable selection bias among their enrollees when compared to people enrolled in non-HMO plans.

[13] Among people who reported to medical conditions, 3.6% of those who were enrolled in an HMO saw a physician in a 2-week period, compared with 3.0% of those covered by indemnity insurance, not a statistically significant difference.

condition, 34.8% of HMO enrollees had seen a doctor in a given 2-week period, compared with 33.2% of those enrolled in indemnity insurance plans.[14]

Health Outcomes

Studies of outcomes between managed and non-managed health care plans also have found mixed results. Clement and others (1994) found that Medicare beneficiaries in HMOs who reported either joint pain or chest pain were less likely to have seen a specialist for care, to have a follow-up recommended, or to have their progress monitored. Less improvement in symptoms was found among the HMO enrollees in one of four outcomes studied. In a 4-year study of chronically ill patients, Ware and others (1996) found that physical and mental health outcomes did not differ between FFS and HMO plans for the average patient, but they did for certain sub-groups of patients. Among elderly patients, declines in physical health were more common among those in HMOs than in FFS plans. Outcomes tended to be better in FFS plans among poor patients, but better outcomes were found in HMOs for non-poor patients. Yelin, Criswell, and Feigenbaum (1996) examined data on health outcomes over periods of up to 11 years for patients with rheumatoid arthritis in FFS insurance plans and prepaid group practices. They found that the "two groups did not differ on any outcome measure on either an annual or long-term basis."

DATA AND METHODS

Access to ambulatory medical care services often is measured in terms of the frequency of contracts with a physician or other health care professional. Another measure of access is the likelihood that a physician office visit will result in a specific service being provided. If the likelihood that a specific service will be performed during an office visit appears to differ according to the kinds of insurance accepted by the physician, we would like to know the extent to which this variation reflects differences in the patients being treated, the physician's practice patterns (including the influence of managed care), or a combination of these factors. This CRS Report uses data from a nationally representative survey of physicians to examine the frequency with which particular classes of medical services were performed during office visits to physicians who participated in different kinds of insurance arrangements. The report focuses on two broad classifications of services identified in the National Ambulatory Medical Care Survey: *diagnostic and screening services and therapeutic and preventive services.*

For this chapter, we analyzed the frequency with which specific services were performed during physician office visits *according to the kind of health insurance plans accepted by the physician.* Most prior studies have looked at the kind of insurance that covered the individual patient; however, in 1995 more than four-fifths of all office visits to primary care physicians by privately insured individuals under age 65 were made to physicians who saw some patients in managed health plans *and* some with non-managed insurance. Studies that focus on the

[14] Although the difference in chronic conditions and 2-week office visits are not large enough to suggest dramatic behavioral differences either by patients or physicians in HMOs compared to indemnity plans, both are statistically significant at the 95% confidence level based on a two-tailed t-test.

kind of insurance that covered the patient would be likely to find differences in treatments or outcomes between patients in prepaid and FFS plans only of a significant proportion of physicians differentiated their treatment decisions based on the kind of health insurance by which the patient was covered. This hypothesis is not generally supported by empirical findings.[15] The methodology employed for this analysis permitted us to see whether the frequency of services differed between physicians who accepted only prepaid insurance such as HMOs or *only* FFS insurance. This classification scheme also allowed us to see whether the frequency with which certain categories of medical services were performed differed between physicians in pure-HMO or pure-FFS practices and physicians who see patients in both prepaid and FFS plans.

The analysis presented here focuses on office visits to physicians who are *primary-care providers* because it is these physician offices in which managed care principles have been most widely adopted. Likewise, in some of the tables that follow, the sample has been restricted to office visits made by patients who were reported by the physician to have no chronic medical conditions. This restriction can help to make clear whether a difference in the frequency with which specific services were provided was the result of differences in physician practice patterns between managed care and non-managed care; differences in the proportion of people enrolled in each kind of plan who were in poor health; or a combination of these two factors.

Data on health care services provided during visits to office-based physicians were collected as part of the 1995 National Ambulatory Medical Care Survey (NAMCS) conducted by the National Center for Health Statistics, a division of the U.S. Department of Health and Human Services. All non-federally employed office-based physicians who were primarily engaged in patient-care activities were eligible to be included in the Ambulatory Medical Care Survey with the exception of physicians whose specialties were anesthesiology, pathology, or radiology. Contracts with patients by telephone, outside the physician's office, in hospital settings (inpatient or outpatient), in institutional settings such as nursing homes, or office visits for administrative purposes (such as paying a bill, filling out insurance forms, or dropping off a specimen) were not included in the survey. Of the 2,587 physicians contacted in 1995, 73% participated in the survey.

The 1995 survey data consist of 36,875 patient record forms collected from 1,833 physicians who participated in the NAMCS. Each record represents one visit by a patient to an office-based physician, and each has been assigned a patient visit weight, which when aggregated across all visits, represent the estimated total of 697 million physician office visits in the U.S. in 1995. For this chapter the analysis is limited to physician visits by people under age 65 with employer-group or other private health insurance. This sub-sample comprised 27,067 patient record forms (73.4% of the total), and represented 254.5 million physician office visits.

Of the 254.5 million office visits by people under age 65 with employer-group or other private health insurance, 168.3 million visits (66.1%) were made to primary-care physicians,

---

[15] For example, many physicians are unaware even whether a patient is covered by private insurance or by a publicly financed program such as Medicaid. Research into state compliance with the early, periodic, screening, diagnosis and testing (EPSDT) requirements for children covered by Medicaid indicates that most physicians performing a physical exam or well-child checkup are unaware of the child's source of health insurance coverage. (Elicia Herz, Ph. D., MEDSTAT Group, Washington DC, personal communication with author.)

including general and family practitioners, internists, pediatricians, and obstetricians/ gynecologists. Just 10% of these visits were made to physicians who accepted only insurance that reimbursed the physician on a FFS basis and who did not participate in either a PPO or HMO. Only 6% of these office visits were made to physicians who only saw patients who were enrolled in an HMO. Thus, relatively small proportions of physician office visits in 1995 were made to physicians who had *no* patients in managed care or to physicians who saw *only* patients who were enrolled in the most strictly managed form of managed care. The vast majority of physician office visits in 1995 - 84% of the total - were made to physicians who treated some patients who were enrolled in a managed care plan, and some who were not.

Patient records on the NAMCS include both the expected source of insurance and the expected source of payment. The categories for expected source of insurance are Blue Cross/Blue Shield, other private insurance, Medicare, Medicaid, worker's compensation, other insurance, and unknown. There are eight source-of-payment categories on the survey instrument:

- blank with no source of insurance reported,
- preferred provided option,
- insured FFS,
- HMO or other prepaid,
- self-pay,
- no change,
- other source of payment, and
- type of payment was not specified but source of insurance was reported.

In this chapter, physician office visits have been grouped according to the sources of payment reported on patient records during the week that each physician participated in the NAMCS. WE used the unique physician identifiers to classify physicians into four groups, based on the kinds of insurance that covered patients seen by the physician. The four groups of physicians were:

- those who saw *only* patients whose insurance reimbursed the physician on a FFS basis with no PPO discounts,
- those who saw patients in both regular FFS plans and in PPO plans, but who saw no patients who were enrolled in an HMO.
- those who saw patients enrolled in HMOs, in PPOs, and in non-PPO plans,
- those who saw *only* patients who were enrolled in an HMO.[16]

This classification allows us to discern not only whether services differed between managed care and non-managed care, but also whether the frequency of services provided during visits to "mixed insurance" physician offices was more like the frequency seen in

[16] The data collected on the Ambulatory Medical Care Survey do not differentiate between group/staff model HMOs and IPA-model HMOs, a distinction that could increase the explanatory power of these data which respect to differences *among* HMOs in the frequency with which specific services were provided during office visits. Nevertheless, because neither kind of HMO typically uses FFS reimbursement, the NAMCS data allow

visits to MHO-only physician offices or like that which occurred during visits to physicians who accepted only pure payments.

RESULTS: SERVICES PROVIDED DURING PHYSICIAN OFFICE VISITS

Physician Office Visits: Patient Demographic Characteristics (Table 1)

Patient demographic and health characteristics, geographic variations in physician practice patterns, and whether the physician has seen the patient before all may influence diagnostic and treatment procedures. These characteristics are arrayed in Table 1 according to the proportion of office visits made by people in each category to physicians who accepted each of four kinds or combinations of health insurance plans.

Age

Children and young adults were less likely than adults 35 or older to have made an office visit to a physician who accepted only FFS insurance arrangements, and were more likely than people in other age groups to have visited a physician office that accepted both HMO and PPO insurance plans. People between the ages of 55 and 64 made up 18.1% of visits to physicians who accepted only FFS insurance arrangements, significantly higher than the overall average of 10.0%; however, they also comprised a higher-than-average share of visits to physicians who treated only patients enrolled in HMOs.

Sex

In 1995, 107 million out of 168 million office visits (63.5%) to primary care physicians by privately insured people under age 65 were made by female patients. Male and female patients had very similar probabilities of visiting a physician who treated only HMO patients, but males made up an above-average share of all visits to physicians who accepted only FFS insurance plans.

Race

Both white and non-white patients had similar likelihoods of visiting a primary care physician who saw only HMO enrollees, but non-white patients had an above-average probability of visiting a physician who accepted only FFS insurance reimbursement.

Health Status: Chronic Medical Conditions

Office visits to physicians who accepted *only* FFS reimbursement included a higher-than-average proportion of visits made by patients with chronic medical conditions, while visits to physician offices that accepted both FFS and PPO plans included a lower-than-average proportion of visits made by chronically ill patients.[17] Visits to FFS-only physician offices made up 10% of all visits by privacy insured patients under age 65, but they comprised 14.8%

---

us to distinguish between kinds of insurance payment that respond to increases in the number of patient visits or volume of services and those that do not.

[17] In the National Ambulatory Care Survey, chronic conditions are defined to include arthritis, arteriosclerosis, chronic obstructive pulmonary disorder, renal disease, clinical depression, diabetes, human immunodeficiency virus/acquired immune deficiency syndrome (HIV/AIDS), hyperactivity, hypertension, and obesity.

of all visits made by patients with one or more chronic medical conditions. Visits to physician offices that participated in both FFS and PPO plans made up 16.1% of all visits by privately insured patients under age 65, but they comprised 14.2% of all visits made by patients with one or more chronic medical conditions.

Table 1. Office Visits to Primary Care Physicians by Privately Insured People Under Age 65

	Visits (000s)	*Percentage of visits that were to physicians who accepted:* FFS only	FFS and PPO	HMO and PPO	HMO Only	Total
Patient demographic						
Under age 18	59,144	7.9%	18.4%	71.5%	2.3%	100%
Ages 18 to 34	36,224	8.4%	11.8%	72.6%	7.3%	100%
Ages 35 to 54	53,413	10.5%	16.4%	65.6%	7.4%	100%
Ages 55 to 64	19,508	18.1%	16.3%	56.8%	8.8%	100%
Female	106,942	8.8%	15.7%	69.8%	5.8%	100%
Male	61,347	12.1%	16.9%	65.4%	5.7%	100%
White	147,423	9.5%	16.9%	67.9%	5.7%	100%
Black or other	20,865	13.8%	10.2%	70.1%	6.0%	100%
Has Chronic Condition(s)	36,434	14.8%	14.2%	64.0%	7.0%	100%
No Chronic Conditions	131,853	8.7%	16.6%	69.3%	5.4%	100%
Physician Location:						
Northeast	29,070	10.9%	4.5%	81.5%	3.2%	100%
Midwest	40,991	10.3%	19.9%	65.6%	4.2%	100%
South	57,684	9.3%	25.6%	61.4%	3.8%	100%
West	45,544	10.1%	9.1%	69.8%	11.1%	100%
Urban	141,671	7.1%	14.2%	72.1%	6.6%	100%
Rural	26,616	25.5%	26.4%	46.9%	1.2%	100%
Patient Seen Previously	151,818	10.3%	16.7%	67.4%	5.6%	100%
Not Seen Previously	16,470	7.5%	10.7%	75.2%	6.6%	100%
Total	168,289	10.0%	16.1%	68.2%	5.7%	100%

Source: CRS analysts of data from the 1995 NAMCS.
Note: Percentages that are significantly different from the column average at 95% or greater confidence are shown in boldface type.

Region

There were significant regional differences in the proportion of office visits that were made to physicians who participated in an HMO. In the West, 11.1% of all visits were made to physicians who treated *only* patients enrolled in an HMO, while in no other region were more than 4.2% of visits made to HMO-only physician offices. In both the Northeast and the West, more than 80% of all office visits were made to physicians who saw some HMO patients, usually along with PPO patients. In the Midwest and Sough, fewer than 70% of all office visits were made to primary care physicians who participated in at least one HMO.

Urban/Rural Location

In 1995, 78.7% of office visits in urban areas were made to physicians who treated at least some patients who were enrolled in an HMO. Only 7.1% of office visits to physicians in urban areas were to office that accepted only FFS reimbursement. In contrast, just 48.1% of office visits in rural areas were made to physicians who treated at least some patients who were in an HMO. More than a quarter of all office visits in rural areas were made to physicians who accepted only insurance plans that reimbursed the provider on a FFS basis.

New or Previously Physician-Patient Relationship

Among office visits to primary care physicians by privately insured people under age 65, 90.2% were made to a physician who had seen the patient before (151,818 out of 168,289). Office visits by patients that the physician had never seen before were most likely to have occurred in among physicians who participated in both HMO and PPO insurance plans. While two-thirds of all office visits by privately insured people under age 65 were made to physicians who saw patients in both HMO and PPO plans, visits to HMO and PPO offices comprised three-fourths of all visits in which the physician had not seen the patient before.

Performance of Diagnostic or Screening Services (Table 2)

Diagnostic or screening services were performed during 74.3% of all office visits to primary care physicians in 1995, but the frequency varied according to the type of insurance accepted by the provider. (Diagnostic and screening services are defined in Appendix II.) Visits to HMO-only physicians had the highest probability of a diagnostic or screening service, at 85% of visits. Office visits to FFS-only physicians had the second highest probability of a diagnostic or screening service (78%). Office visits to physician practices that accepted both FFS and PPO plans had lower-than-average rates of screening and diagnostic services. The pattern was similar among patients with no chronic conditions, except that among this group the proportion visits to FFS-only physicians during which diagnostic and screening services were performed was not statistically different from the average for all office visits by patients with a chronic condition.

Table 2. Diagnostic and Screening Services, Privately Insured Patients Under Age 65

	Were diagnostic/screening services performed?			
Type of insurance accepted by physician	**Visits (000s)**	**Yes**	**No**	**Total**
FFS only	16,848	77.9%	22.1%	100.00%
FFS or PPO	27,075	70.5%	29.5%	100.00%
HMO or PPO	114,703	73.8%	26.2%	100.00%
HMO only	9,662	84.8%	15.2%	100.00%
Total	168,288	74.3%	25.7%	100.00%

Privately Insured Patients under Age 65 Who Had No Chronic Medical Conditions

Type of insurance accepted by physician	Visits (000s)	*Were diagnostic/screening services performed?* Yes	No	Total
FFS only	11,459	71.3%	28.7%	100.00%
FFS or PPO	21,915	65.3%	34.7%	100.00%
HMO or PPO	91,365	69.8%	30.2%	100.00%
HMO only	7,115	81.4%	18.6%	100.00%
Total	131,854	69.8%	30.2%	100.00%

Source: CRS analysts of data from the 1995 NAMCS.
Note: Percentages that are significantly different from the column average at 95% or greater confidence are shown in boldface type.

Diagnostic and Screening Services: Differences by Sex (Table 3)

Overall, diagnostic or screening services were more likely to be performed during office visits made by female rather than male patients, (78% vs. 68%). Both female and male patients were most likely to have received diagnostic or screening services during a visit to an HMO-only physician, but the difference was about twice as large for males (83% in pure-HMO offices vs. 67% in other offices) as for females (86% in pure-HMO offices vs. 77% in other offices). Male and female patients were equally likely to receive diagnostic or screening services in physician offices that accepted only traditional FFS insurance (78% for both sexes). Among female patients, the likelihood of receiving these services was significantly different from the overall average only for visits to pure-HMO physician offices. Among male patients, the likelihood of having a diagnostic or screening service performed was significantly higher than average in both pure-HMO and pure-FFS physician offices, and it was significantly below average in offices that accepted both FFS and PPO plans.

Performance of Therapeutic or Preventive Services (Table 4)

Only 36.5% of office visits to primary care physicians in 1995 included performance of at least one therapeutic or preventive services. (Therapeutic and preventive services are defined in Appendix II.) As was also the case with diagnostic and screening services, office visits to physicians who treated only patients enrolled in an HMO had the highest frequency of therapeutic and preventive services (43.4%), and visits to physicians who accepted both FFS and PPO insurance plans included performance of these services at a rate that was significantly below the overall average.

One possible explanation for differences in the proportion of visits during which therapeutic or preventive services were administered would be differences in the health status of patients seen by physicians in each of the four insurance categories. The bottom panel of Table 4 shows office visits by people who were reported by the physician to have no chronic medical conditions. Among patients with no chronic medical conditions, the rate of therapeutic and preventive services did not differ significantly from the overall average for any of the four insurance classifications.

Table 3. Diagnostic and Screening Services by Sex of Patients

Female patients

	Were diagnostic/screening services performed?			
Type of insurance accepted by physician	**Total Visits (000s)**	**Yes**	**No**	**Total**
FFS only	9,408	77.6%	22.4%	100.00%
FFS or PPO	16,738	75.7%	24.3%	100.00%
HMO or PPO	74,602	77.8%	22.2%	100.00%
HMO only	6,194	85.6%	14.4%	100.00%
Total	106,942	77.9%	22.1%	100.00%

Male patients

	Were diagnostic/screening services performed?			
Type of insurance accepted by physician	**Visits (000s)**	**Yes**	**No**	**Total**
FFS only	7,440	78.3%	21.7%	100.00%
FFS or PPO	10,337	62.0%	38.0%	100.00%
HMO or PPO	40,101	66.3%	33.7%	100.00%
HMO only	3,469	83.3%	16.7%	100.00%
Total	61,347	68.0%	32.0%	100.00%

Source: CRS analysts of data from the 1995 NAMCS.
Note: Percentages that are significantly different from the column average at 95% or greater confidence are shown in boldface type.

Table 4. Therapeutic and preventive Services, Privately Insured Patients under Age 65

	Were diagnostic/screening services performed?			
Type of insurance accepted by physician	**Visits (000s)**	**Yes**	**No**	**Total**
FFS only	16,848	38.6%	61.4%	100.00%
FFS or PPO	27,075	32.2%	67.8%	100.00%
HMO or PPO	114,703	36.7%	63.3%	100.00%
HMO only	9,662	43.4%	56.6%	100.00%
Total	168,288	36.5%	63.5%	100.00%

Privately Insured Patients under Age 65 Who Had No Chronic Medical Conditions

	Were diagnostic/screening services performed?			
Type of insurance accepted by physician	**Visits (000s)**	**Yes**	**No**	**Total**
FFS only	11,459	30.2%	69.8%	100.00%
FFS or PPO	21,915	28.7%	71.3%	100.00%
HMO or PPO	91,365	32.2%	67.8%	100.00%
HMO only	7,115	35.7%	64.3%	100.00%
Total	131,854	31.6%	68.4%	100.00%

Source: CRS analysts of data from the 1995 NAMCS.
Note: Percentages that are significantly different from the column average at 95% or greater confidence are shown in boldface type.

Therapeutic or Preventive Services: Differences by Sex (Table 5)

There was little difference in the proportion of office visits by male and female patients during which therapeutic or preventive services were performed. These services were performed during 37.5% of physician office visits by men and 36% of visits by women. Among female patients, therapeutic or preventive services were equally likely to be administered during a visit to an HMO-only or FFS-only physician practice (41%), while visits to physician offices that participated in both FFS and PPO plans included therapeutic and preventive services at a rate significantly lower than the overall average - (30.7% versus 36.0%). Among men, visits to HMO-only physicians had a higher-than-average frequency of therapeutic and preventive services (48%), while visits to all other physician offices included these services at rates near the overall average of 37.5%.

Table 5. Performance of Therapeutic of Preventive Services by Sex of Patient

Female patients

		Were diagnostic/screening services performed?		
Type of insurance accepted by physician	**Total Visits (000s)**	**Yes**	**No**	**Total**
FFS only	9,408	40.9%	59.1%	100.00%
FFS or PPO	16,738	30.7%	69.3%	100.00%
HMO or PPO	74,602	36.2%	63.8%	100.00%
HMO only	6,194	40.8%	59.2%	100.00%
Total	106,942	36.0%	64.0%	100.00%

Male patients

		Were diagnostic/screening services performed?		
Type of insurance accepted by physician	**Visits (000s)**	**Yes**	**No**	**Total**
FFS only	7,440	35.7%	64.3%	100.00%
FFS or PPO	10,337	34.5%	65.5%	100.00%
HMO or PPO	40,101	37.7%	62.3%	100.00%
HMO only	3,469	47.9%	52.1%	100.00%
Total	61,347	37.5%	62.5%	100.00%

Source: CRS analysts of data from the 1995 NAMCS.
Note: Percentages that are significantly different from the column average at 95% or greater confidence are shown in boldface type.

Multi-variate Analysis: Diagnostic and Screening Services

To evaluate the relationship of each the variables described in Table 1 through Table 5 to the probability that a physician office visit included a diagnostic/screening or therapeutic/preventive service, we processed the data though a regression model.[18] This form

[18] The results presented in this section are from a logistic regression model. We also processed the data through a probit model and found substantively the same results.

of analysis shows the relative impact of each specified characteristic of the patient or physician while all of the other factors are held constant.

Age, Sex and Race

Other things being equal, the probability that a privately insured individual under age 65 had a diagnostic or screening service performed during a physician office visit increases by about 4.6% for each additional year of age, and a female patient was about 33% more likely to have a diagnostic or screening service performed during an office visit than was a male patient. (See the column labeled "Odds Ratio.") A patient's race (defined here as white or nonwhite) was unrelated to the likelihood that he or she had a diagnostic or screening service performed, once other patient and physician characteristics were taken into account.

Region and Urban/Rural Location

Both the region and urban or rural location of a physician office had a statistically significant relationship to the probability that a diagnostic or screening service was performed during a physician office visit. Relative to physician office visits in the Midwest, office visits in the Northeast, South, and West all had a greater likelihood of including a diagnostic or screening service, with the probability ranging from 33% higher in the South to 47% higher in the Northeast. Likewise, visits to physician offices in urban areas were about one-third more likely than those in rural areas to include a diagnostic or screening service, other factors being equal.

Health Status; New or Established Physician-Patient Relationship

Patients who had one or more chronic conditions according to the patient records maintained by the physician were much more likely to have undergone a diagnostic or screening service during an office visit than patients who had no chronic conditions. The rate at which these services were performed was almost 80% higher for a patient with a chronic condition when other characteristics were held constant. Having seen a patient during a previous visit was associated with a lower probability of receiving diagnostic or screening services. Patients who had been seen by the health care provider previously were about 26% less likely to have had a diagnostic or screening service performed than those who were being seen for the first time. Office visits also were more likely to include diagnostic and screening services if the provider was a physician rather than a nurse practitioner, registered nurse, or other provider, however, visits to these other providers accounted for only 4% of all office visits.

Insurance plans Accepted by Physician

For the regression analysis, we used office visits to physicians who accepted only non-PPO FFS insurance plans as the reference group for estimating the probability of a diagnostic or screening service being performed during an office visit. Compared to the reference group, there was no significant difference in the likelihood of a diagnostic or screening service being performed during visits to physicians who accepted both FFS and PPO insurance plans. Visits to HMO-only and HMO/PPO physician offices, however, were both associated with higher rates of diagnostic and screening services, than office visits to pure-FFS offices, other things being equal. An office visit to a physician who participated in both PPO and HMO plans was about 20% more likely to include a diagnostic or screening service than a visit to a FFS-only office, while the likelihood of having these services performed during a visit to an HMO-only physician office was about 40% higher than in a pure-FFS office, other things being equal.

Table 6. Diagnostic and Screening Services, Privately Insured Patients Under Age 65: Logistic Regression Results

Response Variable: Were diagnostic or screening services performed?				
Analysis Variable	**Weighted Mean**	**Parameter Estimate**	**Standard Error**	**Odds Ratio**
Intercept		-2.3615***	0.2572	
Age	29.1	0.0449***	0.00202	1.046
Sex (1 - female)	0.6345	0.2843***	0.0670	1.329
Race (1 = white)	0.8778	-0.0551	0.1060	0.946
Northeast	0.1736	0.3835***	0.1043	1.467
South	0.3241	0.2874***	0.0866	1.333
West	0.2640	0.3262***	0.0931	1.386
Urban Area	0.8336	0.2876***	0.0916	1.333
Has Chronic Condition(s)	0.2189	0.5840***	0.1099	1.793
Patient Seen Previously	0.9035	-0.3066***	0.1146	0.736
Provider is an M.D.	0.9583	1.8145***	0.1499	6.138
Reg. FFS or PPO accepted	0.1569	0.1600	0.1265	1.174
HMO or PPO accepted	0.6645	0.1828*	0.1083	1.201
Only HMO accepted	0.0560	0.3341*	0.1921	1.397

Source: CRS analysis of data from the 1995 NAMCS.
n=6,028 observations
*significant at >=.10
*** significant at >=.01

Multi-variate Analysis: Therapeutic and preventive Services

Age, Sex and Race

When the response variable of the regression model was changed to indicate whether therapeutic or preventive services were performed during an office visit, the relationship of the patient's age was significant, but negative. Each additional year of age reduced by about 1% the likelihood of a therapeutic or preventive service being performed during an office visit. The signs of the variables indicating the patient's sex (female = 1) and race (white = 1) also were negative, but neither of these variables was statistically significant.

Region ad Urban/Rural Location

Relative to being located in the Midwest, an office visit in the Northeast was more likely to include a therapeutic or preventive service, and an office visit in the South was less likely to include these services. Physician office visits in the West had effectively the same likelihood of including therapeutic and preventive services as office visits in the Midwest. As was the case with diagnostic and screening services, therapeutic and preventive services were more likely to be administered during a physician office visit in an urban area than in a rural area, with the probability being about 23% greater in urban settings.

Health States; New or Established Physician-Patient Relationship

The presence of one or more chronic medical conditions had a positive and statistically significant relationship to the probability that therapeutic and preventive services were performed during a physician office visit. Other things being equal, patients with chronic conditions were almost three times as likely to have these kinds of services performed as were patients with no chronic conditions. Office visits to a health care provider who had seen the patient-previously were less likely to include therapeutic and preventive services than visits to a provider who had never before seen the patient. An office visit with an M.D. was much more likely to include therapeutic and preventive services than a visit with a primary-care provider who was not a physician.

Insurance Plans Accepted by the Physician

Relative to visits to physicians who accepted only regular fee-for-service (FFS) insurance plans, neither visits to providers that accepted both FFS and PPO or both HMO and PPO plans had a significantly different likelihood of including a therapeutic or preventive service, other things being equal. As was also the case with diagnostic and screening services, however, office visits to primary-care providers who accepted only HMO insurance plans were significantly more likely than visits to a pure-FFS provider to include a therapeutic or preventive service, once other factors were taken into account. Relative to an office visit to a provider who accepted only FFS insurance plans, a visit to an office that accepted only HMO plans was about 37% more likely to include delivery of therapeutic or preventive services.

Table 7. Therapeutic and Preventive Services, Privately Insured Patients under Age 65: Logistic Regression Results

Response Variable: Were diagnostic or screening services performed?				
Analysis Variable	**Weighted Mean**	**Parameter Estimate**	**Standard Error**	**Odds Ratio**
Intercept		-1.1327***	0.2340	
Age	29.1	-0.00796***	0.00162	0.992
Sex (1 - female)	0.6345	-0.0417	0.0585	0.959
Race (1 = white)	0.8778	-0.1265	0.0850	0.881
Northeast	0.1736	0.2931***	0.0856	1.341
South	0.3241	-0.5034***	0.0768	0.605
West	0.2640	0.0588	0.0781	1.061
Urban Area	0.8336	0.2054**	0.0812	1.228
Has Chronic Condition(s)	0.2189	1.0960***	0.0738	2.992
Patient Seen Previously	0.9035	-0.1733*	0.0936	0.841
Provider is an M.D.	0.9583	0.6921***	0.1602	1.998
Reg. FFS or PPO accepted	0.1569	0.0866	0.1111	1.091
HMO or PPO accepted	0.6645	0.0598	0.0924	1.062
Only HMO accepted	0.0560	0.3176**	0.1444	1.374

Source: CRS analysis of data from the 1995 NAMCS.
n=6,028 observations
*significant at >=.10
*** significant at >=.05
*** significant at >=.01

Discussion

The data reported in Table 1 show that patients with particular demographic and health characteristics are more likely to have visited the offices of primary-care physicians that accept certain kinds of insurance and less likely to have visited physicians office that accept other kinds of insurance. Pure FFS physician offices had a smaller-than-average percentage of visits by children and young adults and a greater than average percentage of visits by adults aged 55 to 64. Pure HMO physician practices also had a lower-than-average proportion of visits by children, but a greater-than-average proportion of visits but adults aged 35 to 64. Male patients, non-white patients, patients with one or more chronic medical conditions, and patients in rural areas each made up a greater-than-average proportion of visits to pure-FFS physician offices. Visits to pure FFS offices had a lower-than-average percentage of visits by patients whom the physician had never seen before, while offices that accepted both HMO and PPO plans had a disproportionately large share of visits by patients who were seeing a particular provider for the first time.

The data presented in Table 2 and Table 3 show consistently higher rates of diagnostic and screening services being performed in pure-HMO physician offices and that the relative difference from the average was much greater for men than for women. In contrast, while men also were more likely to have received a diagnostic or screening service in a visit to a FFS-only office and were less likely to have received these services in a mixed FFS/PPO office, no such differences were found for women. Overall, women were more likely than men to have received diagnostic or screening services during a typical office visit, but among all visits by women the likelihood of receiving diagnostic or screening services was significantly above average only during visits to pure-HMO physician offices. Patients with no chronic medical conditions were less likely to receive diagnostic or screening services than those who had a chronic condition. Patients without a chronic condition were most likely to receive diagnostic or screening services in a HMO-only office.

Table 4 and Table 5 show a different pattern with respect to therapeutic and preventive services than Tables 1 and 2 showed for diagnostic and screening services. Overall, the likelihood of receiving therapeutic or preventive services was similar for male patients and female patients. Visits to pure-HMO offices had a greater likelihood of including a therapeutic or screening services, while visits to mixed FFS and PPO offices had a lower-than average likelihood of including these services. The higher rate in HMO offices was statistically significant only for men while the lower rate in FFS/PPO offices was significant only for female patients. Among patients with no chronic medical conditions, office visits to all four insurance categories of primary care providers had statistically similar probabilities of including a therapeutic or preventive service.

With respect to diagnostic and screening services, office visits to providers who accepted both HMO/PPO or pure HMO plans had a greater likelihood of including these services than did visits to physicians who accepted only FFS insurance plans, even when controlling for the patient's health status and demographic characteristics. In the case of therapeutic and preventive services, however, only visits to pure HMO offices had a significantly higher likelihood of receiving such a services than visits to pure FFS offices. For both diagnostic/screening services and therapeutic/preventive services, the presence of a chronic medical condition exerted a much stronger influence on the likelihood that a patient would receive either kind of service than did the types of insurance coverage accepted by the provider.

The finding that female patients were more likely than male patients to have received diagnostic or screening services regardless of the health care provider's insurance affiliation most likely reflects female patient's greater frequency of visits for exams and check-ups. More than 63% of all office visits in 1995 were made by female patients, and a subset of these visits - such as those for mammograms or pap smears - *always* involve a test or exam. The greater probability of receiving either diagnostic/screening services or therapeutic/preventive services in an HMO-only office compared to a physician office that accepts only FFS insurance plans could be the result of several characteristics of HMOs. Health maintenance organizations have historically emphasized preventive care as a way of promoting good health and potentially reducing health care expenses over the long term. HMOs also frequently screen patients with phone consultations before making an appointment for an office visit. If effective, this would result in a greater proportion of patients who ultimately see a physician in a pure HMO being in need of medical services compared with patients in purely FFS physician offices. Finally, an emphasis on primary care is among the fundamental principles of HMOs, and HMOs are staffed mainly by primary-care physicians. Consequently, it may be that some services performed in the offices of primary care physicians in HMOs are referred to specialists in FFS office settings.

Differences in the frequency with which diagnostic or therapeutic services are performed by any given group of physicians on any given group of patients do not necessarily mean that the rates at which these services are performed in one case or the other is inappropriate. However, while this analysis showed that a patient's health status has a much stronger relationship to the likelihood of receiving services during an office visit than does the provider's insurance affiliations, these too appear to influence the likelihood of some kinds of services be administered. Differences in the rates at which diagnostic and therapeutic services are performed among male and female patients and among office visits to physicians who participate in HMOs or PPOs or do not participate in any kind of managed care naturally raise the question of *why* these differences occur.

Previous research has shown that patients enrolled in HMOs typically have a higher number of physician office visits and fewer inpatient admissions in a given period of time than non-HMO patients, but that they also have less access to specialists and use fewer complex tests and procedures. This analysis presents evidence that, even when controlling for the patient's health status, diagnostic and screening services are most likely to be provided during office visits to primary care physicians in HMO or HMO/PPO practices, and that therapeutic and preventive services are most likely to be performed during office visits to HMO-only physician practices.

APPENDIX 1: STANDARD ERRORS OF ESTIMATES

Table A1. Standard Errors for Estimates Displayed in Table 1

Patient age, sex, race, physician location	Visits (000s)	Standard error (+/-) FFS only	FFS or PPO	HMO or PPO	HMO only
Under age 18	59,144	0.7%	1.0%	1.2%	0.4%
Ages 18 to 34	36,224	0.9%	1.1%	1.5%	0.9%
Ages 35 to 54	53,413	0.8%	1.0%	1.3%	0.7%
Ages 55 to 64	19,508	1.7%	1.7%	2.2%	1.3%
Female	106,942	0.5%	0.7%	0.9%	0.4%
Male	61,347	0.8%	0.9%	1.2%	0.6%
White	147,423	0.5%	0.6%	0.8%	0.4%
Black or other	20,865	1.5%	1.3%	2.0%	1.0%
Has Chronic Condition(s)	36,434	1.2%	1.1%	2.5%	0.8%
No Chronic Conditions	131,853	0.5%	0.6%	0.8%	0.4%
Northeast	29,070	1.1%	0.8%	1.7%	0.6%
Midwest	40,991	0.9%	1.2%	1.5%	0.6%
South	52,684	0.8%	1.2%	1.3%	0.5%
West	45,544	0.9%	0.8%	1.3%	0.9%
Urban	141,671	0.4%	0.6%	0.7%	0.4%
Rural	26,616	1.7%	1.7%	1.9%	0.4%
Physician:					
Has seen Patient before	151,818	0.5%	0.6%	0.8%	0.4%
Has not seen Patient Before	16,470	1.3%	1.5%	2.1%	1.2%
Total	168,289	0.5%	0.6%	0.7%	0.4%

Table A2. Standard Errors for Estimates Displayed in Table 2

Were diagnostic services performed?		
Type of insurance accepted by physician	**Total Visits (000s)**	**Yes/No *Standard error (+/-)***
FFS only	16,848	2.0%
HMO only	9,662	2.3%
FFS or PPO	27,075	1.7%
HMO or PPO	114,703	0.8%
Total	168,288	0.7%

People Who Had No Chronic Medical Conditions *Were diagnostic services performed?*		
Type of insurance accepted by physician	**Total Visits (000s)**	**Yes/No *Standard error (+/-)***
FFS only	11,459	2.6%
HMO only	7,115	2.9%
FFS or PPO	21,915	2.0%
HMO or PPO	91,365	1.0%
Total	131,854	0.8%

Table A3. Standard Errors for Estimates Displayed in Table 3

Female Patients *Were diagnostic or screening services performed?*		
Type of insurance accepted by physician	**Total Visits (000s)**	**Yes/No *Standard error (+/-)***
FFS only	9,408	2.6%
HMO only	6,194	2.8%
FFS or PPO	16,738	2.1%
HMO or PPO	74,602	1.0%
Total	106,942	0.8%

Male Patients *Were diagnostic or screening services performed?*		
Type of insurance accepted by physician	**Total Visits (000s)**	**Yes/No *Standard error (+/-)***
FFS only	7,440	3.0%
HMO only	3,469	4.0%
FFS or PPO	10,337	3.0%
HMO or PPO	40,101	1.5%
Total	61,347	1.2%

Table A4. Standard Errors for Estimates Displayed in Table 4

All Privately Insured People Under Age 65 ***Were diagnostic or screening services performed?***		
Type of insurance accepted by physician	**Total Visits (000s)**	**Yes/No** ***Standard error (+/-)***
FFS only	16,848	2.3%
HMO only	9,662	3.2%
FFS or PPO	27,075	1.8%
HMO or PPO	114,703	0.9%
Total	168,288	0.7%

People with No Chronic Medical Conditions ***Were diagnostic or screening services performed?***		
Type of insurance accepted by physician	**Total Visits (000s)**	**Yes/No** ***Standard error (+/-)***
FFS only	11,459	2.7%
HMO only	7,115	3.6%
FFS or PPO	21,915	1.9%
HMO or PPO	91,365	1.0%
Total	131,854	0.8%

Table A5. Standard Errors for Estimates Displayed in Table 5

Female Patients ***Were diagnostic or screening services performed?***		
Type of insurance accepted by physician	**Total Visits (000s)**	**Yes/No** ***Standard error (+/-)***
FFS only	9,408	3.2%
HMO only	6,194	3.9%
FFS or PPO	16,738	2.2%
HMO or PPO	74,602	1.1%
Total	106,942	0.9%

Male Patients ***Were diagnostic or screening services performed?***		
Type of insurance accepted by physician	**Total Visits (000s)**	**Yes/No** ***Standard error (+/-)***
FFS only	7,440	3.5%
HMO only	3,469	5.3%
FFS or PPO	10,337	2.9%
HMO or PPO	40,101	1.5%
Total	61,347	1.2%

APPENDIX II: MEDICAL SERVICES AND MEDICAL CONDITIONS

The National Ambulatory Medical Care Survey (NAMCS) defines three categories of diagnostic and screening services: exams, tests, and imaging.

Exams, Tests, and Imaging

Breast exam
Pelvic exam
Rectal exam
Visual acuity exam
Other exam

Blood pressure test
Urinalysis
TB skin test
Blood lead level test
Cholesterol measure
Prostate screening antigen (PSA) test
HIV serology
Other blood test
Other test

X-ray
Computerized axial tomography (CAAT scan)
Magnetic resonance imaging (MRI)
Ultrasound
Other imaging
Other diagnostic or screening service

The NAMCS defines two categories of therapeutic and preventive services: counseling/education and other therapy.

Counseling/Education

Diet
Exercise
Weight reduction
Cholesterol reduction
HIV transmission
Tobacco use/exposure
Growth/development
Mental health
Other counseling

Other Therapy

Psychotherapy
Corrective lenses
Physiotherapy
Other counseling

REFERENCES

Clement, D.G., S.M Retchin, R.S. Brown, and M.H. Stegall. Access and Outcomes of Elderly Patients Enrolled in Managed Care. *Journal of the American Medical Association,* v. 271, no. 19, May 18, 1994.

CRS Report 97-482, *Managed Health Care: The Use of Financial Incentives,* by Beth C. Fuchs and Jason S. Lee.

CRS Report 97-913, *Managed Health Care: A Primer,* by Jason S Lee.

Eddy, D.M. Balancing Cost and Quality in Fee-for-Service Versus Managed Care. *Health Affairs, v. 16, no. 3, May/June 1997.*

Fama, T., P.D. Fox, and L.A. White. Can HMOs Care for the Chronically Ill? *Health Affairs,* v. 14, spring, 1995.

Gabel, J. Ten Ways HMOs Have Changed During the 1990s. *Health Affairs,* v. 16, no. 3, May/June 1997.

Gazmararian, J.A. and J.P Koplan. Length of Stay After Delivery: Managed Care Versus Fee-for-Service. *Health Affairs,* v. 15, no. 4, winter, 1996.

Hellinger, F.J. Selection Bias in HMOs and PPOs: A Review of the Evidence. *Injury,* v. 32, summer, 1995.

Hoechst-Marion-Roussel. *Managed Care Digest Series: HMO-PPO-Digest 1996.* Kansas City, MO, 1996.

KPMG Peat Marwick. *The Impact of Managed Care on U.S. Markets.* Washington, DC, 1996.

Mark T. and C. Mueller. Access to Care in HMOs and Traditional insurance Plans. *Health Affairs,* v. 15, no. 4, winter, 1996.

Miller, R.H. and H.S. Luft. Does Managed Care Lead to Better or Worse Quality of Care? *Health Affairs,* v. 16, no. 5, September/October 1997.

Robinson, J.C. Decline in Hospital Utilization and Cost Inflation Under Managed Care in California. *Journal of the American Medicaid Association,* v. 276, no. 13, October 2, 1996.

Safran, D.G., A.R. Tarlov, and W.H. Rogers. Primary Care Performance in Fee-for-Service and Prepaid Health Care Systems. *Journal of the American Medical Association,* v. 271, no. 20, May 25, 1994.

Taylor, A.K., K.M. Beauregard, and J.P. Vistnes. Who Belongs to HMOs: A comparison of Fee-for-Service Versus HMO Enrollees. *Medical Care Research and Review,* v. 52, no. 3, September 1995.

Ware, J.E., M.S. Bayliss, W.H. Rogers, M.Kosinski, and A.R. Tarlov. Differences in 4-Year Health Outcomes for Elderly and Poor, Chronically Ill Patients Treated in HMO and Fee-for-Service Systems. *Journal of the American Medical Association,* v. 276, no. 13, October 2, 1996.

Weiner, J.P., A. Lyles, D.M. Stenwachs, and K.C. Hall. Impact of Managed Care on Prescription Drug Use. *Health Affairs,* v. 10, spring, 1991.

Wholey, D.R., J.B. Christianson, J.Enberg, and C. Bryce. HMO Market Structure and Performance. *Health Affairs, v. 16, no.6,* November/December 1997.

Yelin, E.H., L.A. Criswell, and P.G. Feigenbaum. Health Care Utilization and Outcomes Among Persons with Rheumatoid Arthritis in Fee-for-Service and prepaid Group Practice Settings. *Journal of the American Medicaid Association,* v. 276, no. 13, October 2, 1996.

Chapter 2

THE HEALTH INSURANCE PORTABILITY AND ACCOUNTABILITY ACT (HIPAA): SUMMARY OF THE ADMINISTRATIVE SIMPLIFICATION PROVISIONS*

Celinda Franco

INTRODUCTION

The Health Insurance Portability and Accountability Act of 1996 (HIPAA, P.L. 104-191), 42 USC §1320d) mandates significant changes in the health insurance industry and includes, as a small part of the overall insurance reforms, requirements for the standardization of electronically transmitted health insurance financial claims and administrative transactions. The law requires all health care payers and providers who transmit transactions electronically to use standardized data elements to conduct financial and administrative transactions, such as the submission of claims, processing of enrollments, verification of insurance eligibility, and payment and remittance advice. The Secretary of the Department of Health and Human Services (HHS) is required to develop and adopt the standards to be used to electronically transmit health care transactions. The purpose of these HIPAA requirements is to reduce administrative costs and paperwork; improve the efficiency of the health care system, detect fraud and abuse, and facilitate access to medical information. The Health Care Financing Administration (HCFA) estimates that implementing all of the standards will save the health care system $1.5 billion between 1998 and 2002.

Recording the vulnerable nature of information transmitted electronically, HIPAA required the Secretary of HHS to make recommendations to the Congress by August 1997 on ways to protect the privacy of individually identifiable health information. On September 11, 1997, the Secretary delivered recommendations to the Congress for federal privacy legislation for health information. Under HIPAA, the Congress has until August 1999 to enact a medical records privacy law. During the 105th Congress several medical records privacy proposals

* This report has benefitted from the comments and suggestions of Gina Marie Stevens of the American Law Division

were considered, however, none of the bills were enacted. If the Congress fails to enact a privacy law, the Secretary of HHS is required to promulgate regulations on privacy protections by February 2000. Federal privacy protections are required to be in place before the administrative simplification provisions of HIPAA can be fully implemented.

The standardization provisions of HIPAA require the Secretary to adopt a standard unique identifier for each individual, employer, health plan, and health care provider. Implementation of the unique health identifier for individuals required under HIPAA and ensuring the privacy of individually identifiable health information has become controversial. On July 31, 1998, Vice President Gore announced that the Administration would delay implementation of a unique health identifier for individuals until medical records privacy legislation is enacted. The Omnibus Consolidated and Emergency Supplemental Appropriations for FY1999, H.R. 4328 (P.L. 105-277), included a general provision that prohibited any federal funds appropriated by the law to be used to adopt a final standard providing for a unique health identifier for an individual until legislation is enacted specifically approving the standard.

ADMINISTRATIVE SIMPLIFICATION

Background

Each year the health care industry generates billion of financial and administrative transactions in both paper and electronic form that result from the delivery of health care services. Seeking ways to lower the costs of delivering health care, health care payers and providers have long sought ways to simplify the administration of health care financial transactions. Over the years, many in the health care industry looked to electronic information systems and various computer technologies as potential tools for achieving the administrative simplification of health care transactions. Despite attempts to develop standards for the uniform processing of health care claims and related administrative transactions electronically, payers and providers failed to reach agreement on the standardization of these transactions.

Currently, there are no standardized formats for the electronic or paper transmission of health care information, or standards for identifying providers, health plans, employers or individuals participating in the health care system. There are approximately 400 formats for electronic health claims used in the United States today. The absence of standardized formats for health claims means that payers and providers must frequently invest in multiple computer systems or programs, as well as additional human resources in order to process claims with different format requirements. This increases the administrative costs of health care delivery. The lack of standardization limits the efficient flow of information between payers and providers, increases the complexity and costs of processing of health care claims and other financial and administrative transactions, and hinders efforts to direct fraud and abuse.

Today health care information is used for many purposes by a variety of individuals and organizations within and outside the health care industry. Primary uses of health care information include physicians, clinics, and hospitals that provide care to patients. Patients provide health care information to their physicians to supply historical background so their health care needs can be assessed. Physicians use this information to develop appropriate treatment plans, order diagnostic tests, and maintain an ongoing medical record of services provided to a patient. Hospitals and clinics use health care information to provide patient care ordered by physicians and maintain ongoing records of health care services provided. To receive payment for health care services, providers must bill either patients or health insurers for reimbursement. In order for providers to be reimbursed by health insurers, provider claims often must include certain information about the patient's medical records to justify that the services provided were appropriate. Insurance claims often include such patient-specific information as diagnosis, treatment, and prognosis.

Secretary users of health care information include organizations that pay for health care benefits, such as traditional health insurance companies, managed care providers, and government programs, like Medicare and Medicaid. As a part of their management functions, these health care payers also use health care information to analyze the cost and quality of health care delivered by various providers. Other secondary uses of health information include medical and social science researchers, employers, and public health services, for purposes such as researching the costs and benefits of alternative medical treatments, determining eligibility for social programs, and understanding state and local health care needs. Much of the health care data that is available to secondary users specifically identifies individuals, and may or may not have required the patient's consent to grant access to some secondary users.

The transformation of the health care industry by the expansion of managed care and other integrated delivery systems, has further increased the amount of health care information that is routinely being exchanged between insurers and providers as they seek to inform coverage and payment decisions with health care data. Much of the data being exchanged contains patient-identifiable information about private, often sensitive, health care matters. In the absence of uniform laws protecting the privacy rights of patients, the increased dissemination of health data raises serious concerns about the privacy and security of health care information. This is a particularly important concerns when health care information is transmitted electronically and there may not be adequate security measures in place to protect unauthorized access to patient-identifiable data and misuse of such information.

The Health Insurance Portability and Accountability Act of 1996 (HIPAA, P.L. 104-191, 42 USC §1320d) enacted on August 21, 1996, added a new Part C - Administrative Simplification - to Title XI of the Social Security Act. HIPAA established requirements and standards for the electronic transmission of health information that are intended to improve health care system efficiency and effectiveness, make it easier to detect fraud and abuse, facilitate access to health and medical information by researchers, and reduce administrative costs. Under HIPAA, health information is defined as any information, whether oral or recorded in any form or medium that is created or received by a health care provider, health plan, public health authority, employer, life insurer, school or university, or health care clearinghouse. Health information can relate to the past, present, or future physical or mental health or condition of an individual, the provision of health care to an individual, or the past, present, or future payment for the provision of health care to an individual. HIPAA does not, however, provide for the collection of clinical data or the electronic maintenance of patient medical records. As such, HIPAA's overarching goal in this area is to serve as a catalyst for the health care industry to increasingly use electronic transactions and standard formats so that significant administrative savings can be achieved.

General Requirements for Adoption of Standards

HIPAA requires the Secretary of the Department of Health and Human Services (HHS) to adopt standards for the financial and administrative transactions used in the operation of the health care system to enable health information to be exchanged electronically. The standards mandated by HIPAA apply to all health plans, health care clearinghouses, and health care providers that transmit health information electronically.[1] The standards are required to reduce the administrative costs of providing and paying for health care. Any standard adopted by the Secretary must have been developed, adopted, or modified by standard setting organizations.[2] The Secretary may adopt a different standard if the different standard will substantially reduce administrative costs to health care providers, and the standard is promulgated in accordance with federal rulemaking procedures. If no standard has been adopted by any standard setting organization that is required by HIPAA, the Secretary is required to rely on the recommendations of the National Committee on Vital and Health Statistics (NCVHS) and consult with the standard setting organizations, appropriate federal and state agencies, and private organizations. In general, for any standard adopted by the Secretary, the law further specifies that the following organizations must be consulted: the National Uniform Billing Committee, the National Uniform Claim Committee, the Workgroup for Electronic Data Interchange, and the American Dental Association.

Standards for Information Transactions and Data Elements

HIPAA establishes general requirements for standards for electronic transactions adopted by the Secretary. These include standards for:

- Transactions to allow the electronic exchange of health information, such as health claims and attachments, health plan enrollment and disenrollment, health plan eligibility, health care payment and remittance advice, premium payments, first report of injury, claim status, and referral certification and authorization.
- Unique identifiers for individuals, employers, health plans, and health care providers, with the authorized uses identified.
- Code sets for data elements for standard transactions using established sets of codes for data elements such as tables of terms, medical concepts, medical diagnostic codes, or medical procedure codes.

---

[1] HIPAA defines a *health plan* to include individual or group plans that provide, or pay the cost of, medical care, including group health plans, health insurance issuers, health maintenance organizations, Medicare, Medicaid, a long-term care policy, an employee welfare benefit plan or other arrangement covering employees of two or more employers, military health care programs, the Veterans health care program, the Civilian Health and Medical Program of the Uniformed Services (CHAAMPUS), the Indian Health Service program, and the Federal Employees Health Benefit Program. HIPAA define a *health care clearinghouse* as a public or private entity that processes or facilitates the processing of nonstandard data elements of health information into standard data elements. HIPAA defines a *health care provider* to include a provider of medical or other health services, or any other person furnishing health care services or supplies.

[2] The law defines a standard setting organization as an organization accredited by the American National Standards Institute, including the National Council for Prescription Drug Programs, that develops standards for information transactions data elements, or any other standard that is necessary to, or will facilitate, the implementation of the administrative simplification provisions in HIPAA.

- Security standards for entities that maintain or transmit health information in order to provide "reasonable and appropriate" administrative, technical, and physical safeguards for confidentially and security of the information.
- Electronic signatures specifying procedures for the electronic transmission and authentication of signatures.
- Transfer of information, among health plans for the coordination of benefits, sequential claims processing, and other data elements for individuals with more than one health plan.

Timetables for Adoption of Standards[3]

HIPAA provides timetables for the Secretary, in consultation with standard-setting organizations and providers, to develop and adopt standards for electronic transactions. HHS is required to develop the standards for *electronic transactions* by February 21, 1998, and adopt standards by August 21, 1998. The standards for *claims attachments* are required by February 21, 1999.

HHS issued a proposed rule in the *Federal Register* (v. 63, no. 88, p. 25272) on May 7, 1998, for the standards for electronic transactions and code sets, and the requirements for implementing these standards. The proposed rule would establish the requirements that health plans, health care clearinghouses, and certain health care providers would have to meet. Proposed rules were also issued for the identifier for employers on June 6, 1998 (v. 63, no. 115, p. 32784), and for security standards on August 12, 1998 (v. 63, no. 155, p. 43242).

Requirements for Conducting Transactions

Health plans are required to process a transaction electronically that is submitted electronically, in a standard format, and may not delay or adversely affect transactions submitted electronically. Information that is submitted and received electronically is required to be in standard data elements. Plans can meet the requirements to transmit and receive such data either or by contracting with a health care clearinghouse to cover nonstandard data elements into standard transactions. After the final rules are issued by HHS, health plans or persons to whom the standards apply have 2 years to comply, and small health plans[4] have 3 years. A plan or person may comply voluntarily before the effective date of the standards, and may comply by using a health care clearinghouse to transmit or receive the standard transactions. If a standard is modified, compliance with the modified standard may not be earlier than 180 days after notice of the change.

HIPAA does *not* require providers and payers to electronically transmit claims and related transactions. However, if they transmit or accept transactions electronically, they must be submitted in the standard format adopted by the Secretary.

---

[3] For more information about implementation deadlines established in HIPAA, see Appendix A at the end of the report.

[4] HCFA proposed in the *Federal Register* on May 7, 1998, that small health plans be defined as plans with 50 or fewer participants.

General Penalty for Failure to Comply with Standards

HIPAA establishes a $100 civil monetary penalty per person per violation, and not more than $25,000 in a calendar year per person per violation of a single standard. The procedural provisions of Section 1128A of the Social Security Act apply.[5] There are limitations on when a penalty may be imposed, including instances where the failure to comply with the standards was due to offenses otherwise punishable (described separately, below), or where the person liable for the penalty did not know, and would not have known that the provision had been violated exercising reasonable diligence. In addition, the penalty may not be imposed if the failure to comply was due to reasonable cause and not willful neglect, and was corrected within 30 days of learning that the failure to comply had occurred. The Secretary is given discretion to extend the 30-day correction period, and is permitted to provide technical assistance in certain cases. In cases where the failure to comply was due to reasonable cause and not to willful neglect, the penalty may be waived.

Wrongful Disclosure of Individually Identifiable Health Information

Recognizing the vulnerable nature of information transmitted electronically, HIPAA establishes penalties for knowing misuse of unique health identifiers and individually identifiable health information. The penalties for wrongfully obtaining or disclosing individually identifiable information are: (1) a fine of up to $50,000 and/or imprisonment of not more than one year; (2) if committed under false pretenses, a fine of not more than $100,000, imprisonment of not more than 5 years, or both; and (3) if the offense is committed with intent to sell, transfer, or use individually identifiable information for commercial advantage, personal gain, or to do "malicious harm," a fine of up to $250,000, imprisonment of not more than 10 years, or both.

Effect on State Law

The standards adopted or modified under HIPAA shall supersede contrary provisions in state law pertaining to health information, including provisions of state law requiring medical records to be maintained in written rather than electronic form. State laws on health information include statutes governing the use and disclosure of such information, inspection and copying of health information, procedures for correction and amendment of health information, and maintenance requirements for health information and medical records.[6] The HIPAA standards do not supersede provisions in state law to detect fraud and abuse, to regulate insurance and health plans, for reporting health care delivery or costs, or for regulation of controlled substances. Moreover, HIPAA's requirements cannot be construed to invalidate or limit state laws requiring the reporting of disease, injury, child abuse, birth or death, public health surveillance, or public health investigation or intervention. States may

[5] Section 1128A provides for civil and monetary penalty provisions under Medicare and Medicaid programs.

[6] For a further discussion of the complexities of preempting existing state laws, see *Confidentiality of Individually-Identifiable Health Information, Recommendations of the Secretary of health and Human Services, Pursuant to Section 264 of the Health Insurance Portability and Accountability Act of 1996,* September 11, 1997 (available on the Internet at [http://aspe.os.dhhs.gov/admsimp/pvcrec0.htm]).

continue to require reporting of health information for management and financial audits, program monitoring and evaluation, and licensure or certification.

Processing Payment Transactions by Financial Institutions

HIPAA standards do not apply to the activities of financial institutions related to authorizing, processing, clearing, settling, billing, transferring, reconciling, or collecting payments for a financial institution. The conference report explains that Congress intended that the law would not apply to the use or disclosure of information when an individual utilized a payment system to make a payment for, or related to, health plan premiums or health care. As an example, the conference report describes a situation where the standards of HIPAA would not apply when the exchange of information between participants in a credit card system is made in connection with processing a credit card payment for health care. Another example given of a situation not covered by HIPAA's requirements would be when a financial institution sends a checking account statement to an account holder who uses a credit or debit card to pay for health care services. However, if such a company clears health care claims, then the health care claims activities of the company would be subject to HIPAA requirements.

Changes in Membership and Duties of National Committee on Vital and Health Statistics

HIPAA amends the Public Health Service Act to increase the membership of the NCVHS from 16 to 18 members and requires the Committee to assist and advise the Secretary on issues related to statistical problems bearing on health and health services that are of national and international interest. HIPAA required the NCVHS to report to Congress by August 1997 on the implementation of the standards and requirements provided by the law. The NCVHA submitted this report in July 1997 (available on the Internet at [http://aspe.os.dhhs.gov/ncvhs/reptrecs/htm]). The NCVHS is also required to study the issues related to the adoption of uniform data standards for patient medical record information and the electronic exchange of this information, and report to Congress 4 years after the date of HIPAA's enactment (August 2000).

HHS Recommendations with Respect to Privacy of Certain Health Information

HIPAA required HHS to submit by August 1997, a report with recommendations on federal standards for protecting the privacy of individually identifiable health information to the Senate Labor and Human Resources and Finance Committees and the House Ways and Means Committee. The recommendations for privacy standards were required to address the privacy rights of individuals, procedures to exercise those rights, and uses and disclosure of the information that should be authorized or required under the law. The law established a timetable requiring the Congress to enact legislation to address the privacy issue within 36 months of enactment (August 21, 1999). If the Congress fails to act by that date, the Secretary would then be required by the law to issue privacy protections through final regulation within 42 months of HIPAA enactment (February 21, 2000). These privacy regulations could be preempted by more stringent state law.

The Secretary of HHS submitted the Department's report to Congress on September 11, 1997, at a hearing before the Senate Committee on Labor and Human Resources. The recommendations include five key principles that the Secretary argues must form the foundation for legislation to guarantee the privacy of individually identifiable health information. These principles are:

- Limit, with few exceptions, the use of an individual's health care information to health purposes only;
- Require organizations that are entrusted with health information (including providers and payers, service organizations, organizations receiving information for specified purposes without patient authorization, organizations receiving information with a patient's authorization, and employers) to provide adequate security measures to protect that information from misuse or disclosure;
- Provide patients with new rights to control how their health information is used, such as the ability to get copies of records and propose corrections;
- Hold those who misuse personal health information accountable and provide redress for persons harmed by its misuse through criminal and civil penalties; and
- Balance privacy protections with public responsibility to support national priorities including public health, research, quality care, and reduction of fraud and abuse, including allowing law enforcement access to personal health information within existing law.

Under the HHS recommendations, "health care information" would be defined to include medical records held in any form. The recommendations apply to health care providers and payers, as well as to entities that receive information from providers and payers (vendors or clearinghouses that handle the information). The HHS report also recommended that the sale of patient lists by medical service organizations be made illegal. In addition, HHS recommends that individually identifiable health information should be available without the patient's consent to public health authorities for disease reporting, public health investigation, or intervention, and in certain cases of medical research. Health care information would be considered "identifiable" if there is a reasonable basis to believe that it can be used to identify an individual.

The report recommended that insurers or health care professionals be required to give patients a written explanation detailing who has access to their information; how that information was kept; how they could restrict or limit access to it; how they could authorize disclosure or revoke such authorization; and what their rights would be should an improper disclosure occur. The HHS report also recommended a process for patients to seek corrections or amendments to their health information.

The report recommended that existing confidentiality laws at both state and federal levels that provide more protection remain in force and not be superseded by any new federal legislation. The recommendation concluded that a new federal privacy law should provide a basic level of protection, or "floor" of protection, without preempting more stringent existing laws. Critics of this recommendation argue that there needs to be federal standardization of privacy law because of the lack of uniformity among state laws, and without preemption individuals in states with weak or no privacy protections in place are disadvantaged. Opponents of preemption argue that stricter laws in some states could be lost with a uniform federal law, and therefore state laws should be left in place.

The HHS report also recommended that current state laws that permit disclosure to law enforcement officials for legitimate law enforcement purposes not be changed or limited by federal privacy law. This would include disclosure of medical information, without patient consent, to law enforcement officials for purposes required by state law, such as reporting gunshot wound victims, identification or location of an injured fugitive, or for other "legitimate" law enforcement purposes. This recommendation has been particularly contentious among privacy advocates, who have asserted that law enforcement officials should be required to obtain a judicial warrant or subpoena to gain access to medical records.

The HHS report recommended that individuals or organizations should be subject to criminal felony penalties (including fines and imprisonment) if they knowingly obtain or use health care information without authorization. The penalties would be higher when violations are for monetary gain. Civil monetary penalties would apply when there is a demonstrated pattern or practice of authorized disclosure. Persons whose privacy rights were violated would be able to sue for damages and equitable relief and could obtain attorney's fees and punitive damages if the violation was done knowingly.

While the HHS recommendations were generally regarded as a step in the right direction for establishing minimum federal protections for individually identifiable health information, critics argued that serious concerns remained unresolved.

Issues

Unique Health Identifier for Individuals

According to HHS, the unique identifier for individuals is an essential component of the administrative simplification provisions enacted in HIPAA.[7] HHS contends that the ability to identify individuals in the health system would have benefits, including improved quality of care and reduced administrative costs and that unique individual health information is also essential in the delivery of health care. Currently, many types of health care organizations and insurance companies, integrated delivery systems, health plans, managed care organizations, public programs, clinics, hospitals, physicians, and pharmacies routinely assign individuals identifiers for use within their systems. On the other hand, concerns are emerging about the potential uses and abuses of a unique health identifier for individuals.

The HIPAA law requires the Secretary, in consultation with the NCVHS, to adopt unique identifies for individuals, health care providers, health plans, and employers. The law requires that standards for transactions, the unique health identifier for individuals being one of those, be proposed by February 21, 1998. The law also requires the Secretary to establish specific

[7] For more information, see HHS White paper available via the Internet at [http://aspe.os.dhhs.gov/admnsimp/nprm /noiwp1.htm].

purposes for which a unique health identifier can be used. The development of a standard unique identifier for individuals required under HIPAA has sparked privacy and confidentiality concerns.

The most obvious advantage of a unique individual identifier is that it might contribute to simplification of the health system and potentially reduced costs for institutions and reimbursement systems. Individual identifiers could assist researchers in conducting longitudinal studies, as well as facilitate the linkage of valuable health data about a patient that might be useful in providing improved health care delivery. At the same time, individual identifiers raise serious privacy concerns. Opponents of using an individual identifier argue that, depending on which number were selected as the individual identifier, the use of such a number could increase the ease of linking medical records with other records about an individual, such as financial data or employment information. Some raise the concern that individual identifiers could facilitate access to personal information by unscrupulous employers or insurers who could then use that information to discriminate in hiring individuals with serious or costly health problems, or in some way harm the interests of the individual. Some providers have even argued that concerns about the vulnerability of individually identifiable information may keep some individuals from fully disclosing their health problems to their health care providers.

Some privacy advocates believes that standardized patient identifies should not be employed under any circumstances. Others maintain that, if any identifiers are deemed valuable, they need to be accompanied by strict policy guidance on appropriate use, allowable linkages among records, adequate auditing capability, and appropriate sanctions for misuse.

While there has been considerable consensus on most of the standards required by HIPAA, HHS acknowledges that opinion on the unique identifier for individuals is deeply divided. In an attempt to address the controversy surrounding the use of an individual identifier, HHS has departed from the customary rulemaking process and is holding a series of regional hearings to examine the privacy concerns. The first of these hearings was held in Chicago on July 20-21, 1998. After the remaining hearings are completed and the public comments are assimilated, HHS plans to issue a proposed rule followed by a public comment period. Once HHS considers and responds to comments, it will then publish a final rule to implement a unique health identifier for individuals. The Congress then has 60 days to consider the final rule, and either let it go into effect or disapprove it.

The first regional hearing in Chicago sparked such controversy that on July 31, 1998, the Administration announced its intention to delay the implementation of a unique health identifier for individuals until privacy legislation is enacted.[8] The delay would give officials more time to examine the impact of a unique health identifier.

In response to the concerns about the unique patient identifier, two bills were introduced in the 105th Congress to repeal the requirement for HHS to adopt a standard unique patient identifier under HIPAA. On July 22, 1998, Representative Barr introduced H.R. 4312, the *Medical Privacy Protection Act of 1998*. H.R. 4312 would have repealed section 1173(b) of the Social Security Act, which requires the Secretary to adopt standards for unique identifiers for individuals, employers, health plans, and health care providers. The bill would also have prohibited federal agencies from issuing, using, or establishing a national medical

[8] Brinkley, Joel. Gore Outlines Privacy Measures, but Their Impact is Small. *The New York Times,* August 1, 1998. [http://www.nytimes.com/library/tech/98/08/biztech/articles/01health-numbers-side.html]

identification card, or directing a state to issue or modify an identification card or document in order to satisfy any federal requirement. On July 24, 1998, a similar bill, S. 2342, the *Patient Privacy Rights Act of 1998,* was introduced by Senator Leahy. These bills died in committee without hearings. Th Omnibus Consolidated and Emergency Supplemental Appropriations for FY1999, H.R. 4328 (P.L. 105-277), provided that no funds be used to adopt a final standard providing for a unique health identifier for an individual until legislation is enacted specifically approving the standard.

Privacy Legislation in the 105th Congress

The privacy and confidentiality of health information is an important public policy concern. At the federal level, although health information is protected under several different laws, there is no comprehensive federal medical privacy law. State laws generally define the types of health information considered confidential and the circumstances under which health information can be disclosed. However, existing laws provide a patchwork of protections that are often limited in scope.

Many in Congress have long been concerned with the need to protect the confidentiality and privacy of health information, and privacy legislation has been introduced for a number of years. However, the requirements of the administrative simplification provisions of HIPAA provide greater incentive to consider protections for individually identifiable information. If the Congress fails to enact privacy legislation by August 1999, the Secretary must promulgate such protections through the regulatory process by February 2000.

Privacy protections for individually identifiable health information is at the center of the implementation of the HIPAA law on administrative simplification. While HIPAA requires that entities receiving health information establish security standards that take "real and reasonable" steps to safeguard that information, federal privacy legislation is been by many as necessary to set a uniform, basic level of protections for health information. While there is broad agreement on the underlying principles of privacy from most of the health care industry, there was no consensus reached on many significant aspects of the privacy bills introduced in the 105th Congress.[9] Six bills were introduced to address medical records privacy in the 105th Congress. In addition, 10 other bills were introduced specifically on protecting the privacy of genetic information.[10]

The six bills that were introduced on the general topic of medical records privacy are H.R. 52 (Condit), H.R. 1815 (McDermott), H.R. 3900 (Shays), S. 1368 (Leahy), S. 1921 (Jeffords), and S. 2609 (Bennett). Generally, these bills would have placed restrictions on use and disclosure of personally-identifiable health information, established security and auditing capabilities for records systems, ensured patient access to their records, provided the right to seek corrections, required entities to provide notices of their privacy practices, and established penalties for abuse of privacy rights. The bills varied on how privacy protections would be assured, in what way federal law would have preempted state laws, to what degree use of informed consent or federal statutes would have served as the basis for allowable disclosures,

---

[9] For a more complete discussion of the legislation, see CRS Issue Brief 98002, *Medical Records Confidentiality,* by Irene-Coleman, Coordinator.

[10] For more information on genetic discrimination, see CRS Report 97-873, *Genetic Discrimination Legislation in the 105th Congress: A Bill Comparison,* by Irene Stith-Coleman and Angela Choy.

and what specific safeguards would have been implemented to protect individuals when non-consensual disclosures would be permitted. A number of hearings were held on these proposals, however, none of the bills were enacted in the 105th Congress.

Privacy provisions for health information were also included in much broader legislation designed to regulate health insurance provided through managed care plans, as discussed above.[11] H.R. 3605 and S. 1890/S. 1891, the *Patients' Bill of Rights Act of 1998,* H.R. 4250, the *Patient Protection Act of 1998,* as passed by the House on July 24, 1998, and S. 2330, the *Patient's Bill of Rights Act,* introduced on July 17, 1998, were some of the bills which included provisions designed to protect the confidentiality of health information. All of the bills would have required health insurance plans to allow individuals to inspect and copy protected health information, and H.R. 4250 and S. 2330 would also have allowed patients to amend their protected health information. The bills would have required health care providers and other entities (including law enforcement officials as in S. 2330) to post or provide a notice of confidentiality practices, and required insurers to establish safeguards to protect the privacy of individually identifiable information. H.R. 4250 would have allowed any person who maintains protected health information to disclose it to a health care provider or a health plan in order for a provider or plan to conduct health care operations, but would have prohibited a provider or plan from selling or bartering protected health information as a part of conducting health care operations. Only H.R. 4250 would have explicitly required federal preemption of certain state laws related to protected health information. All of the bills would have imposed civil penalties for failure to comply with the confidentiality provisions of the bills. H.R. 4250 was passed by the House on July 24, 1998, however, the bill was not considered in the Senate even though the bill was placed on the Senate calendar.

There is general consensus among the health care industry that a federal statute that provides baseline medical records privacy protection is necessary and would generally improve safeguards for health information that currently are provided through the existing patchwork of state and federal laws. There also is strong support for a legislative solution to this issue, rather than relying on federal regulations to protect health privacy rights. Yet there is little agreement on many of the specific privacy provisions of the bills that were introduced during the 105th Congress.

The most frequently raised objections to the privacy legislation introduced in the 105th Congress tended to include the following three major legal issues: patient rights to access and amend medical records, limits on law enforcement access, and preemption of existing state laws. Patient rights advocates argued that patients should be informed about information maintained about them, be allowed to amend or supplement their records, and give their consent about disclosures of their information. Provider groups, while recognizing the need to protect individual privacy rights. Argued that the right to see and amend medical records, as well as informed consent requirements for disclosure, would make their compliance burdensome. Some states currently have laws that protect a patient's right to informed consent and limit allowable disclosures without patient consent. In some states disclosure limits on patient information are only provided for certain medical conditions or illnesses,

[11] For a side-by side comparison of the provisions of these bills, see CRS Report 98-643, *Side-by-Side Comparison of Selected Patient Protection Bills: H.R. 4250, H.R. 3605, S. 1890-S. 1891, and S. 2330,* by Jason Lee, Coordinator.

such as AIDS or mental health. However, in many states there are no laws protecting health information disclosures.

The second prominent issue in the debate relates to the need to balance patient control over disclosures of health information with the need for appropriate exemptions from informed patient consent, such as instances where law enforcement officials would need to have access to patient records for evidence of illegal activity. Privacy advocates argue that law enforcement access should not be expanded to allow wider or unlimited access to patient information. Law enforcement officials argue that restricting access to medical records hampers their ability to conduct investigations and collect evidence for criminal prosecutions. In some states law enforcement officials are required to obtain search warrants to have access to medical records, while in most states there are no laws limiting disclosures of health information.

A third contentious issue in the privacy debate is about overriding existing state laws, or preemption. Industry advocates argue that having to comply with varying requirements for health information and medical records in different states is burdensome, and a federal law is needed to standardize these requirements by preempting state law. Privacy advocates argue that in some states existing laws provide greater protections for individually identifiable health information and should not be superseded by federal law. While most health industry advocates agree that a federal law is needed to provide a standard or "floor" of protection, there is no consensus about whether or not federal law should preempt existing state privacy laws.

Conclusion

HIPAA's requirements for administrative simplification were generally welcomed by the health industry after years of failing to agree on standards that would achieve uniformity in financial and administrative transactions. Among the participants in the health industry there has largely been agreement on the standards and requirements being implemented by HIPAA. However, two extremely contentions issues have surfaced and are inextricably linked together in a way that may slow the implementation of the law: the unique individual identifier and the need for federal privacy protections in a standardized and integrated health industry. If legislation to eliminate the HIPAA requirement for a unique individual identifier (as well as the employer, health plan and provider identifiers) is enacted, it may prove difficult to achieve the administrative simplification desired by some. Moreover, the privacy debate has ensured for years with little consensus on the best approach for federal legislation. If the implementation of the unique individual health identifier is delayed until federal privacy protections are in place, then the full implementation of HIPAA's administrative simplification provisions may also be delayed. Therefore, enacting privacy protections for health information may be a high priority in the 106th Congress.

Table 1. Important Dates for Administrative Simplification Provisions

Description of activity	Statutory requirement	Actual implementation date
DHHS Secretary's Recommendations for Privacy Legislation delivered to Congress.	August 21, 1997	September 11, 1997
Four Notices of Proposed Rule Making (NPRMs) have been published in the Federal Register. The NPRMs propose standards for:	February 21, 1998	-
1. National Provides Identifier	-	May 7, 1998
2. Administrative and Financial Transaction and Code Sets	-	May 7, 1998
3. Identifier for Employers	-	June 6, 1998
4. Security Standards to Protect Health Care Information	-	August 12, 1998
NPRM for identifier for health plans	February 21, 1998	Delayed
Adoption of standards for electronic transactions. Final rules will follow publication of the NPRMs, including analysis of and responses to comments. Effective date for health information standards for most health plans will be 24 months after publication of final rules in the Federal Register (36 months for small health plans)	August 21, 1998	Delayed
Hearings on the individual identifier are held by the National Committee on Vital and Health Statistics.	None	July 20-21, 1998, Chicago, IL
Adoption of standards for claims attachments are required.	February 21, 1999	-
Deadline for congressional action on privacy legislation	August 21, 1999	-
If Congress fails to enact privacy protections, deadline for Secretary to issue privacy protection through regulation.	February 21, 2000	-
NCVHS is required to report to Congress on issues related to the adoption of uniform data standards and electronic exchange of health information.	August 21, 2000	-

Chapter 3

HEALTH INSURANCE: EXPLAINING DIFFERENCES IN COUNTS OF THE UNINSURED

Loftin Graham and Madeleine Smith

INTRODUCTION

A central issue in debates about health care reform in the United States has been what to do about the increasing number of the Nation's citizens who are without health insurance. This chapter explains the differences in the more commonly referred to estimates of the uninsured, based on three main surveys: the Survey of Income and Program Participation (SIPP), the National Medical Expenditure Survey (NMES), and the march version of the Current Population Survey (CPS).

Differences in the estimates of the number who are uninsured exist for several reasons:

- sources quote different types of estimates (point-in-time, yearly, and dynamic estimates);
- sources get their estimates from different surveys; and
- sources have different ways of dealing with potential survey inconsistencies.

The most significant differences in estimates of the number of uninsured occur between analysts who believe that the CPS-based estimates represent yearly counts of the number uninsured and analysts who believe that CPS-based estimates represent point-in-time counts. Based on comparisons of CPS estimates with those from SIPP and NMES, it appears that CPS estimates before 1995 more closely reflect point-in-time counts of the number uninsured. Analysis of the March 1995 CPS, which includes a question regarding insurance coverage during the last week, as well as question about coverage during the prior year, should shed light on the time frame issue.

Other variations in estimates of the number uninsured result from different interpretations of CPS responses. Two major differences in interpretation concern assignment of private health insurance status to children and Medicaid coverage. The Employee Benefit Research Institute (EBRI) employs a strict definition of insurance, so the number of uninsured children it reports (11.1 million in 1993) is greater than that reported by the Urban Institute (8.7 million) or Census Bureau (9.5 million). The Urban Institute is more restrictive than the Census Bureau in assigning private health insurance coverage to children, but makes corrections for perceived underreporting of Medicaid coverage, and assigns Medicaid coverage to 4 million children who did not report coverage. As a result, EBRI's estimate of the number uninsured is greater than both the Urban Institute's and the Census Bureau's estimates, and the Census Bureau's estimate is greater than Urban Institute's. Recent changes to the March CPS may mitigate the perceived need for these adjustments, and eliminate differences in estimates of the number who are uninsured prepared by different organizations.

QUANTIFYING THE UNINSURED: TYPES OF ESTIMATES

There are several ways to quantify uninsurance. Some estimates describe uninsurance in terms of the number of people who are uninsured at any given point-in-time during the year. Other estimates describe the number of people who are without insurance for the entire year (not just at any one point-in-time during that year). Still other estimates quantify uninsurance by describing the dynamics of health insurance coverage, usually by quoting the lengths of uninsured spells, or periods without coverage.

Different sources for estimates of the uninsured often use different methods of quantifying uninsurance. An important part of understanding the differences in the numbers is understanding what the estimates represent.

GETTING THE ESTIMATES: SURVEY DIFFERENCES

Estimates used in describing the uninsured often come from different surveys. Not only do different surveys generally produce slightly different estimates due to sampling error, but they often use different methods of measuring the uninsured. There are three main surveys that are used to estimate the number of uninsured in the U.S.: the Survey of Income and Program Participation (SIPP), the National Medical Expenditure Survey (NMES), and the March version of the Current Population Survey (CPS). Table 1 summarizes the main differences between these three surveys and the estimates they are used to produce.

Table 1. Characteristics of Major Sources for Estimates of the Uninsured

Information source	Type of survey	Type of estimate
CPS	Single sample	Yearly
SIPP	Multiple samples (longitudinal)	Yearly and point-in-time
NMES	Multiple samples (longitudinal)	Yearly and point-in-time

Note: Point-in-time estimates refer to the number of people uninsured at the point-in-time when the survey was administered. Yearly estimates refer to the number of people uninsured throughout the entire year.

SIPP and NMES

SIPP and NMES both produce longitudinal data sets; they survey the same respondents multiple times. This allows analysts to track health insurance coverage over time and enables them to produce estimates that discriminate between the portion of the population that is chronically uninsured (i.e. without health insurance for the whole year) and the portion that is only temporarily uninsured. SIPP and NMES can be used to describe the dynamics of health insurance in the Nation, by producing estimates that reflect the extent to which people experience lapses of coverage during the year. Table 2 shows an example of such estimates.

Table 2. Percent of Population with Health Insurance: Length of Coverage Periods (SIPP Estimates)

Length of coverage	1991	1992
Covered for entire year	79.4%	79.7%
Covered for part of year (not entire year)	13.6%	13.0
1 to 4 months	4.1	4.2
5 to 8 months	5.2	4.9
9 to 11 months	4.3	4.0
Never covered	7.0	7.9

Source: Bennefield, Robert L. *Dynamics of Economic Well-Being: Health Insurance, 1991 to 1993;* Census Bureau. Current Population Reports, P70-43.

The NMES was last conducted in 1987. Each family was interviewed four times over a 16-month period. The survey included three major components: a household survey (noninstitutionalized population), a survey of the institutionalized population (those in nursing homes and facilities for the mentally retarded), and a survey of American Indians and Alaska Natives. The second and third components of this survey are unique to NMES. The three components together gathered information on over 50,000 individuals about health status, use of health services, insurance coverage, health care expenditures and other characteristics. Since estimates from this survey are not current, they are not included in this chapter.

The most recent health insurance report from SIPP covers a 32-month period beginning in early 1991 and ending in the middle of 1993. This survey involved a sample of about 20,000 households which were interviewed a total of eight or nine times at intervals of 4 months. Information is collected on health insurance for each month of the period. One can measure the length of each individual's health insurance coverage over the entire 32-month period because the survey captures lapses in coverage. As the most recent available survey involved only half of 1993, there are no estimates for that year. Table 2 shows SIPP estimates for 1991 and 1992.

Current Population Survey

The March CPS is different from SIPP and NMES in that it surveys respondents only once each year on health insurance status.[1] The CPS is also the most commonly reported source for numbers on the uninsured. The Census Bureau, the Congressional Budget Office (CBO), the Congressional Research Service (CRS), the Employee Benefits Research Institute (EBRI), and the Urban Institute use the CPS to produce estimates of the uninsured. The March CPS is a survey of about 60,000 different households (150,000 individuals[2]) across the country. Respondents answer questions about household composition and income, as well as health insurance status.

CPS respondents are asked whether they had employment-based or privately purchased health insurance at any time during the previous year. They are also asked if they had any kind of public health care (Medicaid, Medicare, or military) during the previous year. If respondents answer no to these questions, they are considered uninsured - something that, due to the specific wording of the survey questions, should technically apply to the whole year.[3] Note that the CPS does not ask respondents directly if they were uninsured. While CPS estimates have the advantage of a large sample size, some analysts believe they also have some shortcomings described below, including:

- time-period response inconsistency;
- conflicting responses about child coverage; and
- potential under reporting of Medicaid coverage.
- potential under-reporting of Medicaid coverage.

Time-Period Response Inconsistency

Significant changes were made to the health insurance questions in the March 1995 CPS that were meant to correct some of problems in interpretation of survey responses.[4] One problem that has plagued analysts of CPS data has been uncertainty about the time periods to which survey responses correspond. CPS survey questions are intended to measure yearly health insurance characteristics, and the specific wording of the survey questions seems to elicit this kind of response; however, due to the large differences in yearly uninsured estimates produced by the CPS and those produced by other surveys, some analysts believe that CPS estimates come closer to reflecting health insurance characteristics of survey respondents *at the time of the interview* rather than health insurance characteristics for the whole year. For example, someone that had employment-based coverage for several months of the year but who did not have it at the time of the survey might respond *no* to the question of whether they had employment-based health insurance at any time during the previous year.

---

[1] Each CPS sample includes eight rotation groups, or subsamples. Each rotation group is included in the survey for 4 months, excluded for the next 8 months, and returned to the sample for 4 additional months, after which it is retired. Because of this rotation patterns, each March supplement survey, which covers health insurance questions, includes a 50% overlap in households with the preceding year's March supplement survey.

[2] The CPS gathers information on the nonistitutionalized population of the United States.

[3] Controversy over the time frame issue is discussed below.

[4] These new data are not yet available from the census Bureau.

Most experts concede that CPS survey responses cannot be taken at face value. Uncertainty about time frame has made it difficult for those using the CPS to give a definite answer about what time interval the aggregate responses can be inferred to represent - whether the whole year or only the point-in-time when the survey is conducted. The most accurate description of these estimates might be that they are neither.[5] Comparison with the SIPP estimates for the number of people without insurance for the whole year suggests that CPS estimates may be poor indicators of the number of chronically uninsured people in the country (table 3). Based on the comparison of CPS estimates and SIPP point-in-time estimates, one analyst has even suggested that CPS estimates are closer to point-in-time estimates.[6]

Table 3. Comparison of CPS and SIPP Estimates for Selected Health Insurance Characteristics (1992)

Health Insurance Status	CPS	SIPP (Longitudinal)	SIPP (Point-in-time)*
Percent insured	85.3%	92.8%	85.6%
Percent with private insurance	71.1	82.8%	72.7
Percent with Medicaid	11.2	12.2	10.0
Percent uninsured	14.7	7.2	14.5

* Fourth quarter of the year.
Note: Point-in-time estimates refer to the number of people uninsured at the point-in-time when the survey was administered. Longitudinal estimates refer to the number of people uninsured throughout the entire year.

This potential problem with the CPS affects the estimates of all the organizations that use CPS data to produce health insurance information. To shed light on the time frame question, the March 1995 CPS included a question about the respondent's health insurance status during the past week, but data are not currently available to analyze the time frame question.

Treatment of other Inconsistencies in the CPS

Some other perceived inconsistencies in the CPS lend themselves more easily to correction. Most of the variation in the estimates produced by differing organizations using CPS data can be explained by how each interprets survey responses.

Responses Concerning Child Coverage

One of the most significant inconsistencies in the CPS involves respondents' reports on private health insurance for children. Prior to March 1995, the CPS had two sets of questions related to health insurance for children (see tables 4a and 4b).[7] In 1993, 5.2 million of the

[5] Urban Institute analysts believe the evidence suggests that there is at best a mix of responses among respondents to the CPS: some are reporting their current coverage while others are reporting coverage during the previous year, as requested. (Washington, Colin, et al, *State-Level Databook on Health Care Access and Financing,* 1994. p. 246.)

[6] Swartz, Katharine, Interpreting the Estimates from Four National Surveys of the Number of People without Health Insurance. *Journal of Economic and Social Measurement,* v. 14, 1986. P. 233-242.

[7] Several changes were made to the March 1988 CPS. First, the survey began to ask about employment-based coverage for all persons over 14, when before only workers were asked about such coverage. Second, a second set of questions was added regarding children's coverage. This second set was designed to capture information

58.1 million children under age 15 had conflicting responses on one or more health insurance-related survey questions.[8] One set of responses indicated that the child was insured when the other indicated that he or she was not. The Census Bureau, EBRI, and the Urban Institute deal with these response inconsistencies differently.[9] The Census Bureau is the most generous in assigning health insurance to children with inconsistent responses, and assigns an insured status to all children with inconsistent responses. EBRI and the Urban Institute are more restrictive in assigning private coverage, and EBRI is more restrictive than the Urban Institute.

Table 4a. CPS Health Insurance Questions - Part I

74. There are several government programs which provide medical care or help pay medical bills.

During [previous year] was anyone in this household covered by:

74A. Medicare (for the disabled and elderly)?
74B. [If yes…] Who was that? (Anyone else?)
74C. Medicaid (for the needy?)
74D. [If yes…] Who was that? (Anyone else?)
74E. CHAMPUS. VA, or military health care?
74F. [If yes…] Who was that? (Anyone else?)

75A. Other than government sponsored policies, health Insurance can be obtained privately or through a current or former employer or union. Was anyone in this household covered by health insurance of this type at any time during [previous year]?

[If yes….]
75B. Who was that? (Anyone else?)
[For each person with such coverage….]
75C. Was….'s health insurance coverage from a plan in ….'s own name?
75D. Was this health insurance plan offered through …'s current or former employer or union?
75E. Did….'s employer or union pay for all, part, or some of the cost of this plan?
75F. What other previous were covered by this health insurance policy? (Mark all that apply)
Spouse
Child(ren) in the household
Child(ren) not in the household
Other
No one

Source: Winterbottom, Colin, et al. State-Level Databook on Health Care Access and Financing, 1994 p. 241-242.

Table 4B. CPSS Health Insurance Questions - Part II

80. During [previous year], how many of the children under age 15 in this household were covered by Medicare or Medicaid?
All
Some, but not all (indicate number)
None

81. During [previous year], how many children under age 15 in this household were covered by a health insurance plan (excluding Medicaid or Medicare)?

All
Some, but not all (indicate number)
None

81A. How many of these children were covered by the health insurance plan of someone not residing in this household?
All
Some, but not all (indicate number)
None

Source: Winterbottom, Colin, et al. State-Level Databook on Health Care Access and Financing, 1994 p. 241-242.

about coverage under Medicaid and private insurance provided by someone (e.g., a divorced parent) who lives outside the child's home.

8 *Sources of Health Insurance and Characteristics of the Uninsured: Analysis of the March 1994 Current Population Survey.* EBRI Special Report SR-28, p. 21.

9 CBO and CRS follow Census procedures. The General Accounting Office relies on estimates produced by other organizations.

If responses to the first set of survey questions (see table 4a) indicate that the child is covered by private insurance through someone in the household and responses to the second set of questions indicate no coverage, Urban Institute considers the child covered. For the child to be considered privately insured, EBRI adds the requirement that the head of the household also have private coverage. If the first set of questions indicates no coverage for the child, and the second set indicates that the child is covered by someone outside the household (see table 4b, question 81A), the Urban Institute considers the child covered. EBRI again adds a second requirement: the survey must also indicate that the child is receiving some kind of financial assistance from someone outside the household (through child support or alimony, for example). If responses to the second set of questions indicate that the child is covered by someone in the households and the first set of questions does not indicate coverage, the Urban Institute considers the child covered provided that survey responses indicate that any adult in the child's health insurance unit is insured.[10] Again, EBRI required that the head of household have private health insurance coverage to consider the child covered. Table 5 provides a simple layout of EBRI and Urban Institute requirements for assigning health insurance coverage to children with inconsistent responses.

Responses Concerning Medicaid Coverage

CPS responses about Medicaid any undercount coverage. The number of people participating in the Medicaid program according to the program's administrative data systems is significantly higher than the number of people reporting Medicaid coverage on the CPS. In order to eliminate this perceived undercount in survey responses, the Urban Institute uses a computer simulation program to assign additional Medicaid coverage. This program determines which respondents would be eligible for Medicaid coverage based on state eligibility requirements and then, using computational procedures, assigns Medicaid coverage to some of those that did not report Medicaid on the CPS. This continues until the number of people covered by Medicaid on the CPS matches the number that were reportedly enrolled during the year according to the administrative data. This procedure accounts for much of the difference between the number covered by Medicaid as reported by the Urban Institute and the other two CPS users (Census and EBRI), and tends to produce lower uninsured counts because some of those that were previously uninsured are signed Medicaid coverage (table 6).

[10] This includes both private health insurance and CHAMPUS (Civilian Health and Medical Program of the Uniformed Services, a health insurance program for actives duty military personnel).

Table 5. How Different Organizations Interpret CPS Inconsistent Responses to Questions About Children's Health Insurance Coverage

Survey responses	Source of coverage	Census interpretation	Urban Institute interpretation	EBRI Interpretation
Child covered according to first set of questions, not covered according to second set	Inside household	Covered	Covered	Covered if head of household has private health insurance
Child covered according to second set of questions, not covered according to first set	Inside household	Covered	Covered only if any adult in the child's insurance unit has private coverage	Covered if head of household has private health insurance
	Outside household	Covered	Covered	Covered if child receives some other kind of financial assistance from outside the home (e.g., child support or alimony)

Source: Winterbottom, Colin, et al. *State-Level Databook on Health Care Access and Financing*, 1994; EBRI Special Report SR-28; *Sources of Health Insurance and Characteristics of the Uninsured: Analysis of the March 1994 Current Population Survey*.

Table 6. 1993 CPS Estimates by Different Organizations (in millions)

	Uninsured children	Non-aged uninsured	Children on Medicaid	Non-aged on Medicaid	Total non-aged population
Urban Institute	8.7	35.5	20.2	33.5	225.8*
Census Bureau	9.6	39.4	16.5	29	228.5
EBRI	11.1	40.9	16.6	28.9	226.2*

* Total excludes families with an active military member. Differences in estimates due to organizations' interpretations.

Sources: Census Bureau information from unpublished Current Population Survey, March 1994; EBRI information: *Sources of Health Insurance and Characteristics of the Uninsured: Analysis of the March 1994 Current Population Survey,* EBRI Special Report SR-28, Issue Brief No. 158. p. 5, 7; Urban Institute information provided by Colin Winterbottom at the Institute.

CONCLUSION

Differences in the estimates of the number who are uninsured exists for several reasons:

- sources quote different types of estimates (point-in-time, yearly, and dynamic estimates);
- sources get their estimates from different surveys; and
- sources have different ways of dealing with potential survey inconsistencies.

The most significant differences in estimates of the number of uninsured occur between analysts who believe that the CPS-based estimates represent yearly counts of the number uninsured and analysts who believe that CPS-based estimates represent point-in-time counts. Based on comparisons of CPS estimates with those from SIPP and NMES, it appears that CPS estimates more closely reflect point-in-time counts of the number uninsured. Recent analysis of the number uninsured reported in the literature, and estimates prepared by the Congressional Budget Office, interpret CPS results as point-in-time estimates of the number of uninsured.[11] Analysis of the March 1995 CPS, which includes a question regarding insurance coverage during the last week as well as questions about coverage during the prior year, should shed light on the time frame issue.

Other differences in estimates of the number uninsured result from different interpretations of CPS responses. In assigning health insurance status to children, EBRI employs a strict definition of insurance, so the number of uninsured children it reports (11.1 million in 1993) is greater than that reported by the Urban Institute (8.7 million) or Census Bureau (9.5 million). The difference between the EBRI estimate of uninsured children and the Census Bureau's estimate (1.6 million) carries over directly to their overall estimates of the total number uninsured (see table 6). The Urban Institute is more restrictive than the Census Bureau in assigning health insurance coverage to children with inconsistent responses, and if it were not for their treatment of perceived Medicaid underreporting, the Urban Institute's estimate would fall somewhere between the Census Bureau's estimate and EBRI's. However, by assigning Medicaid coverage to more than 4 million children who did not report it, in an effort to correct for survey underreporting, the Urban Institute's estimate of the uninsured dropped well below estimates from the Census Bureau and EBRI.[12] Changes to the March 1995 CPS may mitigate the need for these adjustments and eliminate differences in estimates of the number who are uninsured prepared by different organizations.

[11] Long, Stephen H., and M. Susan Marquis. The Uninsured 'Access Gap' and the Cost of Universal Coverage. *Health Affairs,* v. II, spring, 1994. P. 211-220; Swartz, Katherine, Dynamics of People Without Health Insurance. *Journal of the American Medical Association,* v. 271, 1994. p. 64-66.

[12] Compare differences in the number of uninsured children and children with Medicaid for Urban Institute and the other two organizations in table 6.

Chapter 4

TAX BENEFITS FOR HEALTH INSURANCE: CURRENT LEGISLATION

Bob Lyke and Christopher Sroka

INTRODUCTION

The 108th Congress is considering a number of new or expanded tax benefits for health insurance. Individual tax credits have been proposed to help people purchase and maintain coverage, as have tax credits for employers. Legislative activity has recently occurred on measures to expand insurance options qualifying for the existing tax credit for trade-displaced workers (H.R. 1528) and to authorize expanded tax-advantaged health savings accounts (H.R. 2596 and H.R. 1). Proponents of these measures generally argue that new tax benefits are needed to reduce the number of uninsured and to address efficiency and equity problems; opponents claim they would primarily benefit higher income taxpayers and do little for most without coverage.

Current law contains significant tax benefits for health insurance. (1) Most important is the exclusion of employer-paid health insurance from the determination of income and employment taxes. Over 2/3 of the noninstitutionalized population under age 65 are insured through employment-based plans; on average, large employers pay about 80% of its cost, though some pay all and others none. The exclusion also applies to health insurance provided through cafeteria plans. (2) Self-employed taxpayers may deduct 100% of their health insurance payments, up from 70% in 2002. (3) Taxpayers who itemize deductions may deduct insurance payments to the extent they and other medical expenses exceed 7.5% of adjusted gross income. While not widely used, this deduction benefits some with employment-based insurance (for the employee share), some self-employed (the remaining 30% of their 2002 cost) and others who purchase individual market policies. (4) Some workers displaced by trade or receiving a pension paid by the Pension Benefit Guarantee Corporation can receive an advanceable, refundable tax credit to purchase certain types of insurance. (5) Coverage under Medicare and Medicaid is not considered taxable income. (6) With some exceptions, benefits received from private or public insurance are not taxable.

By lowering the after-tax cost of insurance, the tax benefits help extend coverage to more people; they also lead insured people to obtain more coverage than otherwise. The incentives influence how coverage is acquired: the uncapped exclusion for employer-paid insurance, which can benefit nearly all workers and is easy to administer, is partly responsible for the predominance of employment-based insurance in the United States. Employment-based insurance has both advantages and disadvantages for the typical worker. The tax benefits also increase the demand for health care by enabling insured people to obtain services at discounted prices. This is one reason health care prices have risen more rapidly than the general inflation rate. Moreover, since many people would likely obtain some insurance without the tax benefits, they can be an inefficient use of public dollars. They also raise questions of equity, largely because the tax savings they generate depend upon the taxpayer's marginal tax rate. When viewed as a form of personal consumption, giving tax incentives for health insurance provides more benefits to higher income families who may not need them. Comprehensive reforms (e.g., capping the employer exclusion or replacing it with deductions and credits) might address these concerns, though they could be difficult to implement and may cause inequities of their own.

MOST RECENT DEVELOPMENTS

On June 19, 2003, the House passed an amended version of H.R. 1528, the Taxpayer Protection and IRS Accountability Act of 2003. One provision would allow certain insurance to qualify for the current-law tax credit for trade-displaced workers if the eligible taxpayer elects to waive requirements for guaranteed issue and no preexisting condition exclusion, provided the taxpayer does not reside in a state with state-sponsored or arranged coverage qualifying for the credit. The waiver provision would apply through December 31, 2004.

On June 26, the House approved H.R. 2596, which would authorize two forms of tax-advantaged savings accounts (health savings accounts and health security savings accounts) and allow limited rollovers for flexible spending accounts; the legislation was then appended to H.R. 1, the Medicare prescription drug bill that the House passed earlier that day.

H.R. 1 would also make the Medicare medical savings account demonstration a permanent program and remove the current enrollment limits and deadlines. S. 1, the comparable bill passed by the Senate on June 27, would extend the enrollment deadline for the current demonstration by one year, through 2003.

BACKGROUND AND ANALYSIS
TAX BENEFITS IN CURRENT LAW

Current law provides significant tax benefits for health insurance. The tax subsidies — for the most part federal income tax exclusions and deductions — are widely available, though not everyone can take advantage of them. They reward some people more than others, raising questions of equity. They influence the amount and type of coverage that people obtain, which affects their ability to choose doctors and other providers. In addition, the tax benefits affect the distribution and cost of health care.

Overview of Current Provisions

This section summarizes the current tax treatment of the principal ways that people obtain health insurance. It describes general rules but does not discuss all limitations, qualifications, and exceptions. An outline of the tax provisions discussed in this section is provided in **Table 1**. To understand possible effects on tax liability, readers may want to refer to the Appendix for an outline of the federal income tax formula. (For example, exclusions are items that are omitted from gross income, while deductions are subtracted from gross income in order to arrive at taxable income.) Section number references are to the Internal Revenue Code of 1986 as amended.

Table 1. Summary of the Tax Treatment of Health Insurance

Plan type	Tax treatment for individual	Tax treatment for employer
Traditional employer-sponsored plan	— Premiums paid by employer are excluded for income and employment tax purposes — Insurance benefits used for health care are excluded from employee's gross income — Premiums paid by employee are deductible if (1) employee itemizes and (2) premiums plus other unreimbursed medical expenses exceed 7.5% of adjusted gross income (AGI). Payments are made through cafeteria plan ("premium conversion") are exempt from income and employment taxes	— Employer contributions deducted as a business expense, and they are not counted for employer's share of employment taxes
Individual market policies	— Premiums are deductible if (1) the individual itemizes and (2) premiums plus other unreimbursed medical expenses exceed 7.5% of AGI	— N/A
Policies purchased by self-employed individuals	— Individual can deduct 100% of premiums (up from 70% in 2002) in determining adjusted gross income; deduction does not have to exceed 7.5% of AGI	— Not exempt from employment taxes
Cafeteria plans	— Premiums and other health benefits are excluded for income and employment tax purposes	— Employer contributions deducted as a business expense, and they are not counted for employer's share of employment taxes
Flexible spending accounts	— All contributions excluded for income and employment tax purposes	— Employer contributions deducted as a business expense, and they are not counted for employer's share of employment taxes
Medical savings accounts	— Employer contributions excluded for income and employment tax purposes — Individual contributions deductible for income tax purposes — Only for self-employed individuals with high-deductible insurance or employees of a small business providing high deductible insurance	— Employer contributions deducted as a business expense, and they are not counted for employer's share of employment taxes
Military and veterans health care	— Benefits and coverage provided under military and veterans health care programs are not considered taxable income	— N/A
Medicare and Medicaid	— Benefits and coverage provided under the Medicare and Medicaid programs are not considered taxable income — Premiums paid for Medicare are deductible if (1) the individual itemizes and (2) premiums plus other unreimbursed medical expenses exceed 7.5% of AGI	— N/A

Employment-Based Plans

Health insurance paid by employers generally is excluded from employees' gross income in determining their income tax liability; it also is not considered for either the employee's or the employer's share of employment taxes (i.e., social security, Medicare, and unemployment taxes). (Sections 106 and 3121, respectively) The income and employment tax exclusions apply to both single and family coverage, which includes the employee's spouse and dependents. Premiums paid by employees generally are not deductible, though they may be counted towards the itemized medical expense deduction or subject to a premium conversion arrangement under a cafeteria plan (both of which are discussed below).

Over two-thirds of the noninstitutionalized population under age 65 is insured under an employment-based plan. On average, large employers pay about 80% of the cost for employment-based insurance, though some pay all and others pay none. Employers typically pay a smaller percentage for family than for single coverage.

Insurance benefits paid from employment-based plans are excluded from gross income if they are reimbursements for medical expenses or payments for permanent physical injuries. Benefits not meeting these tests are taxable in proportion to the share of the insurance costs paid by the employer that were excluded from gross income. (Sections 104 and 105) Benefits are also taxable to the extent taxpayers received a tax benefit from claiming a deduction for the expenses in a prior year (for example, if taxpayers claimed a medical expense deduction for expenditures in 2002 and then received an insurance reimbursement in 2003). In addition, benefits received by highly-compensated employees under discriminatory self-insured plans are partly taxable. A self-insured plan is one in which the employer assumes the risk for a health care plan and does not shift it to a third party.

Employers may deduct their insurance payments as a business expense. The deduction is not a tax benefit but a calculation necessary for the proper measurement of the net income that is subject to taxation. Revenue loss attributable to this deduction is not considered a tax expenditure.

The Joint Committee on Taxation (JCT) estimates the FY2003 federal revenue loss attributable to the exclusion for employer contributions for health insurance, medical care (including that provided through cafeteria plans and flexible spending accounts, described below) and long-term care insurance will be $75.1 billion. The estimate does not include the effect of the exclusion on employment taxes.

Medical Expense Deduction

Taxpayers who itemize their deductions may deduct unreimbursed medical expenses, but only the amount of such expenses that exceeds 7.5% of adjusted gross income (AGI). (Section 213) Medical expenses include health insurance premiums paid by the taxpayer, such as the employee's share of premiums in employment-based plans, premiums for individual private market policies, and part of the premiums paid by self-employed taxpayers. More generally, medical expenses include amounts paid for the "diagnosis, cure, mitigation, treatment, or prevention of disease, or for the purpose of affecting any structure or function of the body." They also include certain transportation and lodging expenditures, qualified long-term care service costs, and long-term care premiums that do not exceed certain amounts. Currently, the deduction is intended to help only those with catastrophic expenses.

The medical expense deduction is not widely used. For most taxpayers, the standard deduction is larger than the sum of itemized deductions; moreover, most do not have unreimbursed expenses that exceed the 7.5% AGI floor. In 1998, about 31% of all individual income tax returns had itemized deductions, and of these only about 15% (i.e., about 4.5% of all returns) claimed a medical expense deduction.

The JCT estimates the FY2003 revenue loss attributable to the medical expense deduction (including long-term care expenses) will be $6 billion.

Individual Private Market Policies

Payments for private market health insurance purchased by individuals are a deductible medical expense, provided the taxpayer itemizes deductions and applies the 7.5% AGI floor as just described. Premiums for the following insurance, however, are not deductible: policies for loss of life, limb, sight, etc.; policies that pay guaranteed amounts each week for a stated number of weeks for hospitalization; and the part of car insurance that provides medical coverage for all persons injured in or by the policyholder's car. Benefits paid under accident and health insurance policies purchased by individuals are excluded from gross income, even if they exceed medical expenses.

About 6% of the noninstitutionalized population under age 65 is insured through these private policies. Likely purchasers include early retirees, young adults, employees without access to employment-based insurance, and the self-employed.

Self-Employed Deduction

Self-employed taxpayers may deduct payments for health insurance in determining their AGI. (Section 162) Their insurance typically is an individual private market policy. The self-employed deduction, an "above-the-line" deduction, is not restricted to itemizers, as is the medical expense deduction. Following enactment of the Omnibus Consolidated and Emergency Supplemental Appropriations Act for Fiscal Year 1999 (P.L. 105-277), the deduction was 60% of insurance payments in 1999 through 2001, 70% in 2002, and 100% in 2003 and thereafter. The deduction cannot exceed the net profit and any other earned income from the business under which the plan is established, less deductions taken for certain retirement plans and for one-half the selfemployment tax. It is not available for any month in which the taxpayer or the taxpayer's spouse is eligible to participate in a subsidized employment-based health plan (that is, one in which the employer pays part of the cost). These restrictions prevent taxpayers with little net income from their business (which may not be uncommon in a new business, for example, or in a part-time business that grows out of a hobby) from deducting much if any of their insurance payments. However, the portion not deductible under these rules may be treated as an itemized medical expense deduction.

Self employed individuals include sole proprietors (single owners of unincorporated businesses), general partners, limited partners who receive guaranteed payments, and individuals who receive wages from S-corporations in which they are more than 2% shareholders. (S-corporation status may be elected by corporations that meet a number of Internal Revenue Code requirements. Among other things, they cannot have more than 75 shareholders or more than one class of stock. S-corporations are tax-reporting rather than tax-paying entities, in contrast to C-corporations that are subject to the corporate income tax.)

In 1998, about 3.4 million tax returns (about 2.7% of all returns) claimed the self-employed health insurance deduction. For FY2003, the JCT estimates the revenue loss attributable to the deduction (including the deduction for long-term care insurance) to be $2.4 billion.

Cafeteria Plans

Health benefits provided through a cafeteria plan are excludable for both income and employment tax purposes. A cafeteria plan is a written benefit plan under which employees may choose between receiving cash and certain nontaxable benefits such as health coverage or dependent care. (Cash here includes any taxable benefits.) Under an option known as a premium conversion plan, employees may elect to reduce their taxable wages in exchange for having their share of health insurance premiums paid on a pre-tax basis; the effect is the same as if employees could claim an above-the line deduction for their payments. Federal employees who participate in the Federal Employees Health Benefits Program (FEHBP) have been able to elect this option since October, 2000; however, the option is not available to federal retirees.

Nontaxable benefits provided through cafeteria plans are exempt from income and employment taxes under the Internal Revenue Code rules applicable to those benefits, such as employer-paid insurance. A separate statutory provision (Section 125) extends these exclusions to situations in which employees are given the option of receiving cash; were it not for this provision, the nontaxable benefit would be taxable since the employees had been in constructive receipt of the cash.

Flexible Spending Accounts

Benefits paid from flexible spending accounts (FSAs) are also excludable for income and employment tax purposes. FSAs and cafeteria plans are closely related, but not all cafeteria plans have FSAs and not all FSAs are part of cafeteria plans. FSAs funded through salary reductions are exempt from taxation through cafeteria plan provisions (since otherwise employees would be in constructive receipt of cash) while FSAs funded by nonelective employer contributions are exempt directly under provisions applying to employer-paid insurance.

Health care FSAs must exhibit some of the risk-shifting and risk-distribution characteristics of insurance. Among other things, participants must elect a specific benefit amount prior to the start of a plan year; this election cannot be revoked except for changes in family status. The full benefit amount (less any benefits paid) must be made available throughout the entire year, even if employees spread their contributions throughout the year. Any amount unused at the end of the year must be forfeited to the employer (thus, "use it or lose it"). FSAs cannot be used to purchase insurance; however, they can be combined with premium conversion plans under cafeteria arrangements to achieve the same tax effect.

In 1999, about 22% of private-sector firms could have a health care FSA, but actual participation was far less.

Medical Savings Accounts

Medical savings accounts (MSAs) are personal savings accounts for unreimbursed medical expenses. They are used to pay for health care not covered by insurance, including deductibles and copayments. Currently, a limited number of MSAs may be established by individuals who have qualifying high deductible insurance (and none other, with some exceptions) and who either are self-employed or are employees covered by a high deductible insurance plan established by their small employer (50 or fewer employees on average). The formal name of MSAs is now Archer MSAs.

Employer contributions to MSAs are excludable for both income and employment tax purposes, while individuals' contributions (allowed only if the employer does not contribute) are deductible for determining AGI. Contributions are limited to 65% of the insurance deductible for single coverage and 75% for family coverage. Account earnings are excludable as well, as are distributions used for unreimbursed medical expenses, with some exceptions. Non-qualified distributions are included in gross income and an additional 15% penalty is applied.

The original medical savings account legislation (the Health Insurance Portability and Accountability Act of 1996, P.L. 104-191), authorized a limited number of MSAs under a demonstration beginning in 1997. Eligibility was to be restricted after the *earlier* of (1) December 31, 2000, or (2) specified dates following a determination that the number of taxpayers with accounts exceeded certain thresholds (eventually, 750,000). Once eligibility was restricted under these tests, MSAs generally would have been limited to individuals who either were active participants (had contributions to their accounts) prior to the cut-off date or became active participants through a participating employer. The Community Renewal Tax Relief Act of 2000 (P.L. 106-554) included an extension of eligibility for new participants until December 31, 2002; it also changed the formal name to Archer MSAs for the retiring chairman of the House Ways and Means Committee. The Job Creation and Worker Assistance Act (P.L. 107-147) extended eligibility for new participants until December 31, 2003.

In October, 2002, the IRS estimated that there would be 78,913 MSA returns filed for tax year 2001; it also determined that 20,592 taxpayers who did not make contributions in 2001 established accounts in the first 6 months of 2002. These numbers are far less than the 750,000 statutory ceiling. (Not all MSAs are counted toward the ceiling; for example, accounts of taxpayers who previously were uninsured are not taken into consideration.) MSAs should be distinguished from Medicare+Choice MSAs, which are discussed below under the tax treatment of Medicare and Medicaid.

Tax Credit for Trade-Displaced Workers

On August 6, 2002, President Bush signed into law the Trade Act of 2002 (P.L. 107-210). The law allows workers displaced by trade to receive a tax credit for purchasing insurance. The amount of the credit is equal to 65% of the premiums paid by the worker for qualified health insurance. The credit is advanceable, meaning that workers can receive the credit when purchasing insurance rather than receiving it after filing their tax returns. The credit is also refundable; eligible workers can receive the credit even if they have zero tax liability for the year. To be eligible for the credit, a worker must be (1) a recipient of a trade readjustment allowance under the Trade Act of 1974; (2) an individual who is not eligible for a trade readjustment allowance because he or she has not exhausted all rights to unemployment insurance; (3) a displaced worker whose current job pays less than the job lost to trade and who is receiving a supplemental wage allowance; or (4) an individual who is over the age of 55 and is receiving a pension benefit from the Pension Benefit Guaranty Corporation (PBGC).

The tax credit for workers displaced by trade can be used for limited types of health insurance. The tax credit can be applied towards premiums paid to continue employer-sponsored health insurance under the Consolidated Omnibus Budget Reconciliation Act of 1985 (COBRA). The credit can also be used to purchase an individual health insurance policy (if the worker was covered by an individual policy at least 30 days prior to becoming unemployed) or to purchase a group policy offered through a spouse's employer. An eligible worker can use the credit to purchase various types of state-based insurance coverage, such as coverage through a state-sponsored high-risk pool, coverage through a health insurance program offered to state employees, and coverage through an arrangement between private entities and the state. State-based coverage must be guaranteed issue, cannot limit coverage due to pre-existing conditions, cannot charge higher premiums than those charged to individuals who do not receive the tax credit, and must offer the same benefits as those provided to individuals who do not receive the tax credit.

Some Members of Congress have stated that the law was not intended to allow states to enter into agreements with private insurers offering individual coverage. However, others argue that the intent of the law was to allow states to enter into agreements with private insurers, even those offering individual coverage.

The tax-credit for trade-displaced workers may serve as a model for a tax credit that is more generally available.

Military and Veterans Health Care

Coverage under military and veterans health care programs is not taxable income, nor are the benefits these programs provide. The tax exclusion (Section 134) applies as well to the Civilian Health and Medical Program of the Uniformed Services (CHAMPUS) and Tricare, which serve military dependents, retirees, and retiree dependents. In 1996, about 2.2% of the noninstitutionalized population under age 65 had military or veterans health care as their primary form of coverage. The FY2003 revenue loss attributable to CHAMPUS and Tricare is estimated to be $1.5 billion.

Medicare and Medicaid

Coverage under Medicare or Medicaid is not taxable income. Similarly, benefits paid from either program are not subject to taxation. Medicare covers over 38 million people, including 96% of those ages 65 and older. Medicaid covers over 41 million people. The JCT estimates the revenue loss attributable to the exclusion of Medicare benefits will be $27.1 billion in FY2002. Medicaid beneficiaries, who must meet certain categorical requirements (aged, blind, or disabled, or specified members of families with dependent children) are generally poor and unlikely to have tax liability.

The employment tax individuals pay for Medicare Part A is not a deductible medical expense. However, premiums paid by individuals who voluntarily enroll in Part A are deductible, provided the taxpayer itemizes deductions and applies the 7.5 % AGI floor as described above. (Medicare Part A is insurance for hospitalization, skilled nursing facilities, home health and hospice care. Individuals age 65 and older may voluntarily enroll in Part A if they or their spouse do not have at least 10 years of Medicare-covered employment.) Medicare Part B premiums are also deductible subject to those same limitations, as are premiums for Medigap insurance. (Medicare Part B is supplementary insurance for doctors' fees and outpatient services. Medigap insurance is private insurance that covers Medicare deductibles, co-payments, and benefits not covered under Medicare.)

Beginning in 1999, legislation allowed a limited number of Medicare beneficiaries to elect Medicare+Choice medical savings accounts instead of traditional Medicare. Contributions to these accounts (made only by the Secretary of Health and Human Services) are exempt from taxes, as are account earnings. Withdrawals are likewise not taxed nor subject to penalties if used to pay unreimbursed medical expenses, with some exceptions. No Medicare+Choice MSA plans have ever been offered.

Some Consequences of the Tax Benefits

Increases in Coverage

By lowering the after-tax cost of insurance, the tax benefits described above help extend coverage to more people. This of course is the intention: Congress has long been concerned about whether people have access to health care. The public subsidy implicit in the incentives (foregone tax revenues) usually is justified on grounds that people would otherwise under-insure, that is, delay purchasing coverage in the hope that they will not become ill or have an accident. Uninsured people are an indication of market failure; they impose spill-over costs on society in the form of public health risks and uncompensated charity care (the free-rider problem). Moreover, if insurance were purchased only by people who most need health care, its cost would become prohibitive for others (the adverse selection problem).

However, the tax benefits also lead insured people to obtain more coverage than they would otherwise choose. They purchase insurance that covers more than hospitalization and other catastrophic expenses, such as routine doctor visits, prescription drugs, and dental care. They obtain coverage with smaller deductibles and copayments. On the other hand, comprehensive coverage and lower cost-sharing are thought to lead to better preventive care and possibly long-run savings for certain medical conditions.

Source of Coverage

Tax benefits influence the way in which insurance coverage is acquired. The uncapped exclusion for employer-paid insurance, for example, which can benefit nearly all workers and is easy to administer, is partly responsible for the predominance of employment-based insurance in the United States. In contrast, restrictions on the itemized deduction allowed for individual private market insurance may be one reason why that insurance covers only 6% of the population under age 65.

Employment-based insurance carries both advantages and disadvantages for the typical worker. Generally costs are lower, and usually individual premiums do not vary by age or risk. (Thus, young and healthy workers may pay more than their actuarial risk would cost, though they are protected as they get older or need additional health care.) However, plans chosen by employers may not meet individual workers' needs (particularly if there are limited options), and changing jobs may require both new insurance and doctors.

Increase in Health Care Use and Cost

The tax benefits increase the demand for health care by enabling insured people to obtain services at discounted prices. This induced demand can be beneficial to the extent it reflects needed health care (that which society deems everyone should have) that financial constraints otherwise would have prevented. It can be wasteful to the extent it results in less essential or ineffective care. In either case, many economists argue, the additional demand is one reason why prices for health care have risen more rapidly than the general rate of inflation.

Whether insurance coverage could be encouraged without increasing the cost of health care has been a matter of debate. Comprehensive reforms that might accomplish this goal include capping the exclusion for employer-paid insurance and replacing both the exclusion and the deduction with a limited tax credit. But these changes could be difficult to implement and may create serious inequities. A 1994 Congressional Budget Office study, *The Tax Treatment of Employment-Based Health Insurance,* provides an overview of the issues and questions these approaches raise.

Many people probably would obtain some health insurance even without the tax benefits. The cost of subsidizing people for what they would otherwise do is an inefficient use of public dollars. Ideally, the tax incentives should lead to insurance being purchased only to the extent it results in better health care for society as a whole. But how they could be revised to accomplish this goal is a difficult question given the different ways insurance is provided, the various ways it is regulated, and the voluntary nature of decisions to purchase it.

Equity

Questions might be raised about the distribution of the tax incentives. Since as a practical matter they are not available to everyone, problems of horizontal equity arise. Workers without employment-based insurance generally cannot benefit from them, nor can many early retirees (people under the age of 65). Even if these individuals itemized their deductions, they can deduct health insurance premiums only to the extent that they (and other health care expenditures) exceed 7.5% of AGI. In contrast, the exclusion for employer-paid insurance is unlimited.

Even if everyone could benefit from the tax incentives, there would be questions of vertical equity. Tax savings from the exclusions and deductions described above generally are determined by taxpayers' marginal tax rate. Thus, taxpayers in the 15% tax bracket would save $600 in income taxes from a $4,000 exclusion (i.e., $4,000 x 0.15) for an employer-paid premium, while taxpayers in the 36% bracket would save $1,440 (i.e., $4,000 x 0.36). If health insurance is considered a form of personal consumption (such as food or clothing), this pattern of benefits would strike many people as unfair. It is unlikely that a government grant program would be designed in this manner. However, to the extent that health insurance is considered a way of spreading an individual's catastrophic economic risk over multiple years, basing tax savings on marginal tax rates might be justified.

CURRENT PROPOSALS

In the 108th Congress, numerous proposals for new or expanded tax benefits for health insurance have been introduced. In general, proponents of new or expanded tax benefits argue that they are needed to extend coverage to the uninsured and to address efficiency and equity problems. Opponents generally argue that tax benefits are unlikely to make much difference for most people who do not now have insurance.

This chapter will not attempt to identify all bills relating to tax benefits for health insurance. For a comprehensive list of bills providing tax benefits for health insurance, Congressional offices can use the Legislative Information System (LIS) available through the CRS home page [http://www.crs.gov].

Tax Credit for Trade-Displaced Workers

Under current law, the tax credit for trade-displaced workers is available only for qualifying insurance, including coverage sponsored by state governments. State-sponsored or arranged coverage must meet certain requirements: it must be guaranteed issue, cannot have limits for pre-existing conditions, and must have the same benefits and no higher premiums as the coverage provided to individuals who do not receive the tax credit.

On June 19, 2003, the House passed an amended version of H.R. 1528, the Taxpayer Protection and IRS Accountability Act of 2003. One provision would allow certain insurance to qualify for the tax credit if the eligible taxpayer elects to waive requirements for guaranteed issue and no preexisting condition exclusion, provided the taxpayer does not reside in a state with state-sponsored or arranged coverage qualifying for the credit. The waiver would apply through December 31, 2004. The bill would not allow the waivers to supersede state laws relating to consumer insurance protections. (H.R. 1528 as introduced had different language regarding these waivers, as did the version reported by the Committee on Ways and Means.)

Proponents of the waiver contend that it is needed to give more options to trade-displaced workers who live in states without qualifying state-sponsored or arranged coverage. Opponents argue that it would allow insurance companies to "cherry-pick" workers whom they would like to cover, as well as the conditions they would cover.

H.R. 1528 would also provide that consumer protection provisions of the current tax credit law would not apply to insurance under state continuation coverage.

Tax-Advantaged Health Savings Accounts

As described above, relatively few tax-advantaged Archer **medical savings accounts** (MSAs) have been established since they first became available in 1997. The slow growth can be attributed to a number of factors including product unfamiliarity, consumer aversion to financial risk, and the reluctance of insurance agents to sell lower-priced policies; however, statutory restrictions undoubtedly have played some role. MSA proponents are urging Congress to expand eligibility and modify restrictions on the required high deductible insurance. In their view, MSAs ought to be encouraged since they can make insurance more affordable, allow a wider choice among doctors, and protect patient rights better than government regulation. Critics generally oppose expansion, arguing that MSAs will result in adverse selection among health plans, underutilization of preventive care, and unwarranted tax breaks for high income families.

President Bush's proposed FY2004 budget would expand and permanently extend the authorization for MSAs. (Under current law, the authorization for new MSAs is set to expire December 31, 2003.) Effective after December 31, 2003, the proposal would:

- repeal limits on the number of accounts;
- make active accounts generally available to anyone with qualifying high deductible insurance (thus repealing restrictions limiting them to employees of small employers and self-employed individuals);

- allow contributions up to the amount of the insurance deductible (thus deleting the 65% and 75% ceilings);
- allow contributions to be made both by employers and account owners;
- lower minimum insurance deductibles from $1,700 to $1,000 for single coverage and $3,350 to $2,000 for family coverage;
- allow MSAs to be offered through cafeteria plans;
- allow the qualifying insurance to provide, without counting against the deductible, up to $100 of preventive care per covered individual per year.

On June 19, 2003, the House Committee on Ways and Means approved an amended version of H.R. 2351 which would authorize tax-advantaged health savings accounts (HSAs) similar to MSAs. The bill was formally reported on June 25 (H.Rept. 108-177). On June 26, the House approved expanded tax-advantaged health savings accounts in H.R. 2596, which had been introduced the day before; the passed legislation was then appended to H.R. 1, the House-passed Medicare prescription drug bill, as provided in H.Res. 299. Under H.R. 2596 (and thus H.R. 1), two tax-advantaged accounts would be authorized, "health savings accounts" and "health savings security accounts." **Health savings accounts (HSAs)** would be for individuals covered by a health plan with an annual deductible of between $1,000 and $2,500 for self-only coverage and between $2,000 and $5,050 for family coverage; out-ofpocket limits could not exceed $3,350 for the former and $6,150 for the latter. Annual contributions equal to the deductible would be deductible by the taxpayer (or excluded by the taxpayer, if paid by the employer). The JCT estimates that HSAs would result in a revenue loss of $5.7 billion over the fiscal year 2004 through 2013 period. **Health savings security accounts (HSSAs)** would be for individuals who are uninsured or who are covered by a health plan with a deductible of at least $500 for self-only coverage and $1,000 for family coverage. Annual deductible contributions of up to $2,000 could be made by individuals with self-only coverage and uninsured individuals with no dependents; deductible contributions of up to $4,000 could be made by individuals with family coverage and uninsured individuals with dependents or who file a joint return. Allowable contributions would be reduced and then eliminated for the former individuals who have incomes between $75,000 and $85,000 and for the latter individuals who have incomes between $150,000 and $170,000. Individuals age 55 and over could make larger contributions. The JCT estimates that HSSAs would result in a revenue loss of $169 billion over the fiscal year 2004 through 2013 period.

Flexible Spending Accounts

President Bush's FY2004 budget would allow up to $500 in unused balances in health care flexible spending accounts (FSAs) to be carried over to the following year without being taxed. Under current law, unused balances must be forfeited to the employer. The proposal would also permit unused balances to be distributed to participants (in which case they would be taxed) or rolled over into certain qualified deferred compensation plans (section 401(k), 403(b), and 457 plans). H.R. 176 (introduced by Representative Royce) and H.R. 1177 (introduced by Representative DeMint) would also allow limited amounts of unused balances to be carried forward to the following year.

On June 19, 2003, the House Committee on Ways and Means approved an amended version of H.R. 2351 which would allow up to $500 in unused health care FSA balances to be carried over, contributed to a qualified retirement or deferred compensation plan, or contributed to a health savings account (which that same legislation would allow). The provision was also included in H.R. 2596, which the House passed on June 26 (see the discussion above for tax-advantaged health savings accounts) and then was appended to H.R. 1, the House Medicare prescription drug bill, also passed that day.

The principal argument for allowing these options is that taxpayers might be more willing to participate in FSAs if unused balances at the end of the year were not lost. Allowing carryovers or rollovers might also discourage participants from spending remaining balances carelessly, just to use them up. FSAs generally do not restrict patients' choice of doctors; thus, some might favor them as a way around limitations of managed care.

However, the options might result in tax breaks that are unwarranted, particularly for higher income families. Some participants might increase their FSA contributions just to take advantage of them. The health care FSA carryover could become another form of MSA, though limited in size and without account earnings that accrue to the employee. It is not clear in the President's proposal when rollovers to deferred compensation plans would occur; employers generally would need time to run nondiscrimination tests to see if additional contributions to these plans would be permissible.

Expanded Tax Deduction

In the 108th Congress, one bill has been introduced that would allow individuals to deduct 100% of their insurance premiums, regardless of whether they itemize (H.R. 198, introduced by Representative Stearns). Another bill would remove would allow itemizers to deduct all of their medical expenses (H.R. 53, introduced by Representative Cox). As discussed above, the deduction allowed under current law is restricted to taxpayers who itemize and is further limited to insurance and medical costs that exceed 7.5% adjusted gross income; thus, most taxpayers cannot benefit from it.

An expanded tax deduction would improve horizontal equity since more taxpayers could receive tax benefits similar to those associated with employer-paid coverage. (An above-the-line deduction has the same income tax effect as the exclusion allowed that coverage.) At the same time, an expanded deduction would not improve vertical equity since the tax benefits generally would be proportional to the taxpayer's marginal tax rate. A $2,000 premium would result in tax savings of $720 for someone in the 36% bracket (i.e., $2,000 x 0.36) but only $300 for someone in the 15% bracket (i.e., $2,000 x 0.15). It might also be doubted whether tax savings of 15% would enable more lower income taxpayers to obtain insurance.

Expanded Tax Credit

President Bush's FY2004 budget includes a refundable tax credit for health insurance for individuals under age 65. Under the FY2004 budget proposal, the credit would equal 90% of the premium and would decrease for higher incomes; the credit would phase out at $30,000 for individuals and at $60,000 for families. The amount of the credit be limited to $1,000 for an adult covered by a policy and $500 for each child, up to two children. Individuals participating in public health plans (such as Medicaid or the State Children's Health Insurance Program) or employer health plans would not be eligible for the credit. The credit would be claimed through the normal tax-filing process. Alternatively, beginning July 1, 2005, an individual could use the credit in advance to reduce payments to the insurance company. The insurer would have then received the credit directly from the U.S. Treasury.

A tax credit could be attractive in several respects. If it were generally available, a credit could aid taxpayers who do not have access to employment-based insurance (or who are dissatisfied with it) and who cannot claim the medical expense deduction. A credit could provide all taxpayers with the same dollar reduction in final tax liability; this would avoid problems of vertical equity associated with the tax exclusion and tax deduction. A credit might also provide lower income taxpayers with greater tax savings than either the exclusion or the deduction; this might reduce the number of the uninsured. If the credit were refundable, it could even help taxpayers with limited or no tax liability.

But the effects of tax credits can vary widely, depending on how they are designed. One important question is whether the credit would supplement or replace existing tax benefits, particularly the exclusion for employer-paid insurance. Another is whether the credit would be the same for all taxpayers or more generous for those with lower incomes. Ensuring that lower income families benefit from any credit may be difficult if they cannot afford to purchase insurance beforehand. Similarly, it might be asked whether the credit would vary with factors that affect the cost of health insurance, such as age, gender, place of residence, or health status. Whether the insurance must meet certain standards for benefits, coinsurance, and underwriting might also be a factor.

Small Employer Tax Credit

The Economic Recovery Act of 2003 (S. 414, introduced by Senator Daschle) would provide a tax credit to small employers. The credit would equal a certain percentage of the amount spent by the employer for employee benefits. The percentage would equal 50% for employers with less than 26 qualified employees, 40% for employers with between 26 and 35 qualified employees, and 30% for employers with between 36 and 50 qualified employees. A qualified employee is a worker who is not covered under a spouse's health insurance or covered under a public insurance program.

In the 108th Congress, several other bills have been introduced that would provide a tax credit to small employers that offer health insurance to their employees (S. 10, introduced by Senator Daschle; S. 53, introduced by Senator Durbin; S. 86 introduced by Senator Clinton). In each bill, the credit would equal a percentage of the cost incurred by the employer for providing health insurance to qualified employees. Each bill has different provisions for calculating the percentage of the credit. Factors determining the percentage include the number of qualified employees in the firm, the average wage of the firm's qualified employees, the share of insurance premiums paid by the firm, and whether a qualified employee is covered by a single or family policy.

LEGISLATION

H.R. 53 (Cox)

Health Care Freedom of Choice Act. Introduced January 7, 2003. Referred to the Committee on Ways and Means.

H.R. 176 (Royce)

A bill to allow amounts elected for reimbursement of medical care expenses under a health flexible spending arrangement that are unused during a plan year to be carried over for such use for subsequent plan years. Introduced January 7, 2003. Referred to the Committee on Ways and Means.

H.R. 198 (Stearns)

Health Care Tax Deduction Act of 2003. Introduced January 7, 2003. Referred to the Committee on Ways and Means.

H.R. 450 (Dunn)

Small Business Health Insurance Affordability Act of 2003. Introduced January 29, 2003. Referred to the Committee on Ways and Means.

H.R. 1177 (DeMint)

A bill to amend the Internal Revenue Code of 1986 to provide additional choice regarding unused health benefits in cafeteria plans and flexible spending arrangements. Introduced March 11, 2003. Referred to the Committee on Ways and Means.

S. 10 (Daschle)

Health Care Coverage Expansion and Quality Improvement Act of 2003. Introduced January 7, 2003. Referred to the Committee on Finance.

S. 53 (Durbin)

A bill to amend the Internal Revenue Code of 1986 to allow small business employers a credit against income tax for employee health insurance expenses paid or incurred by the employer. Introduced January 7, 2003. Referred to the Committee on Finance.

S. 86 (Clinton)

Small Employer Tax Assistance for Health Coverage Act of 2003. Introduced January 7, 2003. Referred to the Committee on Finance.

S. 414 (Daschle)

Economic Recovery Act of 2003. Introduced February 14, 2003. Placed on Senate Legislative Calendar February 24, 2003.

FOR ADDITIONAL READING

Cunningham. Laura E. National Health Insurance and the Medical Deduction. *Tax Law Review*. V. 50 (1995), p. 237-264.

Gruber, Jonathan and Larry Levitt. Tax Subsidies for Health Insurance: Costs and Benefits. *Health Affairs*. V. 19 (2000), p. 72-85.

Gruber, Jonathan and James Poterba. Tax Incentives and the Decision to Purchase Health Insurance: Evidence from the Self-Employed. *The Quarterly Journal of Economics*. V. 109 (1994), p. 701-733.

Kaplow, Louis. The Income Tax as Insurance: The Casualty Loss and Medical Expense Deductions and the Exclusion of Medical Insurance Premiums. *California Law Review*, v. 79 (1991), p. 1485-1510.

Kahn, Charles N. and Ronald F. Pollack. Building a Consensus for Expanding Health Coverage. *Health Affairs*. V. 20 (January/February 2001), p. 40-48.

Pauly, Mark. Taxation, Health Insurance, and Market Failure in the Medical Economy. *Journal of Economic Literature*. V. 24 (1986), p. 629-675.

Pauly, Mark and Bradley Herring. Expanding Coverage via Tax Credits: Trade-Offs and Outcomes. *Health Affairs*. V. 20 (January/February, 2001), p. 9-26.

Sheils, John and Paul Hogan. Cost of Tax-Exempt Health Benefits in 1998. *Health Affairs*. V. 18 (1999), p. 176-181.

U.S. Congress. Congressional Budget Office. *The Tax Treatment of Employment-Based Health Insurance*. Washington, March, 1994.

U.S. Congress. House. Committee on Ways and Means. Subcommittee on Health. *Health Insurance Premium Tax Deductions for the Self-Employed.* Hearings, 104th Congress, 1st session. January 27, 1995. Washington, U.S. Govt. Print. Off., 1996.

U.S. General Accounting Office. *Medical Savings Accounts: Results from Surveys of Insurers* GAO/HEHS-99-34. Washington, December, 1998.

APPENDIX

Listed below is the general formula for calculating federal income taxes. The list omits some steps, such as prepayments (from withholding and estimated payments) and the alternative minimum tax.

1. Gross income
2. *minus* Deductions (or adjustments) for AGI (i.e., "above the line")
3. = Adjusted gross income (AGI)
4. *minus* Greater of standard or itemized deductions
5. *minus* Personal and dependency exemptions
6. = Taxable income
7. *times* Tax rate
8. = Tax on taxable income ("regular tax liability")
9. *minus* Credits
10. = Final tax liability

Chapter 5

TAX SUBSIDIES FOR EXPANDING HEALTH INSURANCE COVERAGE

Gary Guenther

INTRODUCTION

An issue of continuing concern to Congress is the number of Americans who lack health insurance coverage. In 2001, the most recent year for which estimates are available, 41.2 million persons were uninsured,[1] 40.9 million (or 99%) of whom were under age 65. Among the non-elderly population, this is the highest total ever reported by the U.S. Census Bureau, and it marks the first time since 1998 that the number of uninsured under age 65 exceeded 40 million. The number of non-elderly uninsured rose each year from 1987 to 1998 and then declined in both 1999 and 2000, before rising again in 2001. Much of the expansion since the mid-1980s has been due to sustained increases in the cost of health care, which in turn drive up private health insurance premiums.[2]

Congressional concern about the size of the uninsured population has multiple roots. One is the adverse health effects associated with a lack of health insurance coverage. Compared to insured individuals, individuals with no or inadequate health insurance are more likely to postpone or do without needed health care, incur burdensome personal debts for care they receive, be denied access to health care, be hospitalized for preventable health problems, and have a greater likelihood of being diagnosed with late-stage breast, prostate, colorectal, or skin cancer.[3] Another source of congressional concern is the economic costs arising from

[1] There is some question about how many of these individuals can be considered chronically uninsured. The estimate is intended to capture those who were without health insurance during all of 2001. Nonetheless, in recent testimony before the Senate Special Committee on Aging, former Congressional Budget Office Director Dan Crippen claimed that the number of Americans who are uninsured for more than one year at a stretch "is substantially lower then 40 million, perhaps as much as 20 million lower than 40 million." (See "Ex-CBO Head Urges Focus on Uninsured Who Remain Without Coverage Over Time," *Daily Report for Executives*, Bureau of National Affairs, March 11, 2003, p. A-37.)

[2] Harvey S. Rosen, *Public Finance*, 6th edition (New York: McGraw-Hill Irwin, 2002), p. 211.

[3] Kaiser Commission on the Uninsured and Medicaid, *The Uninsured: A Primer* (Washington: Henry J. Kaiser Family Foundation, March 2002), pp. 6 and 8.

being uninsured. According to recent study of the tradeoffs in using tax credits to expand health insurance coverage, the uninsured pay only 30% of the actual cost of their care.[4] The cost of uncompensated medical care received by uninsured individuals is passed on to the insured in the form of higher health insurance premiums; to local, state, and federal governments in the form of higher subsidies for uncompensated care; and to health care providers in the form of reduced incomes.[5] Finally, congressional concern about the uninsured population also reflects a view held by many Americans that health care is a merit good. According to this view, all individuals, regardless of ability to pay, ought to have access to adequate health care. Exponents also argue that if choices must be made, they should be done so on the basis not of a patient's income or wealth but of factors related to the cost-effectiveness of recommended medical care, such as the age and sex of a patient or the appropriateness and cost of prescribed treatments.

These concerns have led policymakers at the state and federal levels of government to search for effective, affordable, and politically feasible ways to expand access to adequate health insurance coverage. While a variety of proposed solutions have been analyzed and debated – including the creation of unrestricted medical savings accounts and a single-payer health care system – recent Congresses have shown a growing bipartisan interest in tax-based approaches to increase this coverage.[6] In the 107th Congress, the Trade Act of 2002 (P.L. 107-210) established a new refundable tax credit for the purchase of health insurance by individuals who receive or are eligible to receive trade adjustment assistance and who are between the ages of 55 and 64 and receive benefits from the Pension Benefits Guaranty Corporation.[7] And numerous bills to create tax deductions or credits for the purchase of health insurance by those not covered under employer or public health plans were introduced. Proposals to establish new tax incentives for health insurance coverage have begun to surface in the 108th Congress.[8] For example, Representative Cliff Stearns has introduced a bill (H.R.

---

[4] Mark Pauly and Bradley Herring, "Expanding Coverage Via Tax Credits: Trade-Offs and Outcomes," *Health Affairs*, vol. 20, no. 1, Jan./Feb. 2001, p. 15.

[5] There is some uncertainty over the amount of uncompensated care received by the uninsured. A central difficulty with many available estimates is that the data used to generate them are flawed. The latest attempt to steer clear of this difficulty is a study by two senior analysts from the Urban Institute. According to the study, uninsured individuals received an estimated $35 billion in uncompensated care in 2001, or about 3% of total personal health care spending. Federal, state, and local governments covered an estimated 87% of that amount through a combination of grants, direct provision of care, appropriated funds, and special payments under Medicare and Medicaid. See Jack Hadley and John Holahan, "How Much Medical Care Do the Uninsured Use, and Who Pays for It?," *Health Affairs*, Web Exclusive: [http://www.healthaffairs.org], visited Feb. 12, 2003, pp. W3-78.

[6] This is not to imply that there are no significant differences between congressional Republicans and Democrats over the use of tax subsidies to reduce the uninsured population. The two sides do not fully agree on some critical issues, such as the merits of targeting subsidies at non-group coverage and the need for reforms of the private health insurance industry to discourage rating and underwriting practices that make it difficult for high-risk, low-income individuals to obtain adequate, affordable coverage. See Robert Cunningham, "Joint Custody: Bipartisan Interest Expands Scope of Tax-Credit Proposals," *Health Affairs*, Web Exclusive [http://www.healthaffairs.org], visited Sept. 18, 2002, pp. W290-W298.

[7] The credit is equal to 65% of health insurance premiums paid by eligible persons for policies covering themselves and qualifying family members. It can be paid in one of two ways. First, the Internal Revenue Service can pay the credit directly to taxpayers when they file their annual tax returns. Second, the IRS can pay the credit directly to a health insurer on a monthly basis, provided the eligible taxpayers first pay their 35% share of the premium.

[8] For a brief overview of legislative proposals in the 108th Congress to expand tax benefits for health insurance, see CRS Issue Brief IB98037, *Tax Benefits for Health Insurance: Current Legislation*, by Bob Lyke and Christopher Sroka, pp. 9-13.

198) to permit individuals to deduct 100% of out-of-pocket payments for health insurance coverage and prescription drugs. And at least four bills (S. 10, S. 53, S. 86, and H.R. 450) to establish a tax credit for small firms that offer health insurance to employees have been introduced.

The Bush Administration also favors a tax-based approach to reducing the uninsured population. In his budget request for FY2004, President Bush proposes that Congress pass a limited, means-tested refundable tax credit for the purchase of non-group health insurance by individuals not covered under employer or public health plans.[9]

The use of tax policy to shrink the uninsured population appeals to some policymakers for a variety of reasons – although proponents of tax subsidies to expand health insurance coverage do not necessarily agree on which reasons are paramount. Foremost among them are a preference for tax incentives to government spending in achieving important social goals; a recognition that existing federal tax subsidies for health insurance coverage are inequitable in that they exclude the non-elderly who are unemployed or drop out of the workforce; and the belief that private insurance companies would be more efficient and effective than government agencies in providing Americans with an agreeable choice of health insurance plans. Others, however, doubt that tax subsidies are an efficient and effective way to achieve substantial reductions in the size of the uninsured population. They tend to favor more direct solutions, such as public health insurance programs for the uninsured.

This chapter summarizes what is known about the factors shaping the cost-effectiveness of tax subsidies for expanding health insurance coverage. It opens with an explanation of the economic justification for government intervention in the market for health insurance. The report then moves on to examine key considerations in designing tax subsidies for expanding health insurance coverage and concludes with a review of the principal findings of recent studies assessing the cost-effectiveness of a variety of proposed tax subsidies, many of which resemble proposals that have attracted attention in recent Congresses. The report will be updated or revised to reflect legislation to expand federal tax incentives for health insurance passed by a full committee in the House or Senate, or to incorporate significant new research findings on the cost-effectiveness of such incentives.

[9] More specifically, the Bush Administration wants to establish a refundable tax credit for the purchase of health insurance by individuals under age 65 who are not covered under public or employer health plans. The credit would subsidize up to 90% of the health insurance premium and would be capped at $1,000 per adult and $500 per child for up to two children. Single filers with no dependents and a modified adjusted gross income (MAGI) of up to $15,000 would be eligible for the maximum credit; the credit phases out completely at a MAGI of $30,000. All other filers with a MAGI up to $25,000 would be eligible for the maximum credit. In the case of a household consisting of two adults and two children, the credit would phase out completely at a MAGI of $60,000. Taxpayers could claim the credit either on their federal tax returns or through reductions in their premium payments equal to the credit they are due. If they choose the second option, health insurers would receive reimbursements from the Treasury Department equal to the amount of the credit. Eligibility for the advance credit would be based on an individual's tax return for the previous year. Health plans eligible for the credit would need to meet minimum coverage criteria. Individuals could purchase these plans through the non-group market, private purchasing groups, state-sponsored purchasing pools, or state high-risk pools.

RATIONALE FOR GOVERNMENT INTERVENTION IN THE MARKET FOR HEALTH INSURANCE

Mainstream economic theory holds that markets are most likely to achieve their best possible outcomes when governments refrain from intervening in their operations. Yet one of the defining characteristics of the U.S. health insurance market is the dominant role played by state and federal health insurance programs and tax subsidies for health insurance.[10] In 2001, for example, spending on Medicare and Medicaid (which provide health insurance for the elderly and a large number of the poor and disabled) and the State Children's Health Insurance Program totaled $454.8 billion; and the federal government lost an estimated $65.7 billion in tax revenues because of the tax exclusion for employer-provided health insurance, according to the Joint Committee on Taxation. On what economic grounds can such involvement be justified?

Conventional economic analysis suggests two possible grounds. On the one hand, mainstream economic theory holds that social welfare is enhanced by the widespread availability of actuarially fair insurance. Most individuals are risk-averse to some degree, and risk-averse individuals are thought to be better off when they can reduce their financial risks by transferring them to entities with a comparative advantage in risk bearing because of their capacity for risk pooling and diversification (e.g., private insurance companies). Thus, most individuals would want to buy enough health insurance, provided the cost reflects their expected annual losses from health problems. Health economists seem to agree that health insurance is likely to yield maximum social welfare gains when coverage is widespread among all risk groups, the potential losses from health problems are large, and the probabilities of suffering such problems cannot be known for specific individuals.

On the other hand, if the market for health insurance were left to its own devices, there would be no certainty that health insurance coverage would produce a net welfare gain. Instead of the emergence of broad, actuarially fair insurance coverage, one might find that available coverage would be excessive in many cases, and too few individuals would have adequate and affordable insurance coverage. Undesirable outcomes such as these may arise because the provision of health care is vulnerable to four market failures: adverse selection, moral hazard, incompleteness, and the existence of free riders in the utilization of medical care.[11]

Adverse selection refers to a process which is likely to emerge in the health insurance market when buyers of particular policies have greater risks of illness and injury than the average potential buyer. It is most likely to materialize when participation in health insurance coverage is voluntary, risk pools are small and dominated by experience rating, and a multitude of insurers vie for market share by offering consumers a range of plans with

[10] For an overview of existing federal tax subsidies for health insurance, see CRS Issue Brief IB98037, *Tax Benefits for Health Insurance: Current Legislation*, by Bob Lyke and Christopher Sroka, pp. 2-7.

[11] The health care market appears riddled with imperfections. In addition to the three problems discussed here, consumers and health insurance companies face imperfect information relating to the skills of doctors, health profiles of patients, and the benefits of treatments and procedures; competition in the provision of health care services is limited; and providers whose principal objective goes beyond the minimization of costs or maximization of profits play a large role in the delivery of health care. For more details on these market failures, see Joseph E. Stiglitz, *Economics of the Public Sector*, 3rd edition (New York: W.W. Norton, 2000), pp. 308-311.

varying benefits. In general, the average buyer of a health insurance plan has an above-average risk of developing serious health problems. Such a tendency is rooted in the fact that a very small share of the U.S. population accounts for a large share of spending on health care in a given year.[12] This disparity, if uncorrected by policy intervention, can touch off an upward spiral in insurance premiums driven by efforts by insurers to raise rates to cover losses from unanticipated claims. In response, individuals with relatively low risks (e.g., young, healthy adults) may choose to become uninsured or switch to cheaper policies offering less coverage, while individuals with relatively high risks (e.g., middle-aged adults who smoke, do not exercise regularly, and are overweight) face the choice of paying premiums far above their expected losses, switching to cheaper policies offering inadequate coverage, or becoming uninsured and relying on charity care as needed. The prevalence of adverse selection in non-group markets gives insurance companies an incentive to engage in a practice known as "cherry picking," where they focus on selling health insurance to those with relatively low risks.

Among health economists, moral hazard refers not to a character defect but to the excessive utilization of health care fostered by having health insurance and the associated efficiency losses. Health insurance can have this effect mainly because insured individuals bear only a fraction of the actual cost of the health care they receive, weakening their incentive to avoid behaviors that are known to contribute to health problems and dulling their awareness of the relationship between the marginal costs and benefits of the care they receive. In theory, insured individuals will consume health care until the marginal benefits match the marginal out-of-pocket costs, which under most policies are equivalent to deductibles and copayments. Generous health insurance coverage can push these costs far below the actual marginal costs of the medical services. Of course, insurance companies are well aware of the damage moral hazard can inflict on their financial viability; so they try to contain or limit it through the imposition of deductibles, co-payments, coverage limits and exclusions, managed care plans, mandatory prior approvals of certain treatments and procedures, and financial incentives for health-care providers to restrict the use of costly procedures.

Moreover, it appears that the health insurance market fails to satisfy a necessary condition of economic efficiency: the existence of what economists call "complete markets." When a market fails to provide a good or service even though individuals would be willing to pay more than the average cost of providing it, economists consider the market to be incomplete. And they regard the lack of completeness as a market failure. Some argue that the private health insurance market is incomplete because it usually does not provide guaranteed renewability or insurance against future health risks, only current ones.[13] Most individuals cannot purchase health insurance at fixed rates and under fixed terms for more than one year in advance. Yet it is thought that many individuals would be willing to purchase insurance against future health risks at a reasonable cost, if it were provided.

Finally, in every state, certain health care providers – mainly public hospitals – have a legal obligation to provide treatment to someone suffering from a life-threatening or serious health problem, irrespective of his or her ability to pay. Although these mandatory-care laws can enhance social welfare by ensuring that everyone receives at least a modicum of health

[12] In 1992, for example, 10% of Americans accounted for 72% of personal health expenditures.

[13] See Leonard E. Burman and Amelia Gruber, "First, Do No Harm: Designing Tax Incentives for Health Insurance," *National Tax Journal*, vol. 59, no. 3, Sept. 2001, p. 480.

care when it is urgently needed, they can also undermine welfare by diluting the incentive to purchase actuarially fair health insurance, especially for low-income individuals with few financial assets to protect. As a result, mandatory-care laws have the unintended effect of laying the foundation for a classic market failure known as the free rider problem. In general, this problem can be seen as a byproduct of the existence of public goods, one of whose defining traits is the impossibility of excluding anybody from consuming them. Laws granting everyone the right to receive emergency care, regardless of ability to pay, effectively endow health care with this trait, thereby giving rise to a free-rider problem. It is not clear how the welfare gains from these laws compare with the welfare losses.

For most health economists, the presence of these market failures provides ample justification for government intervention in the health insurance market. In their view, a central issue for policymakers is not whether to intervene. Rather, it is to devise politically acceptable policy measures that attempt to strike a balance between the welfare losses arising from moral hazard and the welfare gains inherent in the risk spreading provided by actuarially fair health insurance coverage.

Important Considerations in Designing Tax Incentives to Expand Health Insurance Coverage

If the policy objective is to achieve a sizable reduction in the uninsured population and the preferred policy instrument is tax policy, then a critical task for policymakers is to devise tax subsidies that accomplish the goal at an acceptable budgetary cost. Recent research into the probable effects of tax policy on health insurance coverage sheds light on several factors that should be carefully considered in designing such subsidies. Each is examined in some detail below.

Current Federal Tax Subsidies for Health Insurance

This may seem obvious, but one important factor to weigh in devising a tax-based approach to expanding health insurance coverage is the current mix of federal tax subsidies for health insurance coverage. Any such approach cannot avoid being constructed around a decision about whether to jettison, modify, or retain these subsidies. The reason lies in the central role they play in the current system of health insurance coverage for the non-elderly.

Although the present tax code contains a variety of subsidies for health insurance, three in particular have facilitated the emergence of this system: the tax exclusions for employer-paid health insurance premiums, so-called cafeteria plans, and flexible spending accounts.[14] They are related in that each pertains to health insurance coverage obtained through employers. Under these exclusions, it is possible for individuals who receive health insurance through employers to pay no federal or state income and payroll taxes on their own and their employers' contributions for the premiums. In combination, the exclusions substantially lower the after-tax price of health insurance relative to other goods and services workers may

[14] For an overview of current federal tax benefits for health insurance, see CRS Issue Brief IB98037, *Tax Benefits for Health Insurance: Current Legislation*, pp. 1-8.

consume and subsidize the purchase of employment-based group health insurance relative to non-group coverage.[15] These exclusions are so deeply embedded in the current structure of health insurance coverage for the non-elderly that their removal could trigger a significant increase in the uninsured population. In a recent study, Jonathan Gruber, an economist at MIT who has written extensively on the impact of tax policy on health insurance coverage among the non-elderly, estimated that the elimination of the exclusions at the federal and state levels would lead to a 14% drop in the number of employers offering health insurance to employees, which in turn would result in a decrease in the number of individuals covered under employment-based health plans of over 22 million and a 50% decline in total spending on these plans.[16]

Relevant Characteristics of the Non-Elderly Uninsured Population

Policymakers seeking to craft cost-effective tax subsidies to expand health insurance coverage should also take into account characteristics of the non-elderly uninsured population that are relevant to tax policy.

Several such characteristics deserve mention. First, the non-elderly uninsured are disproportionately concentrated in low-income households: in 2001, nearly 38% of uninsured individuals resided in households with annual incomes below $20,000. It comes as no surprise, then, that a very high proportion of uninsured taxpayers fall in lower tax brackets, and that a significant proportion have no federal income tax liability.[17] Second, while most uninsured individuals under age 65 live in households headed by individuals holding full- or part-time jobs, over 75% of uninsured workers are not offered health insurance by their employers.[18] Third, many uninsured workers are employed by small firms: in 2001, over 50% of uninsured workers held jobs with firms having fewer than 100 employees.[19] Finally, the previous characteristics notwithstanding, the uninsured under age 65 do not constitute an isolated, easily identified or targeted, and stable population group. Rather, they are scattered in varying and shifting degrees throughout all income groups and firm sizes. For instance, in 2001, 24% of uninsured individuals lived in households with annual incomes of $50,000 or more, and 23% of uninsured workers were employed by firms with 500 or more employees.[20]

[15] Jonathan Gruber, an economist at MIT, has estimated that the typical worker in the 15% federal income tax bracket, facing a state income tax rate of 5% and a combined payroll tax rate of 15.3%, pays $0.65 after taxes for $1 of health insurance, meaning that the tax price is 0.65. See Jonathan Gruber, *Taxes and Health Insurance*, Working Paper 8657 (Cambridge, MA: National Bureau of Economic Research, Dec. 2001), p. 4.

[16] Ibid., pp. 26-27.

[17] Gruber has also estimated that in 1997, 90% of uninsured taxpayers with tax liabilities belonged to the 15% tax bracket, and 50% had no federal tax liability. See Jonathan Gruber, *Tax Subsidies for Health Insurance: Evaluating the Costs and Benefits*, Working Paper 7553 (Cambridge, MA: National Bureau of Economic Research, Feb. 2000), p.7.

[18] Gruber, *Taxes and Health Insurance*, p. 7.

[19] CRS Report 96-891, p. 6.

[20] EBRI, pp. 11 and 12.

Relevant Features of Health Insurance Market for the Non-Elderly

It is also useful to consider certain features of the existing structure of health insurance coverage for the non-elderly in designing tax-based subsidies to expand health insurance coverage. Of particular interest for policymakers are the dominant role of employers as sources of health insurance coverage, the advantages and disadvantages of group coverage provided through the workplace, and the limitations of coverage provided in the non-group market.

In 2001, nearly 66% of non-elderly Americans received health insurance coverage through employers; another 15% were covered through public health insurance programs; and about 7% obtained coverage through insurance plans purchased in the non-group or individual market. Gruber has noted that in recent decades, more than nine out of 10 privately insured non-elderly individuals received their coverage from an employer – either their own, their spouse's or their parents'. Most workers who are offered insurance by their employers, regardless of wage and salary income, decide to take it, although the take-up rate appears to have declined somewhat in recent years as employers have passed on to employees increases in the cost of enrolling in health plans.[21] The offering of insurance varies considerably by firm size. In general, smaller firms are much less likely to offer coverage: in 2001, a worker in a firm with fewer than 10 employees was almost three times as likely to be uninsured as a worker in a firm with 1,000 or more employees. Nevertheless, small firms paying high average wages are as likely to offer coverage as large firms; and eligibility, coverage, and take-up rates are similar among employees in small and large firms that offer health insurance coverage.[22]

There are noteworthy advantages and disadvantages to tying health insurance coverage to employment. On the one hand, the work place serves as a convenient, almost logical way to pool health insurance risks, since most individuals choose their employers for reasons other than expected usage of medical care in coming years. In general, the larger the employment group, the greater the scope for the risk sharing and community rating that enhances social welfare. Seen from this perspective, employment-based insurance has the potential to preclude the adverse selection prevailing in the non-group insurance market. Furthermore, insurance administrative, underwriting, and marketing costs are lower for large groups than individuals.[23] Large groups also have greater bargaining power in extracting price and other concessions from insurers and health-care providers.

On the other hand, employer-based health insurance serves as an imperfect risk-pooling mechanism in the case of small firms. In a firm with 20 employees, for instance, if two individuals suffer a serious illness, the average cost of health insurance can rise markedly the following year. In addition, making employers the primary source of health insurance coverage for the non-elderly can contribute to efficiency losses by retarding job mobility.

---

[21] David M. Cutler, *Employee Costs and the Decline in Health Insurance Coverage*, Working Paper 9036 (Cambridge, MA: National Bureau of Economic Research, July 2002), pp. 25-27.

[22] Jason Lee, *Are Health Insurance Premiums Higher for Small Firms?*, Research Synthesis Report No. 2 (Princeton, NJ: Robert Wood Johnson Foundation, Sept. 2002), pp. 4-6.

[23] According to one authoritative estimate, health insurance loading fees as a percent of benefits paid fall in the range of 60% to 80% for individual policies, compared to 8% to 15% for groups of 201 to 1,000 persons. These fees cover the operating costs of insurance companies and represent a mark-up over the expected payout of benefits under a policy. See Charles E. Phelps, *Health Economics*, 3rd Edition (Boston: Addison Wesley, 2003), pp. 342-343.

Insured workers may be disinclined to work for another employer out of fear of losing their coverage or having less desirable options for coverage. Another drawback to employer-provided health insurance is that it offers limited renewability. Those who become unemployed may lose their coverage, and there are no federal laws to keep employers from dropping coverage when faced with huge premium increases. Finally, a system of employment-based health insurance coverage can foster production inefficiencies by implicitly favoring large firms over small firms. The source of the inefficiencies is the considerable cost advantages that large firms typically enjoy over small firms in offering the same package of health benefits to employees.[24]

Some proposals to establish new tax subsidies to expand health insurance coverage would rely on the non-group market to achieve their objectives. In 2001, 16.4 million individuals were covered under non-group policies. Coverage under these policies declined gradually between 1993 – when it reached 17.5 million persons – and 2000. Many of those who purchase insurance in the non-group market are self-employed, retired but not yet eligible for Medicare, working part-time, or divorced or widowed.[25] Access to and the cost of non-group coverage depend critically on a person's health status, age, and place of residence. For young adults in good health, premiums can be lower than in the employer-based group market; but for older adults with chronic health problems, premiums tend to be much higher. Generally, individuals in poor health can face formidable obstacles to obtaining adequate and affordable coverage. Insurers often decline to cover persons with pre-existing conditions, impose severe limits on the coverage they will provide for those conditions, or add high premium surcharges to cover those conditions.[26] Many states have responded to these practices by establishing high-risk insurance pools; and some have enacted law barring insurers from excluding coverage of pre-existing conditions. But they seem to have had little impact on trends in the uninsured population in the past 10 to 15 years.

Price Sensitivity of the Demand for Health Insurance

Tax subsidies attempt to boost the demand for health insurance by reducing its tax price (or after-tax cost). This relationship implies that in designing tax subsidies to shrink the uninsured population, it is useful to know how sensitive the decision to purchase health insurance is to reductions in its tax price. Given the structure of the health insurance coverage for the non-elderly, tax policy can work through three basic channels to expand coverage: (1) subsidies to employers to offer coverage; (2) subsidies to employees to accept coverage that is offered; and (3) subsidies to uninsured individuals to purchase non-group coverage. These options suggest that policymakers might consider the responsiveness to tax price changes of the decision by employers to offer coverage, the decision by employees to take up coverage if it is offered, and the decision of uninsured individuals to purchase non-group coverage, together with the ways in which these decisions may feed back on one another.

---

[24] Small firms pay more than large firms for the same health insurance coverage because the costs of marketing and administration are spread over fewer workers in small firms and underwriting costs typically are greater for small firms. See U.S. Congressional Budget Office, *The Tax Treatment of Employment-Based Health Insurance* (Washington: March 1994), pp. 21-22.

[25] Karen Pollitz, Richard Sorian, and Kathy Thomas, *How Accessible is Individual Health Insurance for Consumers in Less-Than-Perfect Health?* (Washington: Kaiser Family Foundation, June 2001), p. 1.

[26] Ibid., p. iv.

Considerable research has been done on the behavioral responses of firms and individuals to changes in the cost of health insurance. A recent study by Gruber reviewed this literature.[27] One of his findings was a striking lack of consensus on the price sensitivity of the three decisions shaping the efficacy of tax subsidies as a policy tool to expand health insurance coverage. But such a lack was not as problematic for policymakers as it may have seemed upon first glance because of important differences in focus, methodology, data, and applicability of results among the studies considered by Gruber. He compared the strengths and weaknesses of available estimates of price sensitivity and identified those he thought were useful for the purpose of forecasting the impact of proposed tax subsidies on health insurance coverage.

On the question of how responsive the decision by firms to offer health insurance to employees was to changes in its tax price, Gruber concluded that the best available estimate of this responsiveness was one of his own. In a 2000 study done with Michael Lettau, he estimated that the price elasticity of employer offering of health insurance fell between -0.3 and -0.4. This implied that a 10% rise in the tax price of health insurance could lead to a decline in the number of firms offering coverage to employees of three to four percentage points.[28]

On the question of how responsive the decision of employees to accept health insurance coverage offered by their employers was to changes in its tax price, Gruber found that the decision seemed to be independent of such changes. In other words, available evidence indicated that employees did not measurably alter their take up of employer health plans in response to changes in their tax price. He noted that this finding was consistent with "a growing body of evidence" that the decisions of employers appear to have much more influence than the preferences of employees over the availability of fringe benefits like health insurance.[29]

And on the question of how responsive the decision of individuals who lack public or employer-provided health insurance coverage to purchase non-group coverage was to changes in its tax price, Gruber noted that only one meaningful study had been done, and that it was too flawed to provide helpful guidance for policymakers. The study estimated a tax-price elasticity of non-group coverage of -0.3, implying that a 10% drop in the after-tax cost of non-group health insurance would lead to a 3% increase in the number of individuals covered under such policies. In his view, the study's shortcomings meant that the estimate should be construed as a "lower bound" on the tax-price sensitivity of the demand for non-group coverage among those not eligible for public or employer health insurance.[30]

Gruber's study indicated that neither firms nor individuals were especially sensitive to reductions in the tax price of health insurance. But it did offer fresh evidence that the offering decisions of firms tended to be more responsive to such reductions than the acceptance decisions of employees. The study also served the purpose of highlighting some of the significant gaps in our understanding of the forces shaping behavioral responses to tax subsidies for health insurance coverage. Of particular interest was a paucity of conclusive evidence on the price elasticity of demand for non-group insurance among those currently

[27] See Gruber, *Taxes and Health Insurance*, pp. 12-25.
[28] Ibid., p. 16.
[29] Ibid., p. 19.
[30] Ibid., p. 22.

lacking public or employer health insurance. Little is also known about the price sensitivity of the uninsured who are not offered health insurance by their employers.

POTENTIAL EFFECTIVENESS AND COST OF SOME PROPOSED TAX SUBSIDIES TO EXPAND HEALTH INSURANCE COVERAGE

Recent proposals to use tax subsidies to achieve substantial reductions in the uninsured population raise the question of what approach is likely to be most cost-effective. Several recent studies have addressed this question. Among other things, they shed light on the critical factors determining the cost-effectiveness of tax subsidies to expand health insurance coverage. The principal findings of these studies are reviewed below.

Lewin Group Study

In 1999, Lewin Group issued a study that assessed the effectiveness and revenue cost of nine proposed tax subsidies for the purchase of health insurance. The proposals ranged from something as simple as a tax deduction for the purchase of non-group health insurance to something as complex as the replacement of current federal tax subsidies for health insurance with individual insurance mandates and refundable tax credits for the purchase of non-group health insurance. Some were modeled after legislative initiatives then being considered in Congress. For each proposal, the Lewin Group used a micro-simulation model of the U.S. health care system (known as the Lewin Group Health Benefits Simulation Model) to estimate the number of persons who would be eligible for the proposed tax subsidy, the change in the number of insured persons in response to its adoption, and its federal revenue cost in 2000 dollars. These estimates then were used to compute the percentage change in the uninsured population relative to 1997 – the most recent year at the time for which figures on the uninsured population were available – and the revenue cost per newly insured person.

The micro-simulation model generated these estimates on the basis of several key assumptions. Two are worth mentioning here.

One assumption addressed the sensitivity of consumers in general to changes in the after-tax price of health insurance – or the tax-price elasticity of demand for health insurance. The proposed tax subsidies lowered the after-tax price of health insurance for eligible individuals, which in turn sparked an overall increase in health insurance coverage among these individuals. Naturally, the magnitude of the increase depended critically on the price elasticity of demand. The study used an elasticity of -0.2, which implied that a 10% decrease in the after-tax price of insurance would trigger a 2% rise in coverage nationwide. Nonetheless, considerable uncertainty surrounded the actual price elasticity. Health economists who had studied the issue came up with estimates ranging from 0.0 to -2.7.[31]

[31] The coefficient for the price elasticity used in the Lewin Group study came from a 1998 analysis by the same organization that analyzed the effect of changes in employee contributions to employer health insurance on the number of workers and dependents purchasing employer-provided health insurance. Other studies have come up with different estimates of the price elasticity of demand for health insurance, but in doing so they employed different estimation methods, for the most part. For a discussion of these studies, see Gruber and Poterba, "Fundamental Tax Reform and Employer-Provided Health Insurance," pp. 159-162.

Another important assumption concerned the number of individuals who would claim or take up the proposed tax subsidies. For subsidies supplementing existing federal tax subsidies for health insurance, the study assumed every eligible individual currently covered by non-group insurance would claim them, whether a deduction or refundable tax credit. The rate at which a tax subsidy was taken up mattered because its revenue cost and overall efficacy depended in part on how many individuals actually took advantage of it. Available evidence in 1999 suggested, however, that the take-up rate for these individuals was significantly less than 100%.[32]

Several of the study's findings have important implications for the potential cost and effectiveness of tax subsidies to expand health insurance coverage. They are highlighted below.

Lewin Group's Findings on Cost-Effectiveness[33]

- The most cost-effective subsidy was a refundable tax credit for the purchase of non-group insurance by taxpayers not covered by employment-based health insurance, Medicare, or Medicaid that was capped at $500 for single persons and $1,000 for families; the cost per newly insured person was $1,246 (2000 dollars).

- The least cost-effective subsidy was one that scrapped existing federal tax subsidies for the purchase of health insurance – except for medical savings accounts – and substituted a fixed refundable tax credit of $800 per adult and $400 per child (capped at $2,400 per family) for the purchase of health insurance by all taxpayers except those who are covered under Medicare or Medicaid; the cost per newly insured person was $10,541 (2000 dollars).

- Refundable tax credits for the purchase of health insurance by low-income working and non-working individuals were more effective but more costly (per newly insured person) than an above-the-line tax deduction for the purchase of non-group health insurance by taxpayers who were not covered by employment-based insurance, Medicare, or Medicaid.

Lewin Group's Findings on Effectiveness[34]

- The most effective subsidy was a plan developed by the Heritage Foundation which would make sweeping changes in the structure of health insurance coverage for the non-elderly. Among other things, it abolished existing federal tax subsidies for health

---

[32] In a 1993 study of the response of self-employed individuals to the creation of a partial tax deduction for their health insurance expenditures by the Tax Reform Act of 1986, economists Jonathan Gruber and James Poterba found that from 1986 to 1989, between 15% and 20% of the self-employed with incomes below $20,000 and about 50% of those with incomes above $50,000 claimed the deduction. From these response rates, they concluded that a lack of awareness of the presence of the subsidy undercut its effectiveness. See U.S. Congress, House Committee on Ways and Means, Subcommittee on Health, *Health Insurance Premium Deductions for the Self-Employed,* hearing, 104th Cong., 1st sess., Jan. 27, 1995 (Washington: GPO,1996), pp. 42-43.

[33] Cost-effectiveness in this context denotes the revenue cost per newly insured person.

[34] Effectiveness in this context denotes the total decrease in the uninsured population, if any.

insurance, substituted a refundable tax credit for health insurance and medical care expenditures, and required all individuals to purchase a minimum level of health benefits and all employers to convert their health benefit plans to wages. The plan resulted in the elimination of the entire uninsured population, which was assumed to total 43.3 million in 2000.

- The least effective subsidy was a 30% refundable, means-tested tax credit for non-group health insurance purchased by taxpayers without access to employment-based health insurance and not covered under Medicare or Medicaid. The credit phased out for single persons with adjusted gross incomes between $25,000 and $35,000, and for married couples with adjusted gross incomes between $40,000 and $50,000. It reduced the uninsured population by 1.5 million persons.

Lewin Group's Findings on Cost

- The most costly subsidy was the Heritage Foundation plan: its net revenue cost was $55.3 billion (2000 dollars).
- The least costly subsidy was the 30% refundable tax credit for the purchase of non-group health insurance by individuals without access to employment-based health insurance and not covered by Medicare or Medicaid: its net revenue cost was $3.3 billion (2000 dollars).

Gruber 2000 Analysis

Gruber's 2000 study and the Lewin Group study had much in common. The Gruber study had a similar focus: the potential effects of alternative tax subsidies for health insurance on the number of uninsured and the federal budget. Like the Lewin Group study, many of the tax subsidies Gruber evaluated were modeled after legislative proposals stirring interest in recent Congresses. And the Gruber study also employed a computerized model of the links between tax policy and the U.S. health insurance market to analyze these effects.

But the Gruber study went beyond the Lewin Group study in that it addressed two important issues raised by tax-based approaches to expanding health insurance coverage which were excluded or given marginal treatment in the Lewin Group study. One issue was the extent to which different income groups benefitted from the proposed subsidies; and the second concerned the impact of the subsidies on the market for group health insurance. The Gruber analysis also differed somewhat in approach (but not in basic methodology). It simulated the effects of a "base case" along a number of dimensions, including the federal revenue cost, the size of the uninsured population, the number of individuals with employment-based health insurance, and the distribution of the net cost of the subsidy among major income groups.[35] Gruber then simulated the effects of other proposed tax subsidies

[35] The base case involved a refundable tax credit for the purchase of non-group health insurance by individuals not covered by Medicare or employment-based health insurance. The credit was limited to $1,000 for single filers and $2,000 for joint filers and head-of-household filers, and it phased out for single filers with adjusted gross

(e.g., a non-refundable tax credit for the purchase of non-group insurance and an above-theline tax deduction for the same purpose) on the same variables and compared the results to those of the base case.

For each proposed tax subsidy, Gruber estimated the revenue cost to the federal government, how many individuals would become insured, how the benefits would be distributed among income groups, and how many individuals with employment-based health insurance would drop it or lose it in response to the subsidy.[36] In simulating these effects, he had to make assumptions about a number of key behavioral variables, including the extent to which those who were uninsured took up the subsidies to purchase non-group coverage, the extent to which those already covered by non-group health insurance claimed the proposed subsidies, and the extent to which firms reacted to the subsidies by eliminating or cutting health benefits for employees. Not surprisingly, the results of Gruber's analysis hinged on the sensitivity of the demand for health insurance coverage to declines in its after-tax price. Gruber assumed a higher price elasticity than the Lewin Group study: -0.53 compared to -0.2. This difference was hardly trivial: a 1% fall in the after-tax price of health insurance in both studies led to an increase in insurance coverage among the uninsured that was 2.6 times greater in Gruber's analysis. While the validity of Gruber's assumed price elasticity is open to question, it should be noted that it was closer to the middle of the range of available elasticity estimates than the one used in the Lewin Group study.

Several results of Gruber's analysis also should be highlighted because they have important implications for the effectiveness and cost of tax subsidies to expand health insurance coverage:

Gruber's Findings on Cost-Effectiveness[37]

- The most cost-effective subsidy was a means-tested refundable tax credit for the purchase of non-group health insurance by individuals not covered by Medicare or employment-based health insurance. Under terms specified by Gruber, the credit could not exceed $500 for single filers and $1,000 for joint and head-of-household filers; and it phased out for single filers with adjusted gross incomes between $45,000 and $60,000 and for joint and head-of-household filers with adjusted gross incomes between $75,000 and $100,000. The cost per newly insured person was $2,239 (1999 dollars).
- The least cost-effective subsidy was a refundable tax credit for out-of-pocket health insurance expenditures by individuals not covered by Medicare: the cost per newly insured person was $5,003 (1999 dollars).

Gruber's Findings on Effectiveness.[38]

- The most effective tax subsidy was a refundable tax credit for all out-of-pocket health insurance expenditures by individuals not covered by Medicare that was

incomes between $45,000 and $60,000 and for joint and head-of-household filers with adjusted gross incomes between $75,000 and $100,000.

[36] Gruber, *Tax Subsidies for Health Insurance: Evaluating the Costs and Benefits,* p. 9.

[37] See footnote #33 for a definition of this concept.

[38] See footnote #34 for a definition of this concept.

limited to $1,000 for single filers and $2,000 for joint and head-of-household filers: it reduced the uninsured population by 12.4 million.

- Running a close second was a refundable tax credit for the purchase of non-group health insurance by individuals not covered by Medicare or employment-based health insurance. The credit was limited to $2,000 for single filers and $4,000 for joint and head-of-household filers and was paid directly to insurers when premium payments were due. It reduced the uninsured population by 12.1 million.

- The least effective subsidy was an above-the-line tax deduction for the purchase of non-group health insurance by individuals not covered by Medicare or employment-based insurance: it lowered the uninsured population by 250,000.

Gruber's Findings on Cost

- The most costly subsidy was a refundable tax credit for out-of-pocket health insurance expenditures by individuals not covered by Medicare that was limited to $1,000 for single filers and $2,000 for joint and head-of-household filers: its net revenue cost was $62.2 billion (1999 dollars).

- The least costly subsidy was the above-the-line tax deduction for the same expenditures: it carried a net revenue cost of $0.9 billion (1999 dollars).

Gruber's Findings on Equity

- The subsidy engendering the largest share of benefits for low-income households was a refundable tax credit for the purchase of non-group health insurance by individuals not covered by Medicare or employment-based health insurance. It was limited to $1,000 for single filers and $2,000 for joint and head-of-household filers and phased out for single filers with adjusted gross incomes between $18,000 and $25,000 and for joint and head-of-household filers with adjusted gross incomes between $30,000 and $50,000. Households with incomes below 200% of the federal poverty level in 1999 received 69% of the net revenue cost of the subsidy.

- The subsidy granting the lowest share of its benefits to low-income households was a non-refundable tax credit for the purchase of non-group health insurance by individuals not covered by Medicare or employment-based health insurance. It was limited to $1,000 for single filers and $2,000 for joint and head-of-household filers. Households with incomes below 200% of the federal poverty level in 1999 received 22% of the net revenue cost of the subsidy.

- On the whole, refundable tax credits for the purchase of non-group health insurance were of much greater benefit to low-income households than either a non-refundable tax credit or a tax deduction.

Gruber's Findings on Employer Health Insurance Coverage

- Only one subsidy engendered an increase (6.6%) in the number of individuals covered by employment-based health insurance: a refundable tax credit for out-of-pocket health insurance expenditures by all individuals not covered by Medicare. Those already covered by employer plans were eligible for the credit.

- The subsidy leading to the smallest decline (-0.9%) in the number of individuals covered by employment-based insurance was a tax deduction for the purchase of non-group health insurance.

- Two almost identical subsidies generated the largest decline (-9.6%) in the number of individuals covered by employment-based insurance: (1) a refundable tax credit for the purchase of non-group health insurance by individuals not covered by Medicare or employment-based health insurance that was limited to $2,000 for single filers and $4,000 for joint and head-of-household filers and phased out for single filers with adjusted gross incomes between $45,000 and $60,000 and for joint and head-of-household filers with adjusted gross incomes between $75,000 and $100,000; (2) a version of the same credit which could be paid directly to insurers in advance of the tax year in which it was claimed.

Gruber's Findings on Key Administrative Issues

- Avoiding mismatches between the timing of health insurance premium payments and the timing of subsidy transfers to eligible individuals with minimal or no household savings had a significant impact on the efficacy of the base case. The reduction in the uninsured population was 37% greater when the base case was simulated on the assumption that such mismatches were prevented than when it was simulated without such an assumption.

Gruber 2001 Analysis

In a follow-up to his 2000 study, Gruber explored the potential cost and effectiveness of what he viewed as three likely directions for the use of tax policy to enlarge the insured population.[39] The directions involved offering new tax subsidies to employers; offering new tax subsidies to employees; and offering new tax subsides for the purchase of non-group insurance to individuals not eligible for public or employer-provided insurance coverage. Gruber assessed and compared the efficiency – as measured by the estimated revenue cost per newly insured individual – of these basic options. His key findings are summarized below.

New Subsidies to Employers

As Gruber has noted, many firms already offer health insurance to employees. So an important consideration in devising new tax subsidies for employers to expand health insurance coverage is which firms would be eligible. If the subsidies are not narrowly or properly targeted, the cost per newly insured individual could quickly reach unsustainably

[39] See Gruber, *Taxes and Health Insurance.*

high levels. Available data on the links between the uninsured and the workplace suggest a relatively simple and efficient solution: offering the largest tax subsidy to the smallest firms paying the lowest wages and phasing it out as firm sizes and average wages rise.

Gruber simulated the effects of just such an approach. He assumed a maximum tax subsidy rate of 0.4 for firms with 10 or fewer employees and average annual wages of $10,000 or less. Such a rate was equivalent to a tax credit for 40% of the cost to the firm of providing health insurance to each employee. In addition, he assumed that the amount of the subsidy was reduced by 2.5% for every additional employee beyond 10, so that it reached zero at 50 employees; and that it was also reduced by any increase in average annual wages beyond $10,000. Gruber found that such a tax subsidy added 2.3 million individuals to the ranks of the non-elderly insured at an annual cost of $4.7 billion, or $2,005 (2000 dollars) per newly insured individual.[40] He also found that by increasing the subsidy rate to 0.6, the annual cost rose by 70% (to $8 billion per year) but coverage expanded by 50%, resulting in a higher cost per newly insured individual: $2,300.[41]

New Subsidies to Employees

Another policy option for expanding health insurance coverage among the non-elderly analyzed by Gruber consisted of a new tax subsidy to employees to take up coverage offered by employers. He determined that it would have little effect on coverage rates and would be relatively inefficient.[42] There were two reasons for this outcome. First, only 5% of those who are offered insurance by employers were uninsured. Second, the decision to take up coverage was insensitive to changes in its tax price. Gruber did note that this option offered the advantage of targeting low-income workers; but it had the disadvantage of not being able to target low-wage firms, as many low-wage workers are employed by firms that pay relatively high average wages and already offer insurance.

New Subsidies for Non-Group Coverage

The final alternative analyzed by Gruber consisted of a new tax subsidy for the purchase of non-group insurance by individuals not covered under public or employment-based insurance. He identified three major hurdles lying in the path of such an approach. One was that about half of uninsured households pay no income taxes. This fact suggested that if the subsidy were a tax credit, it should be made refundable. A second hurdle was that most uninsured households lack access to the liquid assets required to pay insurance premiums before receiving a tax subsidy such as a refundable tax credit. As a result, the effectiveness of a tax subsidy would be greatly enhanced if it were made payable in advance. Finally, non-group coverage was costly; so any tax subsidy would need to cover a large share of premiums if it were to be highly effective.

Gruber simulated the effects of a tax subsidy similar to what the Bush Administration proposed in its budget request for FY2002. He assumed that the subsidy involved a refundable credit of $1,000 for single filers with incomes up to $75,000, and $2,000 for joint and head-of-household filers with incomes up to $100,000. In addition, he assumed that it was not payable in advance. Swayed by such a subsidy, the uninsured population shrank by 4

[40] Ibid., p. 29.
[41] Ibid., p. 30.
[42] Ibid., p. 31.

million persons, and the estimated cost per newly insured came to $3,300 (2000 dollars).[43] Gruber performed another simulation under the assumption that the credit was payable in advance and found that the cost per newly insured fell to about $2,500. Both estimates were well above his estimated cost of a new tax subsidy for employers.

Gruber 2002 Analysis

Still another recent study by Gruber is worth considering, since it focused on the cost and effectiveness of the tax credit for health insurance coverage proposed by the Bush Administration in its budget request for FY2003. He presented his findings in a statement made to the House Ways and Means Committee in connection with a hearing on tax credits for expanding health insurance coverage it held on February 13, 2002.[44] The credit had the following features: it was refundable, available only for the purchase of non-group insurance by those not covered under public or employer-provided health insurance, payable in advance, and limited to $1,000 for single individuals with adjusted gross incomes of up to $30,000 and to $3,000 for families with adjusted gross incomes of either $40,000 (if only one adult purchased insurance) or $60,000 (if more than one adult purchased insurance).

Gruber's analysis again involved the use of a micro-simulation model. This one was similar in design to the one he employed in his 2000 analysis and took into account what was known about the behavioral responses of non-elderly individuals, firms, and insurance companies to changes in the tax price of health insurance. One of his assumptions was that individuals and families who purchased non-group coverage in response to the credit paid average market prices for that insurance.

He estimated that the subsidy would have a total annual cost of $5.2 billion (2001 dollars) and result in a net decline in the uninsured population of 1.9 million, yielding a cost per newly insured individual of nearly $2,800.[45] In addition, an estimated 10.5 million individuals took up the new credit, 3.3 million of whom were previously uninsured. Nearly 2.5 million of the individuals taking up the credit had been covered by employment-based coverage. Of these, 1.5 million persons voluntarily switched to non-group coverage because they found it to be a better deal with the credit, and 1.0 million persons involuntarily switched because their employers dropped health insurance coverage in response to the credit. Some of the individuals who lost employer-provided insurance ended up uninsured, which explained why the net decrease in the uninsured population was 1.9 million persons and not 3.3 million. For these newly uninsured, the cost of non-group coverage proved too high even with the credit.

Some analysts have contended that the adoption of a tax credit for health insurance coverage modeled on the President's proposal but somewhat more generous would trigger a major overhaul of the non-group market, leading to the emergence of new low-cost plans with fewer gaps in coverage and less premium variation by age and geographic location.[46] To explore the cost and efficacy of plans such as these, Gruber performed another two

---

[43] Ibid., p. 33.

[44] U.S. Congress, House Ways and Means Committee, *Health Care Tax Credits to Decrease the Number of Uninsured*, hearing, 107th Cong., 2nd sess., Feb. 13, 2002 (Washington: GPO, 2002), pp. 123-128.

[45] Ibid., p. 125.

[46] For a discussion of policy debate over this possible outcome, see Mark V. Pauly and Len M. Nichols, "The Nongroup Health Insurance Market: Short on Facts, Long on Opinions and Policy Disputes," *Health Affairs*, Web exclusive [http://www.healthaffairs.org], Oct. 23, 2002, pp. W325-W344.

simulations. In one, he assumed that half of all persons buying non-group coverage with the credit were able to do so at prices 25% below average market prices; and in the other, he assumed that the same group of individuals were able to obtain coverage at prices 50% below average market prices. His results suggested that the greater the decrease in non-group premiums under the credit, the larger the decline in the uninsured population and the greater the displacement of those previously covered by employment-based insurance.[47] Specifically, with a 25% reduction in non-group premiums, the total cost per year was $5.4 billion (2001 dollars), and the uninsured population fell by 2.2 million persons at a cost per newly insured of $2,503. By contrast, with a 50% reduction in premiums, the total annual cost came to $6.0 billion (2001 dollars), and the uninsured population declined by 3.6 million persons at a cost per newly insured of $1,663.

CONCLUSIONS

A central challenge for policymakers interested in using tax policy to achieve a substantial and lasting reduction in the uninsured population is to devise a tax subsidy that can accomplish this goal without having undesirable effects on the allocation of economic resources, the distribution of disposable income among households, and the cost of tax administration. Generally, tax policy can and does affect the price and terms of health insurance coverage. The material examined here has important implications for the use of tax policy to expand this coverage. Its significance can be illuminated in a series of questions focusing on factors to consider in designing tax subsidies to expand health insurance coverage.

- **Is the subsidy a tax deduction or a tax credit?** Many uninsured individuals reside in low-income households. Gruber has estimated that up to 90% of uninsured taxpayers with tax liabilities belonged to the 15% income tax bracket in 1997. Tax deductions become more valuable as a taxpayer's marginal tax rate increases. But generally, one dollar of a tax deduction has a lower revenue cost than one dollar of a tax credit.

- **If the subsidy is a tax credit, is it refundable?** Gruber has also estimated that 50% of uninsured taxpayers have no tax liability – though the proportion may be smaller today owing to the reduction in marginal tax rates and the creation of 10% bracket under the Economic Growth and Tax Relief Reconciliation Act of 2001 and the increase in wages and salaries since 1997, the year to which Gruber's estimate applies. Non-refundable tax credits are valuable only if a taxpayer has a tax liability against which it can be claimed. Refundable tax credits, by contrast, are valuable to all low-income taxpayers because they can be claimed regardless of whether there is a current tax liability.

- **If the subsidy is a refundable tax credit, is it fixed or proportional in amount?** Another factor shaping the effectiveness of a tax subsidy to expand health insurance

[47] Gruber, *Health Care Tax Credits to Decrease the Number of Uninsured*, pp. 127-128.

coverage is the share of premiums it covers. As many uninsured individuals reside in low-income households, the greater the share of individual and family premiums met by the subsidy, the greater the rate at which the subsidy is likely to be taken up by the uninsured. Fixed refundable tax credits may cover smaller and smaller portions of premiums as health care costs rise over time. In addition, premiums in the non-group market vary by age, sex, and geographic location, and in the group market by size of employer or risk pool. And premiums in the non-group market tend to be lower for young adults in good health and higher for older adults in poor health.

- **Who is eligible for the subsidy?** Recent studies suggest that the most cost-effective subsidies are apt to be ones that are narrowly targeted at groups with large proportions of uninsured individuals. Tax subsidies targeted at low-income households headed by someone not covered by employer-provided or public insurance are likely to have a lower revenue cost per newly insured individual than subsidies with a broader reach, such as a tax deduction for all out-of-pocket expenditures for health insurance. But there is some evidence that targeting firms in the hope of inducing them to offer coverage to employees may be more effective than targeting individuals who lack coverage. Gruber has estimated that over three-quarters of uninsured workers are not offered health insurance by their employers. In addition, eligibility matters because of the different ways that firms, individuals, and private insurers can respond to tax subsidies for health insurance.

- **Does the subsidy address key administrative issues?** Yet another factor affecting the cost and efficacy of proposed tax subsidies to expand health insurance coverage is administrative issues that could impede their smooth implementation. At least three can be mentioned here. One concern is possible mismatches between the timing of health insurance premium payments and the timing of subsidy transfers to eligible individuals. Because relatively few uninsured households appear to have sufficient liquid assets to draw upon in paying health insurance premiums, making the subsidies payable in advance of the due date for filing tax returns may enhance their efficacy. A related concern is the rate at which eligible individuals might take up tax subsidies that are payable in advance. Experience with the federal earned income tax credit suggests that low-income taxpayers are reluctant to claim advanceable tax credits because many fear they will end up facing a tax liability when they file their tax returns.[48] Finally, there is some concern that the IRS lacks the resources to efficiently administer any advanceable tax subsidy for health insurance coverage.[49] It should also be kept in mind that there appear to be significant trade-offs between ease of administration and precision of targeting in tax subsidies to expand health insurance coverage.

- **Does the subsidy address barriers to coverage of high-risk groups in the private insurance market?** Persons with relatively high risks of certain health problems are

[48] Gruber, *Taxes and Health Insurance*, p. 32.

[49] See George Guttman, "Another IRS Burden: The New Health Insurance Credit," *Tax Notes*, March 3, 2003, pp. 1322-1324.

likely to find it difficult to obtain affordable and adequate coverage in the non-group market. Premiums vary widely by age, sex, and region. And in many states, insurers are free to exclude pre-exiting conditions from coverage or to severely restrict coverage for these conditions. These underwriting practices raise the question of whether a tax subsidy to expand health insurance coverage should include regulations aimed at curbing these practices.

- **What is the ultimate policy objective of the tax subsidy?** The design of cost-effective tax subsidies to expand health insurance coverage also depends in part on the ultimate policy objective. If the main goal is to improve equity in access to federal tax subsidies for health insurance, a tax deduction for personal expenditures on health insurance by those ineligible for existing subsidies may suffice. Or if the main goal is to reduce substantially the uninsured population, then a proportional, advanceable, refundable tax credit targeted at uninsured workers not offered health insurance coverage by their employers may suffice. But if the main goal is to achieve universal coverage, then it may be necessary to couple a subsidy such as a refundable, advanceable, means-tested tax credit with reforms of the private health insurance market and a requirement that all individuals purchase health insurance or all firms provide health insurance to their employees.

II. CURRENT ISSUES

Chapter 6

HEALTH INSURANCE FOR FEDERAL EMPLOYEES AND RETIREES

Carolyn L. Merck

INTRODUCTION

The Federal Employees Health Benefits Program (FEHBP) covers 8.6 million individuals, including 2.2 million federal and postal employees, 1.9 million federal annuitants, and 4.5 million dependents. Premiums in FY2001 totaled over $21 billion, of which enrollees and the U.S. Postal Service paid $10.3 billion.

In 2001, total annual premiums for self-only policies averaged about $3,100; family policies averaged $7,000. Premiums will be about 13.3% higher in 2002, and the maximum government share will be $2,544 for self-only coverage and $5,809 for family coverage. On average, annual premium increases have exceeded 9% since 1998, bringing cumulative increases since then to nearly 50%.

The Office of Personnel Management (OPM) renews contracts annually with participating fee-for-service plans (one commercial carrier, six plans sponsored by employee organizations, and six plans limited to certain federal agencies). The program includes over 200 health maintenance organizations (HMOs) which may renew their contract annually or center the program on a noncompetitive basis. HMOs enroll 30% of all participants, including 39% of employees and 17% of annuitants. The number of participating HMOs has declined substantially in recent years although total HMO enrollment has not declined. Plans withdrawing cite small enrollments and a variety of business reasons.

The FEHBP law does not mandate a standard plan benefit package, although OPM has the authority to impose certain coverage requirements, such as child immunizations, cancer screenings, organ transplants, and prescription drugs (enrollee costs for drugs vary widely among the plans). OPM requires plans to limit enrollees' annual out-of-pocket expenses, but there is no standard definition of the expenses that count toward that limit. Clinton Administration directives required inclusion of patient consumer protections and parity for coverage of mental and physical health care. Fee-for-service plan premiums are based on actuarial estimates of the cost of claims, a reserve margin, inflation, and predictions of utilization rates. OPM pays HMOs the capitated rate paid by other large employers in the community.

Enrollees who disagree with their plan's denial of a claim must first seek a redetermination from the plan. If the redetermination results in denial, the enrollee may appeal that decision to OPM. If OPM upholds the denial the enrollee may sue OPM, not the plan, in federal court. If the enrollee prevails in court, the plan will pay for the denied care, but no compensatory or punitive damages may be awarded.

Retirees choose among the same plans at the same premiums as workers. At age 65 most federal retirees are eligible for Medicare Part A, may elect Part B, and may keep their FEHBP enrollment, in which case FEHBP usually pays Medicare's deductibles, coinsurance, and certain other costs. Medicare covers some services not covered by FEHBP fee-for-service plans (e.g., skilled nursing facility care), and FEHBP plans cover some things excluded from Medicare (e.g., outpatient prescription drugs). FEHBP enrollees with Medicare have little or no out-of-pocket costs for care covered by both programs.

ORIGINS AND PURPOSE OF THE PROGRAM

In 1959, the Congress passed the Federal Employees Health Benefits Act ("FEHBA," P.L. 86-382) establishing the FEHBP. A major purpose of the Act was to enable the federal government to attract and certain competent personnel on a competitive basis with private sector employers.

As of July 1, 1960, participation in FEHBP became available on a voluntary basis for federal civilian employees and their immediate family members (spouses and dependent children). Civil service workers who retired on or after that date could continue to participate if they had been enrolled before retirement.[1]

The original law set out broad outlines for the structure of the program and gave the Civil Service Commission (now, OPM) overall administrative responsibility and the authority to contract with private health insurance carriers and federal employee and postal organizations to provide, for fixed, predetermined premiums, benefits the agency judged appropriate to the needs of federal workers and retirees at affordable prices.[2] This design places all risk paying covered claims on the carriers, not on the federal government.

---

[1] The original law did not cover individuals who had already retired from their federal jobs when it was enacted. To provide coverage for this group, Congress enacted P.L. 86-724 (the Retired Federal Employees Health Benefits Program, "RFEHBP") on September 8, 1960. The RFEHBP covers a closed and declining group of retired federal workers (fewer than 7,000).

[2] The FEHBA defines a *carrier* as a voluntary association, corporation, partnership, or other nongovernmental organizations engaged in providing, paying for, or reimbursing the cost of, health services under group insurance policies or contracts, medical or hospital service agreements, membership or subscription contracts for a premium or other periodic charge payable to the carrier, including a health benefits plan sponsored or underwritten by an employee organization. It defines a *health benefits plan* as a group insurance policy or contract, medical or hospital service agreement, membership or subscription contract, or similar group arrangements provided by a carrier for the purpose of providing, paying for, or reimbursing expenses for health services. In general, OPM contracts with a *carrier* and the carrier offers a *plan* that has certain benefit features. In most cases, a single carrier offers a single plan. However, some HMOs operate as carriers that have one contract with OPM under which several plans may be offered in different locations.

Active federal workers and retirees participate in the FEHBP under the same terms and conditions; they have the same choice of plans and benefit packages and the same premiums. This mixed-age population allows for cross-subsidization of costs within the program. Premiums paid by younger workers, who, as a group, generally use comparatively little health care, subsidize the premiums of older retirees who tend to use more health care.

FEHBP's Multiple Plan Design

Enrollment of Plans

When Congress designed the FEHBP to offer federal workers and annuitants a choice among different types of health plans, the intent was primarily to serve the varying needs of a group of workers and retirees that is larger, more diverse, and more geographically disbursed than that covered by most private firms. Another goal of the program was to allow enrollees to choose and change plans according to their needs. In the original legislation, Congress identified the general types of plans that would constitute the FEHBP and gave OPM the authority to enroll plans to achieve variety in coverage and costs. Under this design, carriers do not compete to participate in the program, but those in the program compete to attract enrollees on the basis of service and quality as well as benefits and price.

It is sometimes suggested that program costs might be reduced if plan enrollment were competitive and if a key selection criterion were price. However, cost minimization has never been the primary reason for the multiple plan design of FEHBP. The 1959 Senate committee report accompanying the original legislation noted that, "Reasonable competition among different types of programs will provide federal employees with a better program. Unrestricted competition could make the program administratively unwieldy and ineffective."[3] (For a discussion of the effects of choice on program costs, see **Appendix 1,** *The Potential Effects of Choice in FEHBP*).

Enrollment of Workers and Annuitants

New federal employees hired into permanent positions (working either full time or part time) may join a FEHBP plan at the start of their employment. Workers not previously participating may enroll during an open enrollment season.[4] At the time of retirement, workers have a one-time opportunity to continue to participate as an annuitant (provided the worker participated in any of the plans at least 5 years immediately before retirement and is retiring with a civil service annuity commencing immediately upon retirement). If a retiring worker does not elect coverage, it is permanently forfeited.

---

[3] Federal Employees Health Benefits Act of 1959, Senate Committee Report 86-468, p.4.

[4] In general, workers hired as *temporary employees* may not participate during the first year of such service; however, after completing one year of temporary service, workers continuing in temporary appointments may participate (provided they have no break in service of more than 5 days) but receive no government contribution toward the premium. Permanent, career employees working *part time* may participate but are eligible for only a partial government contribution toward the premium depending on the number of hours the employee works during a pay period.

Annual open seasons start in early November and run for 1 month. Workers and annuitants enrolled in the program may change plans only during an open season, although, at any time, enrollees may drop coverage or change from a self-only policy to a family policy, or vice versa. There are no restrictions regarding preexisting conditions for employees joining the program, for participants who change plans, or for their eligible dependents enrolled or added under a family policy. Participants who take no action to change plans during an open season are automatically continued in the plan in which they are already enrolled. In recent years, fewer than 3% of all participants have changed plans during open seasons, and fewer annuitants than active workers generally change plans.

Categories of Plans Eligible to Participate

Since the beginning of the program, FEHBP law has specified four categories of participating plans. It limits two of those categories to one carrier each. In 1959, the Congress envisioned that most program participants would have a choice of two plans and that some might have four available choices. The four types of plans included in the program are:

- One governmentwide "service benefit plan," defined as a fee-for-service plan under which the plan would pay providers directly for covered services. Originally, the plan paid the customary charges for a service in the area, and enrollees paid no deductibles or coinsurance for basic benefits; the plan is required to offer two levels of benefits. This plan slot was originally modeled on the design of the Blue Cross and Blue Shield plans and has always been filled by Blue Cross and Blue Shield;[5]
- One governmentwide "indemnity plan," defined as a fee-for-service plan under which the plan reimburses the insured individual for "reasonable fees" for covered services as determined by the carrier; enrollees were charged with deductibles and coinsurance. The plan is required to offer two levels of benefits. Originally, under this plan the enrollee would pay the provider and file a claim for reimbursement from the carrier. This plan slot was filled by the Aetna Life Insurance Company from the start of the program until it voluntarily withdrew from the program in 1990; since then there has been no plan filling this slot;
- Plans sponsored by employee organizations, limited to those organizations that applied and were approved within certain time periods (these are fee-for-service plans);
- An unspecified number of "comprehensive medical plans" which, in FEHBP, are HMOs. The law describes these as including (a) group practice prepayment plans in which three or more physicians of different specialities practice in a common center; (b) individual practice prepayment plans in which physicians agree to provide

[5] Blue Cross and Blue Shield is a national organization that represents and lends its name to individual health insurance plans throughout the country. In order to be part of the Blue Cross and Blue Shield System and use its name and logo, affiliated plans must follow certain policies and requirements of the national organization. There are currently 44 affiliated plans operating in different geographic areas; benefit packages and prices differ among the plans. For purposes of FEHBP participation, the national organization negotiates with OPM for one benefit package and premium and all affiliates participate and offer the federal benefit package at the same premium. The national Blue Cross and Blue Shield organization is not an insurance issuer and does not process and pay claims.

services for specified payments under a plan sponsored by an organization that has successfully operated such a plan before seeking participation in FEHBP; or (c) a mix of a group and individual practice prepayment comprehensive plans.

Evolving Plan Designs and Managed Care as Cost Containment

The distinctions among these four types of FEHBP plans were once more clear than they are today. All FEHBP fee-for-service plans currently include deductibles and coinsurance or copayments. In the early 1990s, the rapidly rising cost of fee-for-service health care led OPM to encourage those plans to implement cost containment measures. Today, all FEHBP fee-for-service plans offer preferred provider organization (PPO) networks, which are arrangements under which enrollees who choose from a restricted list of providers pay a lower copayment or a lower coinsurance rate than if they choose a provider not in the PPO network, although not all plans have PPOs in every area of the country or include in the PPO every type of specialized care. PPO arrangements achieve savings for the plan by entering into contracts with providers to furnish care to plan enrollees for discounted fees. (The benefit to the provider is assurance of a group of covered patients.) Thus, although FEHBP fee-for-service plans still allow enrollees to choose their health care provider, their PPO arrangements, where available, provide strong financial incentives for enrollees to limit their choice of providers to those participating in the plan's PPO network.

For plan year 2002, the Blue Cross and Blue Shield plan is making two important changes in the design of its fee-for-service offerings. First, the "high option," which Blue Cross and Blue Shield has offered since the start of the program, will be ended and the approximately 98,000 individuals who have been enrolled in it will be moved to the standard options, unless they elect another plan during the 2001 open season (November 12-December 10). Their premiums and benefits will be those applicable to the standard option.[6] Second, Blue Cross and Blue Shield will offer a new "basic" option under which there is no annual deductible, no discount mail order drug program. And no payment or reimbursement for care received from providers not in the PPO

As a cost containment measure, in 1990, Congress added to the law a requirement that FEHBP fee-for-service plans adopt preadmission certification and case management procedures for inpatient hospital care.

Contrary to the trend among fee-for-service plans to offer incentives for enrollees to use restricted networks of providers, some HMOs currently offer more provider choice than they had previously, largely as a result of enrollee dissatisfaction with the restricted provider choices available to them. Some HMOs have established point-of-service arrangements under which enrollees willing to pay somewhat higher amounts can use providers outside the HMO.

Participating Plans

OPM has about 220 contracts will carriers for 2002, including Blue Cross and Blue Shield (which offers two benefit levels and is the only carrier sponsoring an FEHBP fee-for-service plan that also sells health insurance in private markets); six employee organization fee-for-service plans open to any employee or annuitant nationwide (three of which offer a two benefit levels), and six fee-for-service plans limited to employees of certain small federal

[6] The reserve funds from the discontinued high option plan will be merged with the reserve frauds for the standard option plan.

agencies (but available within that agency nationwide). The remainder are HMOs. (Some HMOs operate plans in more than one location, but they are covered by one contract and are defined by OPM as one plan).

The number of HMOs participating in the FEHBP grew slowly in the early decades of the program, accelerating in the 1980s and early 1990s. According to the General Accounting Office (GAO), 369 HMOs participated in the FEHBP in 1994 followed by a nearly 30% increase to 476 plans in 1996.[7] After that year, the number of HMOs in the program began to decline to the point that, in 2002, there are about 200 such plans. In general only 1% or 2% of FEHBP enrollees or 5% of HMO enrollees have been affected by plans leaving the program in any given year, and, in each year, at least a few new plans entered the program. According to program administrators, plans leave for a variety of reasons, including an inability to attract sufficient numbers of enrollees, maintain competitive premiums, and predict and control utilization and risk. General volatility in the managed care industry and plan mergers and consolidations are also important factors. Withdrawals have not been due to disputes regarding payment adequacy, benefit requirements, or other government administrative requirements. (OPM pays HMOs the rate the plan charges other large employers in the community and does not impose rate discounts on HMOs).

Comparing the number of HMOs in FEHBP from year to year may be misleading because many of the plans that have withdrawn had very small enrollments. For instance, according to the GAO study, about half of the plans that withdrew in 2000 had fewer than 300 enrollees. Additionally, when plans merge or consolidate service areas there may appear to be a reduction in the number of participating plans, but coverage may not be affected. However, many plans remaining in the program have dropped coverage in certain service areas. Despite the decline in the number of HMOs in the FEHBP since 1996, total enrollment has not declined. In 1995, when there were about 430 HMOs in the program (using the GAO definition of a plan), about 1.2 million workers and retirees were enrolled in an HMO; in 2001, when there were about half that number of HMOs participating, nearly 1.7 million were enrolled. Thus, although there are currently far fewer HMOs in the program than in previous years, the plans currently in the program have, on average, larger enrollments.

Enrollment by Plan Type

Over a decade ago, 1989, 24% of FEHBP participants were enrolled in an HMO. In the late 1990s, HMO enrollment leveled off at about 30% of FEHBP participants. Active workers are more likely to choose an HMO than retirees: In 2001, 39% of active workers were enrolled in an HMO and 61% were enrolled in a fee-for-service plan; only 17% of all annuitants were enrolled in an HMO compared with 83% in a fee-for-service plan.

In 2001, 49% of FEHBP policyholders were enrolled in Blue Cross and Blue Shield, and 65% were enrolled in one of the three largest fee-for-service plans (Blue Cross and Blue Shield, Mailhandlers, and the Government Employees Hospital Association, "GEHA"). Seventy-seven percent (77%) were enrolled in either Blue Cross and Blue Shield or an HMO.

[7] *Federal Employees' Health Program: Reason Why HMOs Withdrew in 1999 and 2000*, GAO/GGD-00-100, May, 2000. This report uses a different definition of an HMO "plan" than does OPM. OPM counts as one plan all geographic areas served by an HMO that is covered by one contract with OPM. GAO counted individual plans of an HMO separately when different benefits or premiums applied to enrollees in different geographic areas.

As a practical matter, all current FEHBP participants have a choice among seven fee-for-service plans (four of which offer two options) and the HMOs in their area. The choice of HMOs may vary from none to several, depending on where the participant lives.

Benefits and Cost Sharing

Congress included multiple plans in FEHBP in order to offer enrollees a choice of plans with different benefit packages at different prices. FEHBP law does not mandate coverage of specific benefits but lists only broad categories of care and services that plans might include.[8] Under FEHBP's legislative authority, OPM is authorized to negotiate benefit packages with carriers in order to make available plans that provide the kinds of services sought by federal employees and annuitants at affordable rates.

Covered Services

All FEHBP fee-for-service plans cover the broad categories of services that comprise a competitive benefit package: inpatient and outpatient hospital care, physician services, surgical services, diagnostic tests, and emergency care.

Beyond the basic inpatient and outpatient services noted above, OPM, through its negotiating authority, currently requires that plans cover prescription drugs; childhood immunizations; certain cancer screenings and treatment; and a range of organ transplants. All plans must limit enrollee out-of-pocket expenses for covered care to some extent. In recent years, presidential directives have required FEHBP plans to implement patient consumer protections, certain coverage rules for mental health and substance abuse treatment, and error reduction strategies. Although FEHBP plans have typically excluded coverage for "alternative medicine benefits" such as acupuncture and biofeedback, for 2002, OPM encouraged plans to cover these procedures as well as chiropractic and other plan management treatments.

Although not required, limited dental benefits are available under most plans, and limited amounts of home health care and restorative therapies may be offered in the fee-for-service plans. Coverage of care in skilled nursing facilities, vision care, and hearing care are available only through HMOs.

[8] From time to time, the Congress has included in OPM appropriations legislation prohibition of abortion coverage under FEHBP, and that prohibition is currently in effect. In addition, certain requirements included in federal laws applicable to private health plans also apply to FEHBP, such as Titles VI and VII of P.L. 104-204, which (a) require that new mothers, in consultation with their physician, have the option of remaining in the hospital for at least 48 hours after delivery, (b) require that women have the option of remaining in the hospital for at least 48 hours after a mastectomy, and (c) prohibit annual or lifetime dollar limits on mental health benefits that are less generous than similar limits for other benefits. OPM imposed these requirements on FEHBP plans in its annual call letter for the 1998 contract year, issued on March 31, 1997. In P.L. 105-277 (FY1999 Omnibus Consolidated and Emergency Supplemental Appropriations Act) Congress required FEHBP plans to include prescription contraceptives under their prescription drug coverage (unless the plan chose not to do for religious or moral reasons). This requirement was renewed in appropriations legislation for FY2000 and FY2001; the Bush Administration requested the language not be included in FY2002 appropriations legislation, but did not request that plans be prohibited from offering such coverage; Congress chose to continue to include the requirement.

All FEHBP plans list in their brochures their "general exclusions," which typically include experimental care; treatment for sexual dysfunction; care provided by immediate relatives; and care or services deemed *by the plan* not to be medically necessary (see below). However, not every excluded medical procedure or service can be listed, and enrollees might assume incorrectly that a certain service would be covered if it is not listed.

Prescription Drug Coverage

Although prescription drugs might be considered a basic covered service, the law does not require coverage of drugs, and some plans did not cover them until required to do so by OPM in 1990. Because drugs are a costly component of the FEHBP program, most plans now use pharmacy benefit managers and drug formularies; contract for reduced prices at preferred pharmacy retail outlets; and offer mail order services with low enrollee cost sharing. (The Blue Cross and Blue Shield basic option does not offer a mail order program). Pharmacy benefit managers administer a plan's drug benefit and establish a formulary and negotiate formulary drug prices with drug manufacturers. Formularies are essentially lists of drugs covered by a plan. Formularies generally use three levels of enrollee copayments in order to create financial incentives for enrollees to use the least costly product. Generic drugs require the lowest copayments; "preferred" name brand drugs require a higher copayment than generics, and "non-preferred" brand name drugs or brand name drugs for which a generic alternative is available have the highest copayments. Some HMOs administer their own formulary and dispense prescriptions themselves, usually charging flat copayments, which vary depending on whether the drug is generic or a brand name. However, OPM requires that a covered drug be included for any condition treatable with pharmaceuticals.

Prescription drug coverage and enrollee out-of-pocket costs for prescriptions differ significantly. Although OPM limits enrollee coinsurance to 50% of the cost of a drug under that plan, several different factors determine how much an enrollee pays. These factors include: whether the plan has a separate drug deductible and the amount of the deductible; prices negotiated by the plan's pharmacy benefit managers for the drugs included in the plan's formulary; the type of drug purchased by the enrollee (e.g. generic, preferred brand name, or nonpreferred brand name); whether the drug is purchased through a mail order program, at a preferred or participating pharmacy, or at another retail outlet; whether prior approval was obtained before purchase of certain drugs; and, in some plans, for Medicare-eligible enrollees, whether the individual has Medicare "Part B" coverage or not, even though Medicare does not cover outpatient prescription drugs.[9] Drug benefits under FEHBP fee-for-service plans can be so complex that the explanation of the rules governing the benefit and enrollee cost sharing typically fills three or more pages of a plan's brochure.

[9] In two fee-for-service plans, enrollees age 65 or over are charged lower coinsurance rates for their prescription drugs if they are enrolled in Medicare Part B. For retirees enrolled in Part B (which covers physician and most outpatient care), the FEHBP plan pays only the portion of covered charges not paid by Medicare (generally, the enrollee's deductible and coinsurance). Thus, for nondrug benefits, it is to the FEHBP plan's financial benefit if enrollees participate in Medicare Part B. These reduced FEHBP plan costs for nondrug benefits may more than offset the costs of lower enrollee coinsurance for outpatient drug benefits.

Medical Necessity

All plans in the FEHBP restrict coverage to care and services that *the plan determines are medically necessary,* and each plan brochure includes a statement of the plan's policy regarding medical necessity. OPM does not define medical necessity. In all cases, the ultimate authority for making this determination resides with the plan, not the enrollee's physician. The language regarding the criteria for medical necessity are similar among the fee-for-service plans and specify that services, drugs, supplies, or equipment provided by a hospital or other covered provider must be:

- appropriate to prevent, diagnose, or treat the enrollee's condition, illness, or injury;
- consistent with standards of good medical practice in the United States;
- not primarily for the personal comfort or convenience of the patient, the family, or the provider;
- not part of or associated with scholastic education or vocational training of the patient; and
- in the case of inpatient care, cannot be provided safely on an outpatient basis.

These criteria are usually followed by a qualification saying that, even though a provider participating in the plan may prescribe, recommend, or approve a service or supply, that does not, in itself, make it medically necessary or covered by the plan.

The medical necessity criteria used by HMOs differ substantially among the those plans, but are usually less explicit than those noted above for fee-for-service plans. In addition, although the fee-for-service plans, all of which are available nationwide, use national standards of medical practice as a norm for making a judgment about medical necessity, the HMOs tend to use standards of practice applicable in the community they serve.

Patient Consumer Protections

In November 1997, President Clinton's Advisory Commission on Consumer Protection and Quality in the Health Care Industry reported its recommendations for a patient's bill of rights. President Clinton endorsed the report and, among other things, directed OPM to ensure that all FEHBP plans would be in full compliance by the end of 1999. Although most FEHBP plans were already in substantial compliance, starting in 2000, all FEHBP contracts require the following:

- direct access to woman's health care providers for routine and preventive woman's health services;
- use of the "prudent layperson" standard when determining the coverage of emergency care in situations where enrollees must use non-preferred providers;
- direct access to a qualified specialist in the plan's provider network for individuals with complex or serious medical conditions requiring frequent care;
- extensive information about plan characteristics and performance, provider network characteristics, and care management; and

- a prohibition on "gag" clauses in provider contracts that could limit physician/provider communication about medically necessary treatment.

According to OPM, 0.02 percentage points of the average 9.3% increase in plan premiums from 1999 to 2000 were a result of these new mandated requirements. In addition, starting in plan year 2000, enrollees who must change plans involuntarily because their plan drops out of FEHBP may receive transitional care. Transitional care is provided and paid for by the plan for up to 90 days (or through postpartum care) for individuals who are undergoing treatment for a chronic or disabling condition or are in the second or third trimester of pregnancy when the plan ceases FEHBP participation.

Mental Health and Substance Abuse Parity

Historically, coverage for mental health and substance abuse treatment has been subject to separate and stricter limitations than physical health care under FEHBP plans as well as most private plans. Typical limitations have included total annual and lifetime limits on benefits, caps on the number of inpatient days of care and the number of outpatient therapy visits, and separate of psychopharmacological drugs and drugs management.

P.L. 104-204 (making FY1997 appropriations for the Department of Veterans Affairs and Department of Housing and Urban Development and amending certain other laws governing health insurance plans, including those in the FEHBP) took the first steps toward mental health parity by prohibiting health insurance plans that provide mental health coverage from imposing more restrictive annual and aggregate lifetime dollar limits on mental health care than on physical health care. (The Act did not require plans to cover mental health care). Group health plans (or health insurance coverage offered in connection with group health plans) that covered mental health and medical/surgical conditions *and* that had annual or aggregate dollar limits for medical/surgical conditions were required to established either an inclusive limit for all benefits (e.g., $1 million lifetime limit for all benefits) or separate but identical limits for mental and physical health services. These requirements were effective for plan years beginning on or after January 1, 1998, and FEHBP plans were required to comply with them.

Beginning in 1999, OPM required FEHBP plans to cover prescription drugs for mental conditions under their regular prescription drug coverage and to include office visits and laboratory tests for managing use of such drugs under the regular medical provisions of the plan.

In spite of these new requirements, some health insurance plans, including FEHBP plans, continued to limit coverage of mental health care by imposing higher copayments, higher coinsurance, and/or higher deductibles for mental health care than for other health care. Many plans imposed limits on the number of visits to mental health providers that were not imposed for physical illness.

On May 24, 1999, President Clinton announced his intention to require all FEHBP plans to provide coverage for mental illnesses comparable to that for physical ailments, and, on June 7, 1999, he announced a series of initiatives to reform mental health coverage under all insurance plans. As a result of these Presidential directives, FEHBP plans are not permitted to cover fewer outpatient visits or inpatient hospital days for treatment of mental disorders than would be covered for physical health care, and plans may not charge higher copayments or coinsurance for mental health care than for physical health care. According to OPM, these requirements accounted for 1.28 percentage points of the average premium increase of 10.5% from 2000 to 2001.

Enrollee Deductibles, Coinsurance Rates, and Copayments

Since 1982, all fee-for-service plans in FEHBP have had annual deductibles for outpatient care, although the Blue Cross and Blue Shield basic option starting operation in 2002, requires no annual deductible. Generally, under family enrollments, the deductible is satisfied if the amount of the deductible applicable to two individuals is met even if only one family member has used care or if there are more than two enrolled family members. Annual deductibles for fee-for-service plans with deductibles in 2002 range from $100 to $500 per person, but most are $250 or $300 per person. Four of the seven governmentwide fee-for-service plans have a lower deductible for enrollees using the plan's PPO network providers; three plans include a separate deductible for prescription drugs; six plans include a separate deductible for inpatient stays in non-PPO hospitals; and three plans with a low, basic, or only one option charge an inpatient deductible for PPO and non-PPO inpatient hospital stays.

Under fee-for-service plans, enrollee copayments and coinsurance rates are generally lower when an enrollee uses health care practitioners or facilities that participate in the plan's PPO.[10] *Copayments* are flat dollar amounts (e.g., $15) that generally apply to simple care, such as an outpatient doctor visit, and usually apply only to visit to a PPO physician. A *coinsurance rate* is a specified percentage of the plan's allowed maximum payment or the provider's charge for a service (whichever is lower). Coinsurance rates, rather than copayments, usually apply to an office visit to a non-PPO physician. Coinsurance rates also apply to PPO practitioners and facilities for procedures that are more complex than an office consultation (such as surgery in a hospital outpatient department), but coinsurance rates are lower for PPO physicians and member facilities than for those not in the plan's PPO network. For example, an enrollee having cataract surgery would pay a lower percentage (coinsurance rate) of the plan's allowed amount for both the physician's fee and the charge for the facility in which the surgery takes place (e.g. the hospital outpatient department) if both the physician and the facility were members of the plan's PPO than if a non-PPO physician and facility were used. In general, high option plans have lower copayments and lower coinsurance rates than low option plans. However, all FEHBP fee-for-service plans, except the new Blue Cross and Blue Shield basic option, pay something for covered care and services regardless of the provider.

Most HMOs do not require deductibles and typically charge enrollees a copayment for certain services. HMOs often do not pay anything toward care that is furnished by a provider

---

[10] The 2002 standard option of the Blue Cross and Blue Shield governmentwide fee-for-service plan has three provider status levels and associated enrollee cost sharing amounts: the lowest cost-sharing amount applies if the enrollee uses a "preferred" provider; a higher amount if the enrollee uses a "participating" provider (or "member" if it is a facility rather than a practitioner); and the highest amount if the enrollee uses a "non-participating" provider or member. Only the non-participating providers or members may bill the enrollee for the balance of charges above the amount the plan pays. The 2002 Blue Cross and Blue Shield basic option includes only preferred providers and nonparticipating providers.

who is not part of the plan's network. HMOs with "point-of-service" options may pay part of the costs of out-of-network care, but the enrollee's coinsurance rate may be high.

Plan Limitations on Covered Costs

Fee-for-service plans apply enrollees' *coinsurance rates* (not copayments) to the maximum payment they "allow" for a service, often defined as the "usual and customary" charge or the provider's charge, whichever is lower. For example, a non-PPO physician might charge $100 for a procedure, but, based on charges for that procedure by other physicians in the area, the plan might establish $80 as the maximum allowable payment. If the plan's coinsurance share is 80%, it would pay 80% of $80, and the insured individual would be responsible for the balance of the bill, including enrollee coinsurance (20% of $80, or $16) plus the $20 balance above the plan's maximum.[11] Because usual and customary limits are established for thousands of services and procedures, an individual generally does not know in advance what a plan's limit is, although some plans will provide the information over the phone.

Enrollee Catastrophic Cost Protection

OPM requires plans to limit enrollee out-of-pocket expenditures for covered services used within a plan year.[12] (Limits do not apply to services not covered by the plan). Currently, the annual out-of-pocket catastrophic limits under fee-for-service plans range from $2,000 to $4,000 when PPO network providers are used and from $3,000 to $6,000 when out-of-network providers are used.[13] HMOs generally have lower catastrophic coverage limits than do fee-for-service plans. However, because most HMOs have low enrollee cost sharing requirements, protection against major out-of-pocket costs for covered care is less likely to be an issue.

OPM does not specify the kinds of out-of-pocket expenses that may be accumulated and counted toward reaching the out-of-pocket limit. Countable expenses differ among the fee-for-service plans and may differ between options within a plan. For instance: None of the plans/options includes in countable expenses amounts enrollees using out-of-network providers might pay in excess of the plan's usual and customary limit (often referred to as "balance billing"); most plans/options do not count the plan's deductibles (e.g., the annual deductible, separate inpatient hospital deductible, or separate prescription drug deductible); most plans/options, including HMOs, do not count any or certain of the enrollee's share of covered prescription drug costs; most plans/options do not count an enrollee's coinsurance for

---

[11] Enrollees in the Blue Cross and Blue Shield standard option who use participating providers but not preferred providers may not be billed for a balance; those using non-participating providers may be billed for the balance.

[12] OPM estimates that a little more than 1% of all enrollees hit the out-of-pocket expenditure limit in their plan in 2000.

[13] For example, if an enrollee had incurred countable out-of-pocket costs for covered care from PPO providers equal to his or her plan's limit of $3,000 for PPO care, the enrollee would have no coinsurance or other cost sharing for additional care used that year if the additional care is provided through the plan's PPO. If the additional care is from out-of-network providers, the enrollee would be required to pay any cost-sharing requirements until the plan's higher limit for non-PPO providers is reached.

covered out-of-network mental health/substance abuse treatment; most plans/options do not count enrollee copayments for in-network care; one plan does not count enrollee coinsurance for covered care in out-of-network inpatient hospitals or outpatient facilities.

Government/Enrollee Premium Sharing

FEHBP premium costs are shared by enrollees and the government (the employer). For many years the formula for calculating the enrollee premium was based on the average cost of the "high option" of the "big six" plans. In BBA 97 (Balanced Budget Act of 1997) Congress established a new formula effective January 1, 1999. Under this formula, the maximum amount paid by the government is an amount equal to 72% of the average premium of all participating plans (weighted by the number of plan participants), but no more than 75% of the premium of any individual plan. This formula is applied separately to self only and family plans. On average, participants pay 28%, but no less than 25%, of the premium of the plan they choose. Seventy-two percent (72%) was chosen as the government's share because that was the percentage the government was paying in 1996 under the old formula, and Congress agreed to freeze the premium-sharing ratio at that level.

This premium-sharing procedure would work as illustrated in the following examples for someone buying a self-only policy: In 2002, the maximum annual government share is $2,544 for self-only coverage, which is 72% of the weighted average annual premium of self-only policies for all plans. If an individual chose to enroll in "Plan X" for which the total premium was $2,500, the government would not pay the full $2,544 because 75% of the plan's cost, $1,875, is less. Thus, the government's share would be $1,875 and the enrollee would pay the balance, or $625 (25% of the total premium). Alternatively, assume an enrollee chose a more costly plan, "Plan Y," for which the total premium was $3,800. The government's share would be the maximum amount of $2,544 because 75% of $3,800, or $2,850, would be more than the maximum. The government's share of the total premium, $2,544, would be 67% of the total premium.

The 75% cap on the government's share of the premium is an important component of the premium-sharing formula because it sets a minimum premium requirement on enrollees. If there were no requirement for enrollees to pay part of the premium, a plan night adopt a minimal benefit package with a premium cost of less than 72% of the average premium, and, as result, the government's share would cover the full premium. One consequence of elimination of the minimum enrollee premium share might be attraction to the low-cost plans of healthier participants who feel they don't much insurance protection, leaving higher risk persons concentrated in higher cost plans resulting in "risk segmentation" within the program. If this were to occur, the higher premium plans could be forced to raise premiums further to cover their enrollees' claims. Another consequence might be that, in later years, as enrollees move to the low cost plans, the weighted average premium would decline causing a decline in the government's maximum payment. On the one hand, this scenario would result in a decrease in the cost of the program to the government. On the other hand, risk segmentation among the plans in the program could be exacerbated causing enrollees needing more than minimal coverage to face larger out-of-pocket premium costs.

General Design and Cost-sharing Concepts

Although FEHBP is sometimes referred to as a "defined contribution plan," it does not comport precisely with common characterizations of such a design. Under the defined contribution concept, an employer or other sponsor provides enrollees a fixed sum with which they may purchase health insurance, adding their own funds if they prefer more costly coverage. The defined contribution approach to setting (and controlling) employer/sponsor costs is often associated with the theoretical concept of "managed competition" that has been advanced by some health economists as a way to contain the rate of increase in health care costs.[14]

The managed competition model differs from FEHBP in two important ways. First, a managed competition program would require plans to offer an identical core benefit package and to compete for enrollees on the basis of price as well as efficiency and service. FEHBP has no requirement for coverage of a core benefit package. Plans do not compete to participate in the program, but they compete for enrollees on the basis of benefits as well as efficiency, service, and price.

Second, because FEHBP requires enrollees to pay a minimum of 25% of the premium of any plan in which they enroll, enrollees cannot reduce their premium costs to zero by choosing a very inexpensive plan for which the government's contribution might cover the full premium. Moreover, unlike the general characterization of a defined contribution plan, the FEHBP premium-sharing formula results in a different employer payment for the different plans, up to the maximum dollar amount.

Eligible Population and Enrollee Characteristics

The population eligible to participate in FEHBP is a heterogeneous group. It covers (a) younger workers who, as a group, tend to use little health care; (b) older workers and retirees under age 65 who are not yet eligible for Medicare and who use more health care than the younger population; and (c) retirees (and employees) age 65 or over who, as a group, use the most health care and who, in general, are also eligible for Medicare.[15]

FEHBP is the largest employer-sponsored group health insurance program in the United States. The 4.1 million enrolled policyholders, including 2.2 million federal and postal employees and 1.9 million federal annuitants (including survivor annuitants), represent about 8.6 million individuals, including current spouses and dependent children under age 22. (Policyholders include adult children age 22 to 25 and certain former spouses of employees and annuitants. Under continuation-of-coverage rules, these groups may purchase, at full-price plus a 2% charge for administrative costs, any of the policies available under FEHBP.) About 44% of FEHBP participants have self-only policies, and 56% have family policies that cover a spouse and/or eligible dependent children.

---

[14] For discussion of alternative health insurance program designs in the context of Medicare, see CRS Report RL31068, *Medicare Structural Reform: Background and Options,* by Jeniffer O'Sullivan, Hinda Ripps Chaikind, and Sibyl Tilson.

[15] To participate in FEHBP as a retiree, an individual must be eligible for a federal annuity immediately upon separation from federal service. Thus, workers separating from service before eligibility for an immediate annuity are not eligible to participate in FEHBP even if they receive a deferred federal annuity at age 62.

OPM estimates that about 14% of all workers and retirees eligible to participate in FEHBP choose not to enroll. Among eligible active workers, an estimated 569,000, or 20%, have elected not to enroll. Those choosing not to enroll are presumed to include primarily younger, lower-paid workers who believe they do not need or cannot afford health insurance and those who are covered through a spouse's employer's policy.

According to the most recently available data, FEHBP policyholders who were active workers in 2000 were about 46 years old, on average. The average annual salary of nonpostal workers was about $52,000, and the average postal worker salary was about $39,000. The average age of all retired and survivor annuitants was 72 years, and their average annual annuity was about $21,000. The age range of annuitants is broad. Federal workers can retire on disability at any age (certain length of service and disability criteria must be met), and regular retirement and special early retirement are available as early as age 50 in specified circumstances. About 30% of federal annuitants receive annuities as survivors of deceased workers and retirees. Most survivor annuitants are surviving spouses; their average age was nearly 76 years in 2000; their average survivor annuity was $13,000 (**Table 1**).[16, 17]

Table 1. Selected Characteristics of FEHBP Policyholders (March 2000)

FEHBP policyholders	4.1 million
Active federal and postal employees	2.2. million
Average age	46 years
Average annual federal salary	$52,000
Average annual postal worker salary	$39,000
All annuitants	1.9 million
Average age	72 years
Average annual annuity	$21,000
Survivor annuitants	0.5 million
Average age	76 years
Average annual annuity	$13,000

Source: Unpublished data from OPM.

PAYMENTS TO PLANS

Payments to Fee-for-Service Plans

FEHBP fee-for-service plans are paid a premium by the federal government for each FEHBP policyholder. Premiums differ only for individual versus family coverage and are not adjusted for age, gender, health status, geographic location, or any other factors.

[16] The salary and income data reported here include only the federal or postal salary and federal civil service annuity. Total household income for workers and retirees may include income from other household members and other income sources.

[17] Surviving children under age 18, or age 22 if in school full time, are eligible for child survivor annuities and are eligible to participate in FEHBP while eligible for that annuity.

Experience-Rated Premiums

All fee-for-service plans (and a small number of comprehensive plans) are "experience rates," meaning the premiums are based on the claims experience of the federal enrollees in the plan in preceding years. Experience-rated plan premiums have three components: a subscription charge, a contingency reserve margin, and an OPM administrative reserve charge.

Subscription Charge

This component is the basic premium that OPM negotiates with each fee-for-service carrier annually. It includes: (a) the amount necessary to cover the plan's claims; (b) the plan's documented administrative costs including overhead; and (c) the plan's "service charge" or "profit."[18] To estimate claims costs for an upcoming plan year, actuaries for the plan and actuaries for OPM review the plan's claims experience for the population enrolled in the past year and estimate the effects of benefit changes proposed by the plan or requested by OPM, if any, and anticipated enrollment changes. Every carrier's administrative costs and overhead are subject to periodic audits.

The "service charge" (profit) paid to fee-for-service plans by OPM is calculated according to derailed regulations (48 CFR Subpart 1615.9). There is no guaranteed minimum amount, but the maximum is 1.1% of projected incurred claims and administrative costs. OPM contract officers monitor plan performance throughout a plan year and maintain data which are used to evaluate plan performance and determine profit. Profit is based on six factors:

1) Contractor performance regarding such responsibilities as accurate and timely claims processing, handling of claims disputes, and general beneficial innovations;

2) Contract cost risk factors, including group size (smaller enrollments receive credit for higher risk), and certain demographics and the plan's willingness to assume risk;

3) Federal socioeconomic programs, such as programs to deter drug abuse;

4) Capital investments (this is a general federal acquisition factor but seldom applicable under FEHBP);

5) Cost control, such as contractor-initiated efforts to improve benefit design, cost-sharing, or innovative peer review procedures;

6) Independent development of administrative systems that improve cost efficiency and for which the contractor assumed the development costs.

Each of these profit factors is scored with regard to the plan's performance in the previous year, and the sum of the scores determines the profit percentage.

---

[18] OPM's payment of the "service charge" is unrelated to whether the plan is a "nonprofit" or "for-profit" business. The fee-for-service plans sponsored by employee organizations are nonprofit businesses, although some of the Blue Cross and Blue Shield plans are for-profit, some are mutual plans, and some are nonprofit. OPM pays a service charge to the national Blue Cross and Blue Shield organization which distributes the money to its

The "profit" margins for FEHBP fee-for-service plans are not large, but the plans in the program experience little risk because they may make up losses experienced in the past year through increases in premiums in the following year (or with OPM's approval, under certain circumstances, they may draw down surplus contingency reserves.) Plan income in excess of that which had been estimated when premiums were set for a given year may be carried forward and used to limit premium increases in the following year.

Contingency Reserve Margin

A contingency reserve fund is maintained in the U.S. Treasury by OPM for all FEHBP plans. OPM is authorized to levy a surcharge of up to 3% of a plan's premium to establish and maintain contingency reserves. The balance for fee-for-service plans is maintained at an amount equal to about 1 to 3 months of claims. Fee-for-service plans may use their contingency reserves to offset larger than anticipated claims, or, if the fund balance becomes larger than necessary, it can be drawn down and used to offset a premium increase in the subsequent year.

Since January 1989, FEHBP fee-for-service plans have had their federal premium funds disbursed throughout the year under a letter-of-credit arrangement whereby the plans drawn funds in their accounts as claims are paid.

OPM Administrative Reserve Charge

This amount finances the administrative costs of the OPM. The law sets the maximum at 1% of the total subscription costs (premiums) of the plans, although generally the costs are less than 1%.

Payments to Health Maintenance Organizations

Community-Rated Premiums

OPM pays HMOs a capitated payment for each federal enrollee and bases its payment on the rates the plan charges for enrollees in the two largest nonfederal employer-sponsored groups in that community, plus negotiated upgrades to the community benefit package. HMOs may compute their community rate using factors such as age and sex. OPM requires large HMOs to document the basis of their charges to nonfederal participating employers in the community. The profit rate HMOs receive based on the community rate may be larger than that available to fee-for-service plans under FEHBP.

Contingency Reserves. OPM maintains in the U.S. Treasury contingency reserve funds for community-rated plans, and may charge up to 3% of a plan's premium to establish and maintain the fund. However, unlike that for experience-rated fee-for-service plans, *the contingency reserve fund for community-rated plans can be used only by OPM* (not the plan) if OPM approves an adjustment during a "reconciliation" process that usually takes place in the month of March. For instance, HMOs generally estimate their rates in the spring and negotiate their contracts with OPM in August. The plan year begins the following January. If there are changes in the program or in the community benefit package between the time the plan estimated the rates and implementation of the plan in January, OPM reconciles those

affiliated plans. OPM pays fee-for-service plans a service charge as a performance incentive in accord with federal acquisition regulations.

changes with the previously established premiums and negotiates an adjustment. (OPM allows adjustment only for specified reasons, excluding a plan's underestimate of costs based on group demographics.)

Because payments to HMOs are not based on claims, the government does not use the letter-of-credit draw-down approach to disburse funds to the plans, but pays the plans specified amounts in installments throughout the year.

PREMIUM INCREASES: 1983 THROUGH 2001

Table 2 shows the average annual rates of increase in FEHBP plan premiums from 1983 through 2001. The data take into account the average premium weighted to reflect the size of the population enrolled in each plan and the share of enrollees with individual and family coverage. (The data do not include the estimated increase for 2002 because OPM will not know until after the November 2001 open season how enrollment patterns will change; it's possible that the realignment of the Blue Cross and Blue Shield options could result in more enrollees switching plans than usual.)

The average annual increase in FEHBP premiums from 1983 through 2001 was 6.7%. In 1983 the weighted average premium (including both self only and family coverage) was $1,643, and in 2001 it was about $5,263.

The rates of increase in premiums in **Table 2** include both the government's and the enrollees' shares. Premium increases experienced by individual enrollees would be different from the overall average premium increase because some plans' premium increases are below average and others above, and, from year to year, various plans may be permitted to draw on their premium reserves or may be required to build their reserves. As noted above, OPM negotiates fee-for-service plan premiums annually, and rates of increase reflect the actual claims experience of each plan in the prior year, the expected trend rate for claims in the coming year, and the balancing of those factors with the value of the benefit package and the reserve level. Premium increases for HMOs reflect the increase in the rates the plans change in the community.

In the 1980s, premiums of the plans in the FEHBP fluctuated widely for a number of reasons. *Many of these fluctuations result from the unique administrative structure, premium-setting procedures, and reserve fund requirements of FEHBP; therefore the year-to-year rates of increase are not directly comparable to increases in costs or spending for other health care programs.*

First, beginning in 1982, OPM foresaw unprecedented increases of up to 35% in premiums and required that fee-for-service plans reduce the anticipated rate of increase by about half. Like many plans sponsored by private sector employers at that time, some FEHBP fee-for-service plans offered "first dollar coverage." The reductions sought by OPM were accomplished largely by requiring all fee-for service plans to include an annual deductible and to require enrollees to pay coinsurance when they use care, features now common in the industry. As a result, premium increases from 1981 to 1982 were about half the rate OPM had estimates.

Table 2. Weighted Average Annual Increases in FEHBP Premiums: 1983 through 2001

Year	Percent change in the average premium from previous year
1983	-
1984	10.6
1985	-1.1
1986	-11
1987	17.5
1988	25.9
1989	20.3
1990	8.8
1991	4.7
1992	7.4
1993	8.3
1994	2.9
1995	-3.8
1996	-0.3
1997	1.7
1998	7.2
1999	9.5
2000	9.3
2001	10.5
Average annual rate of increase:	*6.7%*

Source: OPM, Office of Actuaries.

Next, in 1985 and 1986, a complex situation arose with regard to the use of contingency reserve funds. At that time, these funds were managed by the individual plans and were not held within the government. Because reserves in several plans had become very large, in 1986 some of those plans rebated reserves to the program ($600 million to the government and $400 million to enrollees) and others significantly reduced their 1986 premiums to draw down their reserves. During the 1985 open season, some persons transferred to the plans that had chosen to lower their 1986 premiums, and, as a result, the overall weighted average premium showed an 11.4% decline from 1985. The large increases that occurred from 1987 to 1989 were partially due to moving back to plans whose premiums had not been reduced to draw down the large build-up of reserves. In 1989, OPM took over management of the reserves, which are now held in U.S. Treasury accounts, and major premium fluctuations due to increasing or decreasing reserve balances can no longer occur.

The fluctuations in FEHBP premiums that occurred in the 1980s due to the reserve situation mask what might have occurred otherwise during that time period. With regard to health care costs in the economy as a whole, from 1980 to 1990 national expenditures per capita for health care increased at an average annual rate of 9.8%, well beyond the general rate of inflation; national health expenditures increased as a percent of gross domestic product (GPD) from 8.9% to 12.2%. In the late 1980s, employer-provided health insurance premiums rose annually at double digit rates.

However, the rate of increase in spending for health care slowed appreciably during the mid-1990s. Per capita spending nationwide for health care rose at less than 5% per year from 1994 through 1998; total national health expenditures rose annually by 5.5% or less during that time period. The annual rate of increase in premiums for employer-provided insurance fell from an increase of 18% during 1989 to 0.8% during 1996. The FEHBP premium increases in **Table 2** show that the federal employees' program followed those general trends.

There are indicators that health care costs are on the rise again, both nationally and in the FEHBP. A Kaiser Family Foundation survey of employer-sponsored health plans found that, on average, premiums among surveyed employers rose 11% from the spring of 2000 to the spring of 2001 compared with 4.8% from 1998 to 1999 and 8.3% from 1999 to 2000.[19] FEHBP premiums, rose, on average, by 9.3% from 1999 to 2000 and by 10.5% from 2000 to 2001. (FEHBP premiums are usually determined in August for the following calendar year.) According to OPM, FEHBP premiums in 2002 will be about 13.3% higher on average than 2001 premiums, with fee-for-service plans rising by 13% and HMOs increasing by 14%.[20] Agency officials note that the cumulative increase in premiums since 1998 is nearly 50%.

In the FEHBP as well as other health insurance programs, increased health care utilization and costs for prescription drugs are exerting substantial pressure on health insurance premiums and program costs. Rising prescription drug costs are responsible for about 40% of the recent increase in FEHBP premiums. About 4 percentage points of the 10.5% increase in the average premium from 2000 to 2001 was attribute to greater use of prescriptions and more costly drugs. Claims for prescription drugs constitute about 20% of total claims under the FEHBP.

OPM reports that other factors contributing to rising claims costs and therefore higher premiums under FEHBP include the aging of the enrolled population (both workers and retirees) and the concomitant increase in health care utilization, use of costly new medical technologies, and overall price inflation in the economy. OPM cannot isolate the cost effect of utilization of technologies alone, but notes that, to some extent, increased utilization of technologies is related to increasing utilization of health care in general.

As noted above, mandated benefits regarding patient protections and mental health provisions raised premiums by 0.02% (in 2000) and 1.28% (in 2001) respectively in the first year in which they were in effect. Prescription contraceptive coverage was required by law for the first time in 1999, but that requirement had no effect on costs because most plans had already elected to cover contraceptives without a requirement to do so.

A factor that may contribute to increased costs in the future under FEHBP is that a large number of federal retirements is expected in the next few years as federal workers hired during the growth in federal government employment that started in the late 1960s and continued in the 1970s begin to retire. Assuming that retiring workers are replaced with new workers, there will be an increase in the population eligible to enroll in FEHBP, and retiree longevity may continue to increase, also adding to the enrolled population. These factors would cause the total cost of the program to rise, but they may not have an effect on average premiums if the government replaces retiring workers with young, new employees who use

[19] *Employer Health Benefits: 2001 Annual Survey*. The Henry J. Kaiser Family Foundation and the Health Research and Educational Trust, 2001.

[20] This increase would be $4.32 biweekly for persons with individual coverage and $11.57 biweekly for family coverage. The weighted average increase will not be available until after the November 2001 open season when enrolles may change plans.

little health care and whose lower rates of utilization offset rising utilization by the older enrollees. However, if the government does not replace retiring workers, average premiums could rise as the enrolled group ages.

Premium Amounts in 2002

As shown **Table 3,** in 2002, among plans with only one option or the lower of two options, total annual fee-for-service premiums, including both enrollee and government/employer shares for individual enrollment, range from a low of $2,668 to a high of $4,110; premiums for family enrollment (two or more persons) range from $5,791 to $8,713. Among the higher option for plans with two options annual premiums for individual enrollment range from $3,613 to $6,793; premiums for family enrollment range from $8,274 to $14,657. Within a fee-for-service plan, family policies generally cost about twice as much as a self-only policy, probably because annuitants tend to choose fee-for-service plans and annuitants purchasing family coverage are typically two-person households.

In 2002, the maximum government annual payment for any FEHBP plan for nonpostal participants is $2,544 for an individual policy and $5,809 for a family policy. Thus, for example, the government's share of the premium of the highest-priced, high option plan, which costs $14,657, would be $5,809, and the enrollee's out-of-pocket cost for the premium would be $8,848 for the year.

HMO premiums vary substantially in different geographic localities; although some are less costly than the fee-for-service plans, many are more costly, particularly for family coverage. For most HMOs, family coverage costs about 2½ to 3 times that of self-only coverage, largely because younger FEHBP participants are more likely to choose an HMO than older participants, and younger people with children have larger households. Among the seven largest HMOs, premiums for self-only coverage in 2002 range from $2,493 to $3,748; premiums for family coverage range from $5,834 to $9,369.[21]

Table 3. FEHBP Fee-for-Service Governmentwide Plans: Annual Total Premiums (Enrollee plus government share, 2002)

Plan	Individual policy	Family policy
Lower or only option (7 plans)		
lowest premium	$2,668	$5,791
highest premium	4,110	8,713
Higher option (4 plans)		
lowest premium	3,613	8,274
highest premium	6,793	14,657
Maximum gov.share*	2,544	5,809

Source: Office of Personnel Management
*Nonpostal participants. Maximum USPS share for postal employees in 2002 is $2,772 for individual coverage and $6,330 for family coverage.

[21] These seven HMOs include: three Kaiser Permanente plans (two in California and one in Washington, D.C.), Aetna U.S. Healthcare (Washington, D.C. metropolitan area), GHI (New York and New Jersey), Health Net (California), and HMSA (Hawaii).

FINANCING AND COSTS

The government's share of active workers' FEHBP premiums is paid by the government agency for which the employee works. The money for agency payments is appropriated annually to every agency's salary and expense accounts, and, for federal budget purposes, is categorized as discretionary spending. The government's share of nonpostal annuitants' premiums is appropriated annually to OPM and is categorized in the federal budget as direct, or mandatory spending. The government's share of premiums for all nonpostal enrollees is paid from general revenues. The U.S. Postal Service (USPS) pays the employer share of FEHBP premiums with funds taken in by the USPS from postal rate receipts, although the postal unions and the USPS collectively bargain the cost-sharing ratio for active workers.[22]

The cost of FEHBP in FY2001 was over $21 billion. Of this amount, $10.3 billion was estimated to come from outside the government, including $5.8 billion from federal and postal employees and annuitants for their share of premiums and $4.5 billion from the USPS for the employer's share of postal workers' and retirees' premiums. General tax revenues financed the $11 billion balance.

Assuming total program costs in 2002 are 13.3% higher than in 2001, and assuming that the enrolled population in 2002 remains similar to enrollment in recent years (i.e., 4.1 million policyholders and 8.6 million covered individuals, including 4.5 million family members of policyholders), the average annual cost per policyholder in 2002 would be about $5,878, and the average cost per covered person would be about $2,802.

ADMINISTRATION

The Role of OPM

The original FEHBA gave OPM responsibility for administering the FEHBP. OPM is authorized to contract with insurance carriers; approve qualified health benefits plans for participation in the program; negotiate with plans about benefit and premium levels; determine the times and conditions for open seasons during which eligible individuals may elect coverage or change plans; make information available to employees concerning plan options; and administer the financing of the program. OPM is responsible for maintaining the funds that hold contingency reserves for the plans and the fund that receives premium payments from enrollees and employing agencies and from which premiums are disbursed to participating plans.

Annuitant participation. OPM supervises all health insurance activities for annuitants. OPM determines whether retiring employees or survivor annuitants meet the requirements to continue health insurance coverage; takes the action necessary to terminate, accept, or continue enrollment; oversees the automatic deduction of premiums from monthly annuity checks and credits the premiums, along with the applicable government contribution, to the proper account; processes all enrollment changes; notifies affected carriers of enrollment changes; and keeps enrolled annuitants advised of rate and benefit changes within their plan.

[22] In 2002, employees of the USPS pay about 11%of the premiums of standard or basic option plans.

Contract negotiations; dissemination of plan information. An important aspect of OPM's responsibilities is the annual negotiations with plans. Under the law, each contract is for a uniform term of at least 1 year but may be automatically renewed from year to year in the absence of a termination notice by either the plan or OPM. OPM has never asked a plan to leave the program.

OPM begins the annual negotiations by sending out in March or April a "call letter" requesting participating plans to submit their benefit and rate proposals for the next year. HMOs seeking to enter the program for the first time apply to OPM for admission at this time. The call letter includes any changes in the services OPM seeks to make available for federal workers and annuitants, as well as notification of services that OPM discourages. (For example, in 1997, OPM directed plans not to expand their dental coverage.)

Next, OPM reviews proposals for rates (premiums) for the fee-for-service plans in relation to the cost of covered services, managed care initiatives, the plan's past experience, health care utilization patterns of the enrolled group, and health care cost inflation in general. Pursuant to the negotiations, OPM and the plans (including both fee-for-service plans and HMOs) agree to specific terms and conditions each party is obligated to meet in the next contract year, which runs concurrently with a calendar year. Descriptions of both covered and excluded services are incorporated into the final contracts, and the plans print brochures describing the benefits and costs according to a standard format specified by OPM. The brochures are binding statements of benefits and exclusions that plans must follow as parties to FEHBP contracts. OPM then announces an open season (which generally runs for 1 month, beginning in early November).

OPM prints and distributes to personnel offices and annuitants a guide describing the major features and premiums for all participating plans. This guide includes the findings of surveys of enrollee satisfaction with the different plans and includes information about the factors participants should consider in making their selection. Personal advice is not provided, although OPM's internet web site provides information about how to select a plan [www.opm.gov/insure]. Employees are responsible for obtaining from their personnel office a copy of OPM's general guide and the detailed brochures of the specific plans in which they are interested. Annuitants are responsible for obtaining detailed plan brochures by calling the individual carriers and requesting that a brochure be mailed to them. Information about the different plans is also available on OPM's web page on the Internet [www.opm.gov/insure].

Following is the annual cycle of OPM's activities regarding plan contracts.

End of March-early April	Call letter distributed to plans
May 31	Plan responses due to OPM (Electronic format)
June through August	Contract negotiations
September-October	Print and distribute OPM guides and plan brochures
November-December	Open season
Early December-January 1	Enrollment data distributed to plans
January 1	Plan year starts
March	Reconciliation of HMO premiums

The Role of Federal Agencies

Personnel offices in every federal agency manage participation in FEHBP for their employees according to procedures prescribed by OPM. They administer the annual open seasons; adjust coverage and payroll withholding when workers' family or employment situations change and when new workers enter. Agencies are responsible for withholding employee premium payments, adding the government's share (which is appropriated to agencies annually), and providing documentation of these actions to OPM. They keep records and information on withholdings from employee salaries and agency contributions, enrollment statistics, and other necessary data.

The Role of Carriers

The carriers process and pay claims, answer enrollee questions, respond to claims disputes, print annual open season brochures according to the OPM-specified format, and maintain data regarding enrollment, claims, and other financial information required by OPM. In addition, carriers assume all insurance risk.

Administrative Costs

The only administrative costs of the federal government for FEHBP that can be identified explicitly are the costs of OPM's headquarters staff. This staff include the actuaries and employees who negotiate with carriers, monitor plans and contracts, and generally oversee all aspects of program administration. OPM adds a charge to each plan's premium, limited by law to 1% of the premium, to cover these administrative costs. Generally the charge is less than 1%. There is no separate accounting for the costs associated with agency personnel who carry out administrative tasks associated with FEHBP as well as the other pay and benefit programs for federal workers.

Plan carriers' administrative costs are included in their premiums. To the extent that plans compete for enrollees on basis of premiums, they have an incentive for administrative efficiency. However, OPM does not ask for detailed administration cost data, although it periodically audits certain overhead charges.

Grievances and Appeals

All FEHBP plan brochures include an explanation of the procedures enrollees should follow if they disagree with the plan's denial of coverage or rate of payment for a covered service. The first appeal is to the plan for reconsideration. An enrollee must submit a written request for reconsideration within 6 months of the denial of coverage. Within 30 days of receiving the request for reconsideration, the plan must approve the claim, request additional information, or provide the participant with a written statement of the grounds and rationale for denial. If additional information requested by the plan is not received within 60 days, the decision is made with the information the plan has on hand.

If the plan decides against the enrollee, and he or she continues to question the decision, a written appeal can be filed with OPM within 90 days of the plan's second denial or recommendation. OPM will review the facts of the case in the context of the plan's contract with the government as outlined in the plan brochure and provide the enrollee a written determination. In certain cases, OPM may ask for review by an outside physician. (These are usually physicians who, under contract with OPM, also review applications for federal civil service disability retirement.) If OPM determines that, under the terms of its contract with the plan, the enrollee is entitled to coverage of the care or service in question, the law requires that the plan provide or pay for the care as ordered by OPM. If OPM's decision is against the enrollee, he or she can file an appeal *against OPM* in federal district court (as specified in law) but cannot file suit directly against the plan. The suit must be brought no later than December 31 of the third year after the year in which the contested service was provided.

When an enrollee prevails against OPM in court, the award is only for the specific benefit in question. Thus, the plan will pay for the denied service or will provide the service, but neither the plan nor OPM can be sued for compensatory or punitive damages. The decision of the court is final.

QUALITY/ACCREDITATION

To be an FEHBP plan, a carrier must be licensed to sell group health insurance under state law in every area of a state in which it operates as an FEHBP plan. To qualify as one of the two nationwide fee-for-service plans, the carrier must be licensed to sell group health insurance in every state.

OPM requires participating HMOs to meet certain requirements. HMOs must have an internal quality assurance program that sets standards for quality of care and responsiveness to enrollee inquiries; collect and analyze data on condition-specific patient outcomes; administer a uniform patient satisfaction survey and respond to results; provide data from the Health Plan Employer Data and Information Set (HEDIS), and meet other specified requirements. In addition, OPM requires HMOs to credential and periodically re-credential participating providers.[23] Under statute, HMOs participating in FEHBP must inform OPM of changes to their service areas and to demonstrate availability of plan providers within these service areas to FEHBP enrollees.

The open season brochure distributed by OPM includes data on enrollee satisfaction with participating health plans that is obtained from the plan satisfaction surveys. Each participating plan is rated on features such as access to providers, choice of providers, out-of-pocket costs, adequacy of coverage, waiting times, the quality of care received from the plan's doctors and other medical professionals, and the results of care. The brochure also indicates whether a participating HMO has been accredited by the National Committee for Quality Assurance (NCQA) and the nature of the accreditation.[24]

---

[23] American Association of Health Plans, *The Regulation of Health Plans*. Washington, February 3, 1998.

[24] The NCQA PPO accreditation process evaluates (a) the PPO's access and service to patients, and (b) the PPO's accurate assessment and representation of the qualifications of participating providers. PPO are assigned one of four accreditation outcomes: Full accreditation for 3 years (the plan has excellent programs for continuous quality improvement and meets specified NCQA standards); 1-year accreditation (plan has well-established programs for quality improvement and consumer protection and meets most NCQA standards and NCQA provides a list of recommended improvements); provisional accreditation indicates that a PPO's service and

OPM's call letter for 2001 notified HMOs that in 2002 they would be required to begin to seek accreditation from a nationally recognized organization such as NCQA. The call letter for 2002 asked HMOs with 500 or more enrollees to provide OPM with an accreditation plan along with their benefit and rate proposals. Fee-for-service/PPO plans were also asked to submit a business plan outlining the steps they plan to take toward achieving accreditation.

Relationship to State Laws

The fee-for-service plans available to federal employees and annuitants nationwide preempt state laws regarding benefits. Enrollees in these plans have the same benefit coverage regardless of where they live. OPM requires HMOs to provide their FEHBP enrollees with the mandated benefits of the state in which they live. However, OPM has the authority to override state-mandated benefits if it determines that to do so would be in the best interest of federal enrollees.

Relationship to Medicare

Medicare Eligibility Rules

Although most federal workers and annuitants continue their enrollment in the FEHBP after they become eligible for Medicare at age 65, Medicare becomes an important component of their overall health insurance coverage. The Medicare Program consists of three parts: Part A covers inpatient hospital care; post-hospital stays in skilled nursing facilities;[25] some home health care; and hospice care for the terminally ill. Part B covers all care by physicians and certain other practitioners; outpatient facility costs (e.g., hospital outpatient departments and ambulatory surgical centers); outpatient diagnostic tests; and home health care not covered under Part A.

Part A and B cover health care on a fee-for-service basis under which beneficiaries choose a health care provider, and Medicare pays the provider for covered services to the beneficiary. (An annual deductible and other beneficiary cost sharing may be required.) Persons covered by both Parts A and B may elect to enroll in a Medicare managed care plan instead of using traditional fee-for-service Medicare. Enrollees in Medicare's managed care program (also known as Part C, or Medicare+Choice) receive care through an HMO, which may offer care and services not covered under Parts A and B (such as eye exams and outpatient prescription drugs).

Upon turning age 65, individuals eligible for Social Security retirement or spousal benefits become eligible for Part A of Medicare and may elect to enroll in Part B. Persons of any age eligible for Social Security disability benefits are eligible for Medicare after having received disability benefits for 24-months; persons of any age insured under Social Security

clinical quality meet some, but not all of NCQA's basic requirements; denial of accreditation is an indication that a PPO did not met NEQA's requirements during its review.

[25] Medicare does not cover long-term care in nursing homes which provide custodial and personal care services for residents.

(and their spouses and dependent children) requiring treatment for end-stage renal disease may also quality for Medicare.

When the Social Security System was enacted in 1935, federal employment was not covered under that system because federal employees already had a retirement system (the Civil Service Retirement System, enacted in 1920). Thus, because federal employees were excluded from Social Security, they were also excluded from Medicare when it was enacted in 1965. However, in 1982 Congress included federal employees under Medicare, effective for all workers in federal jobs on or after January 1, 1983, when they began paying the hospital insurance payroll tax that finances Part A of Medicare.[26]

Medicare Part A coverage begins for eligible individuals at age 65, regardless of employment status.[27] Persons eligible for Medicare based on Social Security coverage or post-1982 federal employment pay no premium for Part A coverage. Individuals age 65 or over not eligible for Medicare Part A may purchase Part A coverage by paying a monthly premium of $175 for individuals with 30-39 quarters of Social Security-covered employment or $319 for those with fewer than 30 quarters of covered employment. (These premiums levels are applicable to 2002.)

Medicare Part B is not tied to Social Security and is elective for anyone age 65 or older; all participating beneficiaries pay a monthly premium of $54 per person in 2002. (Persons who delay enrollment in Part B until they are older than 65 pay a higher premium as a late enrollment penalty, although that penalty does not apply to individuals as long as they continue to work in their federal job after age 65 or who have coverage under FEHBP through a federally employed spouse.)

Medicare Participation by FEHBP Enrollees

Table 4 shows the Medicare coverage status of FEHBP policyholders who were annuitants age 65 or older in March, 2000. (About 40,000 active federal employees age 65 and over are not included in the data.) FEHBP policyholders included 1.411 million annuitants age 65 and older. Among this group, about 180,000 persons (13% of all annuitants in FEHBP) had no Medicare coverage, presumably because they retired from the federal government before 1983 and never worked long enough in Social Security-covered employment to become eligible for Medicare, were not married to a Medicare-eligible spouse, and had not elected to purchase Medicare coverage. A total of 1.231 million FEHBP policyholders age 65 and over had Medicare coverage, including 1.061 million who were enrolled in both Parts A and B; 132,000 who were enrolled in Part A only; and 39,000 who were enrolled in part B only.

[26] To become eligible for Medicare benefits at age 65, workers in federal jobs when Medicare coverage became effective were not required to pay into Medicare for the same quarters of coverage generally required for Social Security retirement benefits. Anyone in a federal job on January 1, 1983, could court federal employment prior to that date toward the quarters of employment necessary to qualify for Medicare.

[27] In the Social Security Amendments of 1983, Congress gradually raised the age for eligibility for Social Security retirement benefits from 65 to 67, phased-in for people born from 1938 to 1960. However, the eligibility age for Medicare remain at age 65.

Table 4. Medicare Coverage of Federal Annuitants Age 65 and Over in March 2000 (in millions of FEHBP policyholders)

Total FEHBP enrolled annuitants age 65+	1.411
With no Medicare coverage	0.180
With Medicare coverage	1.231
Part A and Part B	1.061
Part A only	0.132
Part B only	0.039

Source: Unpublished data from OPM.

Comparison of Covered Services and Patient Cost-Sharing under Medicare and FEHBP Fee-for-Service Plans[28]

Care and services covered by FEHBP fee-for-service plans and Medicare overlap to a major extent, although Medicare covers some services not included in all FEHBP plans, and FEHBP plans cover some things not covered by Medicare. Table 5 (and the discussion that follows it) compares Medicare and FEHBP fee-for-service coverage for major categories of health care and services; it shows enrollee out-of-pocket cost sharing for different categories of services; and it illustrates how coverage under Medicare and FEHBP are coordinated for a retired federal employee age 65 or over for whom Medicare would be "first payer" and FEHBP would be "second payer." (The general rules regarding coordination of coverage and "first payer" and "second payer" status are discussed in the following section.)[29]

[28] Medicare beneficiary cost-sharing as discussed in this section refers to payments that are the responsibility of the beneficiary, whether the beneficiary makes those payments or purchases a Medicare supplemental policy which pays the beneficiary's share. Either way, the costs are generally borne largely by the beneficiary.

[29] The information provided here focuses on Medicare beneficiaries who participate in traditional fee-for-service Medicare and in an FEHBP fee-for-service plan, which characterizes the arrangement of the vast majority of FEHBP annuitants with Medicare. If an annuitant participates in an FEHBP HMO, that plan's coverage and payment of Medicare cost sharing may vary, as noted in the following section. Although federal annuitants with Medicare may elect to participate in two HMOs, one a Medicare+Choice HMO, which would be first payer, and another an FEHBP HMO, which would be second payer, such a choice is unusual and may not be an optimum arrangement. The plans would provide many of the same benefits and, in a given geographic area, may have largely the same provider networks (in some cases, the same carrier might be a Medicare+Choice plan and an FEHBP HMO).

Table 5. Medicare and FEHBP: Comparison of Major Coverage Categories and Patient Payment Responsibilities in 2002

(fee-for-service coverage)[a]

Service	Covered by Medicare Part A or Part B? Patient payment responsibility?	FEHBP retired enrollees *with* Medicare: Covered by most FEHBP FFS plans? Patient payment responsibility?	FEHBP enrollees *without* Medicare: Covered by most FEHBP FFS plans? Patient payment responsibility?
Inpatient Coverage			
Inpatient hospital care: **(a) room and board, general nursing care, meals;** **(b) other hospital services and supplies* (excludes physicians).** **[Includes rehabilitation hospitals certified as acute care facilities and providing specialized rehabilitation therapies.]** *** e.g., Operating and recovery rooms, drugs, tests, x-rays, scans, dressings, anesthetics, other supplies.**	Yes, Part A. $8.12 inpatient deductible per benefit period. [b] Coverage includes (a) room and board, general nursing care, meals and (b) other hospital services and supplies. No additional patient payment for first 60 days; $203 daily copayment for days 61-90 and $406 daily copayment for lifetime reserve for lifetime reserve days 91-150. Patient pays full charges for over 150 days, unless the beneficiary uses his or her 60 "lifetime reserve days" for inpatient days beyond 150, but reserve days may be used only once.	Yes, but Medicare coverage as first payer would apply. FEHBP plan pays the Medicare deductible and daily copayments.	Yes, Overall annual deductible varies by plan. (a) Preadmission certification required; generally unlimited days of coverage, with review and case management. Patient payments vary among plans and plan options, including: Patient may pay copayment or deductible per admission (may be as little as $100, but amount varies for PPO and non- PPO facilities), or coinsurance rate per day (10% to 35%), or both for non-PPO facilities, or neither for PPO facilities. (b) Patient payment responsibility for other hospital services, and supplies varies widely depending on plan, plan-option, and PPO membership. Patient may pay as little as $100 per admission (PPO facility) or as much as a high copayment plus coinsurance for itemized services and supplies in nonparticipating facility. If coinsurance is required, rates vary from 10% to 35% per vice or item depending on plan, plan option, and provider PPO membership. Patients may be billed by nonparticipating facilities for full charges above the amounts paid by the plan.
Skilled nursing facility care (post-hospital stay)	Yes, Part A. Medicare pays in full for days 1-20. Patient pays $101.50/day copayment for days 21-100; no coverage over 100 days per benefit period.	No. Patient pays Medicare $101.50/day copayment after 20 days; some FEHBP plans pay that copayment for *limited* days after 20.	No. Patient pays full charges.
Home health care ordered by a physician	Yes, Part A.* Medicare pays for medically necessary intermittent skilled nursing care and services of a physical or speech therapist. Those services may be supplemented by	Yes, but Medicare coverage as first payer would apply.	Yes, but with limitations such as: nursing care only, limited hours per visit, limited visits per year. plan payments may be subject to an annual cap which varies by PPO or non-PPO provides agency. Patient payments may begin after plan has paid an initial

Service	Covered by Medicare Part A or Part B? Patient payment responsibility?	FEHBP retired enrollees *with* Medicare: Covered by most FEHBP FFS plans? Patient payment responsibility?	FEHBP enrollees *without* Medicare: Covered by most FEHBP FFS plans? Patient payment responsibility?
	occupational therapy, aide services, and medical social services. No patient deductible or coinsurance. * Certain home health care is paid by Part B, with no patient cost-sharing.		amount. In general, patients pay coinsurance based on the plan's allowable amount per. visit.
Hospice care for terminally ill patients	Yes, Part A. $5 maximum copayment for outpatient drugs and 5% of Medicare approved amount (MAA)[c] coinsurance for respite care days.	Yes, but Medicare coverage as first payer would apply.	Yes, for approved hospice, but some plans limit plan payments. Patient pays and required plan copayment per admission and/or coinsurance, or all costs over plan maximum.
Physician and outpatient Coverage			
Physician and surgeon services	Yes, Part B. $100 annual deductible. Patient pays coinsurance of 20% of MAA.	Yes, but Medicare coverage as first payer would apply. FEHBP plan pays patient coinsurance.	Yes. Patient pays copayment for PPO physicians or coinsurance for non-PPO physicians (coinsurance rates vary among plans and plan options from 10% to 35% of charge up to plan's usual-and-customary maximum).
Hospital outpatient departments	Yes, Part B. Patient copayment is a fixed dollar amount per procedure (varies by facility location), but no less than 20% of MAA.	Yes, but Medicare coverage as first payer would apply. FEHBP plan pays patient copayment.	Yes. Patient pays coinsurance rates vary among plans, plan option, and facility PPO membership from 10% to 35%.
Ambulatory Surgical Centers	Yes, Part B. Patient pays coinsurance of 20% of MAA.	Yes, but Medicare coverage as first payer would apply. FEHBP plan pays patient coinsurance.	Yes. Patient pays coinsurance; rates vary among plans, plan option, and facility PPO membership from 10% to 35%.
Durable medical equipment, orthotics and prosthetics	Yes, Part B. Patient pays coinsurance of 20% of MAA; patient may be billed for charges above the MAA if the supplier does not accept Medicare assigned payments.	Yes, but Medicare coverage as first payer would apply. FEHBP plan pays patient coinsurance.	Yes, but coverage may be limited or excluded for some orthopedic and prosthetic devices. Patient pays coinsurance; rates vary among plans, plan options, and PPO membership of supplier from 10% to 35%.
Outpatient prescription drugs	No, generally. Certain oral cancer drugs and injected drugs that cannot be self-administered are covered.	Yes, FEHBP coverage applies (unless covered by Medicare). Patient pays copayment or coinsurance; amounts vary by type of drug, formulary status, place of purchase, and use of mail order plan; maximum coinsurance is 50% of drug cost.	Yes. Patient pays copayment or coinsurance; amounts vary by type of drug, formulary status, place of purchase, and use of mail order plan; maximum coinsurance is 50% of drug cost.
Outpatient clinical laboratory tests; X-rays, MRIs, CAT scans, EKGs	Yes, Part B. Patients pays nothing for clinical lab tests. Patients pay coinsurance of 20% of MAA for other tests.	Yes, but Medicare coverage as first payer would apply.	No. Patient pays coinsurance; rates vary by plan, Plan options, and facility PPO membership from 10% to 35%.

Service	Covered by Medicare Part A or Part B? Patient payment responsibility?	FEHBP retired enrollees *with* Medicare: Covered by most FEHBP FFS plans? Patient payment responsibility?	FEHBP enrollees *without* Medicare: Covered by most FEHBP FFS plans? Patient payment responsibility?
Preventive care; cancer screening	Yes, Part B. Coverage, frequency of coverage, and waiver of deductible and coinsurance (20%) may vary by type of test, beneficiary age, and risk status. Covered services include: mammograms; pap smears, pelvic examinations and clinical breast examinations; bone mass tests; influenza immunization; pneumococcal shot (one); hepatitis B vaccination (if at risk); prostate cancer screening; and certain glaucoma tests (starting 2002). No coinsurance for associated clinical lab tests.	Yes, but Medicare coverage as first payer would apply. However, FEHBP may apply if Medicare frequency or risk rules preclude coverage.	Yes. Coverage and frequency of coverage may vary by type of test and age. Most plans cover: mammograms; pap smears, examinations an clinical breast examinations; bone mass tests; influenza immunization; pneumococcal shots; lyme disease vaccine; tetanus boosters; hepatitis B vaccination (if at risk); prostate cancer screening; colorectal cancer screening; and all childhood immunizations. Some (not all) plans cover adult routine physical exams and associated tests; all plans cover children's routine physical exams, but amount covered may be limited [per year. Patient pays coinsurance for all procedures and associated clinical lab tests.
Mental health care	Yes, Part A. Inpatient; Part B, outpatient. Inpatient Part A coverage: Inpatient stays in a psychiatric hospital are limited to 190 days per lifetime. Inpatient stays for mental health care in a general hospital are the same as for physical illness. Patient deductible per benefit period and coinsurance per day for inpatient care are the same as for physical illness. Patient coinsurance for physician/approved provider care while an inpatient is 20% of MAA. Outpatient Part B coverage: Patient copayment for services provided in hospital outpatient departments or clinic is the same as physical health care in that facility. Patient coinsurance for outpatient physician-approved provider services is 50% of MAA (regardless of setting). Partial hospitalization services: Medicare covers a structured program of active, intense outpatient treatment for mental illness that might otherwise require hospitalization. Patient payments for this program are same as outpatient services.	Yes, but Medicare coverage as first payer would apply. FEHBP plan would pay deductibles and coinsurance as for physical illness for services covered by the FEHBP plan. (Second payer coverage for partial hospitalization coverage is limited.)	Yes. FEHBP required plans to provide parity in coverage of mental and physical health. Plans may not limit the number of outpatient visits or inpatient hospital days for treatment of mental disorders to fewer than would be provided for physical health care. Patient coinsurance or copayments may not be higher for mental health care than for physical health care. Coverage of partial hospitalization may be limited.

Service	Covered by Medicare Part A or Part B? Patient payment responsibility?	FEHBP retired enrollees *with* Medicare: Covered by most FEHBP FFS plans? Patient payment responsibility?	FEHBP enrollees *without* Medicare: Covered by most FEHBP FFS plans? Patient payment responsibility?
Routine dental care	No.	Yes, FEHBP coverage applies. Coverage limited to fee schedule payments per procedure. Patient pays full balance.	Yes. Same as enrollees with Medicare.
Routine eye and hearing tests, eye glasses and hearing aids	No.	No. Same as enrollees without Medicare.	No, generally. May cover a diagnostic hearing test by an MD; patient pays coinsurance and balance above plan allowance.
Annual cap on patient out-of-pocket expenditures	No.	Yes, FEHBP coverage applies. Annual cap amount for covered services varies plan, plan option, and by PPO membership of providers used. Expenditures countable toward the limit generally *exclude* plan deductibles; charges above the plan's allowable amount; enrollee share of prescription drug costs; copayments for routine care; coinsurance for mental health/substance abuse treatment.	Yes, same as enrollees with Medicare.

[a] FFS: Fee-for-service plans. Enrollees choose a health care provider who is paid for individual services furnished.

[b] Benefit period: A benefit period starts the day an individual is admitted to a hospital or skilled nursing facility and ends when he or she has not received hospital or skilled nursing care for 60 days in a row.

* MAA: Medicare approved amount, usually determined under a prospective payment system or a fee schedule.

Table 5 also shows the variety of coverage and cost-sharing arrangements under the different FEHBP fee-for-service plans. It does not illustrate coverage and costs applicable to most or typical FEHBP participants, nearly half of whom were enrolled in one plan in 2001 (Blue Cross and Blue Shield standard option).[30]

The most common criticisms of the Medicare fee-for-services program are (a) that its coverage is not comparable to modern employer-sponsored group health insurance, and (b) that Medicare beneficiaries face higher out-of-pocket costs than do persons with private group insurance. FHEBP plans are often cited as examples of good employer-sponsored group insurance.

Comparison of Medicare and FEHBP coverage and cost sharing shows that these generalizations do not always hold true, with the major exception of Medicare's lack of outpatient prescription drug coverage. In regard to non-drug benefits, Medicare includes better coverage of certain types of care that are typically used by older persons than do FEHBP plans (e.g., care in a skilled nursing facility or home health care). In addition, for some care or services in certain settings, FEHBP enrollees could pay more out-of-pocket than would a similarly situated Medicare beneficiary.

In general, FEHBP enrollees can limit their out-of-pocket costs through their choice of providers, assuming their plan has a PPO in their area and assuming the PPO includes a provider of the type of care the enrollee needs. Some providers (including both hospitals and physicians) that furnish specialized care do not participate in PPOs because they do not need such network memberships to generate business, and they do not compete for patients on the basis of price. However, participation in Medicare is virtually universal among providers of covered health services, and Medicare's payment systems limit payments from Medicare as well as from beneficiaries, even for specialized services.[31] Thus, when certain specialized care is need or a specialized facility is used, Medicare beneficiaries may pay less than a FEHBP enrollee without Medicare would pay for the same care.

The following discussion highlights some key differences between Medicare Parts A and B, and FEHBP fee-for-service plans.

Comparison of Coverage and Enrollee Cost-sharing for Inpatient Hospital Stays

Both Medicare and FEHBP cover inpatient hospital stays. However, the cost of a hospitalization to a FEHBP enrollee *who is under age 65 and not eligible for Medicare* depends in large part on whether the hospital participates in the enrollee's plan's PPO network. A FEHBP enrollee requiring hospitalization may minimize out-of-pocket costs by choosing a network hospital, thereby paying considerably less than the $812 deductible for an inpatient stay (in 2002) for which a Medicare beneficiary would be responsible. Under some FEHBP plans, a short stay in a PPO facility might require minimal patient cost sharing. (For example, under the Blue Cross and Blue Shield standard option, an enrollee hospitalized in a preferred member facility would pay $100 for room, board, and general care and $100 for other hospital services). However, if an FEHBP enrollee used a hospital that did not participate in his or her plan, the costs to the enrollee could be more than the Medicare

[30] Table 5 does not reflect the new Blue Cross and Blue Shield basic option, which is available as of January 1, 2002. That option is the only fee-for-service plan in FEHBP under which the plan will pay nothing, and has no coinsurance arrangement, for services provided by non-preferred providers.

[31] See: CRS Report RL31067, *Medicare Payment System Design: An Overview,* by Carolyn L.Merck, Jennifer O'Sullivanm, and Sibyl Tilson.

deductible because the enrollee could be required to pay coinsurance for daily hospital care as well as for other hospital services, and the enrollee could be billed by the hospital for the balance of charges above the amount paid by the plan.

In addition to room, board, general care and other hospital services, hospital stays generally include the care of physicians, surgeons, anesthesiologists, radiologists or other health care professionals and practitioners. Because physician/practitioner services are not covered under Medicare's Part A hospital benefits, a Medicare beneficiary would pay for those services under Part B and would be responsible for 20% of Medicare's approved fees for such services. A FEHBP enrollee might have coinsurance rates of less than Medicare's 20% coinsurance if those professionals were members of the patient's FEHBP plan's PPO. However, even though the *hospital* might participate in the patient's FEHBP PPO, other professionals who provide services to the hospital's patients might not. Thus, a FEHBP patient could face non-PPO coinsurance rates for physician/practitioner services above the 20% coinsurance required by Medicare. Additionally, coinsurance for FEHBP enrollees under age 65 and not eligible for Medicare might be based on a higher allowed payment amount than Medicare's approved fees, in addition to which the FEHBP enrollee might be billed for the balance between the plan's payment limit and a non-PPO physician's practitioner's charge.

Comparison of Coverage and Enrollee Cost-sharing for Care in a Skilled Nursing Facility

Medicare covers up to 100 days of care in a skilled nursing facility for beneficiaries with a preceding 3-day hospitalization for the same condition. Covered costs include board and room as well as skilled nursing care and a variety of restorative therapies (e.g., physical therapy; speech therapy). Beneficiary cost-sharing is required for days 21 through 100, but coverage ends after 100 days. (Physician care for beneficiaries in skilled nursing facilities is covered under Medicare Part B and is billed and paid separately under the general physician payment rules applicable under Medicare and/or the FEHBP plan.)

In comparison, FEHBP fee-for-service plans do not cover skilled nursing facility care, although in some cases, plans/options may cover therapy at certain hourly or other rates (board and room are not covered). Although skilled nursing facility care may not be covered by FEHBP fee-for-service plans, some pay a Medicare beneficiary's copayment for about 10 days after the first 20 days for patients who remain in the facility for more than 20 days. Some plans may cover inpatient care in rehabilitation hospitals that provide restorative therapies, although the plan may require the hospital to be certified as an acute care hospital and admission must be pre-certified and medically necessary.

Skilled nursing facility care (including board and room) is a major category of coverage that is available under many FEHBP HMOs but that is not available in the fee-for-service plans.

Comparison of Coverage and Enrollee Cost-sharing for Home Health Care

Home health care is another service for which Medicare provides more extensive coverage at less cost to the patient than do FEHBP plans. A variety of therapy services as well as skilled nursing care is covered under Medicare's home health benefit as long as the individual is homebound and the care is medically necessary.[32] Medicare's home health services are focused on conditions generally characteristic of older persons, and Medicare requires no beneficiary cost sharing for home health services.

In comparison, the home health care benefit offered in most FEHBP plans does not require that the patient be homebound, but it covers nursing care only (no therapy services) and, typically, there are limitations on the number of visits an enrollee may receive per year and on the length of each visit. A FEHBP plan may pay for services only after the patient has paid a certain amount and/or may cap the amount it pays for a patient's home care per year. As a result, cost-sharing for home health care may be substantial for an enrollee without Medicare.

Comparison of Coverage and Enrollee Cost-sharing for Hospice Care

Hospice care for the terminally ill is covered under both Medicare and FEHBP plans. Under Medicare, hospice care is virtually cost-free to beneficiaries. Although some FEHBP plans require no enrollee cost sharing, some require a copayment per admission and/or coinsurance, or limit the amount the plan will pay in total.

Comparison of coverage and enrollee cost-sharing for physicians and outpatient services and suppliers. Coverage under FEHBP and Medicare are similar for physician care and for services provided in outpatient facilities such as hospital outpatient departments and ambulatory surgical centers. Both programs cover diagnostic tests and purchase of certain medical equipment and devices.

In general, Medicare beneficiaries pay 20% of Medicare's approved amount for physicians and outpatient facilities (except for hospital outpatient departments, for which a new payment system is in transition, and clinical laboratory tests for which Medicare requires no cost sharing). FEHBP cost-sharing for such services may be more or less than 20% of the plan's approved amount (which may be more or less than Medicare's approved amount) and depends largely on whether the enrollee uses PPO providers.

Although both FEHBP and Medicare cover purchase of certain medical equipment, prosthetics, and orthotics, Medicare covers more orthotic devices than most FEHBP plans.

Coverage of Outpatient Prescription Drugs and Annual Limitations on Enrollee Out-of-pocket Costs

Prescription drug coverage is a major outpatient benefit OPM requires all FEHBP plans to offer that is not offered by Medicare. Because drugs are a costly component of the FEHBP, most plans now use formularies, pharmacy benefit managers, and preferred pharmacy retail outlets in order to contain costs, and most plans offer mail order services with low enrollee cost sharing for maintenance drugs. Formularies generally use three levels of copayments in order to create financial incentives for enrollees to use generic products by charging low copayments for them, higher copayments for "preferred" name brand drugs, and the highest copayments for non-preferred brand names.

Limitation on enrollee annual out-of-pocket costs for covered benefits ("catastrophic" expense limits) is required by OPM for all FEHBP plans but is not currently a feature of Medicare. Medicare restructuring proposals that have been considered by the Congress in

---

[32] Medicare's home health benefit does not cover long-term care for persons requiring personal assistance with activities of daily living.

recent years have included proposals to limit beneficiary cost sharing for medical benefits, and recent proposals to provide outpatient prescription drug coverage for Medicare beneficiaries have included limitation on beneficiary drug expenditures. However, the Congress is not currently activity considering a plan that would include a combined limit on beneficiary expenditures for medical care and prescription drugs such as provided under FEHBP. As discussed earlier in this chapter, FEHBP fee-for-service plans and options vary greatly in the type and amount of expenses that are countable toward the catastrophic limit. For instance, four of the seven fee-for-service plans *exclude* from the catastrophic expense limit all enrollee cost-sharing for outpatient prescriptions drugs; three plans/options exclude some portion or amount of enrollee drug costs.

Rules for Coordination of Coverage for Annuitants

When a retiree eligible for Medicare also has coverage under a group plan sponsored by a former employer, private or public, Medicare's coordination of benefits policy specifies that Medicare is the "first payer" and the employer plan is the "second payer."[33] This ordering of payers means that when a Medicare beneficiary who is retired from his or her federal job uses health care, the bill for the care is sent first to Medicare, which pays for covered care according to its payment rules, excluding any applicable Medicare deductibles and coinsurance. Next, the bill is sent to the FEHBP plan which pays for care not covered by Medicare (assuming it is covered under the FEHBP policy).

The column in Table 5 titled "FEHBP retired enrollees *with* Medicare" illustrates the situation in which a federal annuitant has Medicare coverage, including both Part A and Part B, and Medicare is the first payer. If the annuitant elects not to participate in Part B, the column titled "FEHBP enrollees *without* Medicare" under "Physician and Outpatient Coverage" would apply.

Medicare as First Payer; FEHBP as Second Payer

When FEHBP plans are second payer, they pay the Medicare deductibles, copayments and coinsurance for their enrollees, and they waive their own deductibles, copayments, and coinsurance (although these policies vary when an FEHBP HMO is the second payer plan.)[34] However, FEHBP plans do not waive their deductibles or coinsurance for things they cover but Medicare does not. For instance, an FEHBP plan would pay the first $100 of outpatient services used in a year by an enrollee with Medicare Part B (the Part B annual deductible), and it would pay the 20% coinsurance required for most outpatient care under Part B. If the FEHBP plan annual deductible were $250 and it required enrollees to pay coinsurance of 20% of the charge or the plan's approved amount for an outpatient service, the deductible and the coinsurance would be waived by the plan, and the enrollee would have no out-of-pocket

[33] In certain cases, a beneficiary's group health insurance, liability, workers' compensation, or no-fault coverage pays first and Medicare pays second. Also, special rules apply to coordination of coverage for renal dialysis for persons with end stage renal disease. These special rules are not addressed in this report.

[34] The general rules regarding first or second payer status of Medicare and FEHBP plans for persons with coverage under both programs are the same regardless of whether the annuitant's FEHBP plan is a fee-for-service plan or an HMO. However, when an FEHBP HMO is second payer, its policies may differ regarding payment of Medicare deductibles and coinsurance (it may depend on use of HMO network providers). HMOs functioning as second payer may not waive their required copayments.

costs. However, because outpatient prescription drugs, for example, are not covered by Medicare, FEHBP plans generally do not waive their drug copayments, coinsurance, or, if applicable, their separate drug deductible.

Special Rules for Coordination of Payments for Inpatient Hospital Care

As indicated in Table 5, an annuitant with FEHBP and Medicare Part A would incur no out-of-pocket costs for a stay as an inpatient in a hospital. The hospital would receive payment in full for all services according to Medicare payment rules and the Medicare deductible would be paid by the FEHBP plan.

For annuitants age 65 or over without Medicare Part A (of whom there are about 180,000), a 1990 amendment to the FEHBA (P.L. 101-508) limited FEHBP fee-for-service plan payments for inpatient stays by enrollees age 65 or older who do not have Medicare part A to the Medicare payment for that stay, inclusive of room and board and all other care and services (Medicare's diagnosis related group or "DRG" payment amount). This policy does not apply to skilled nursing facilities, home health care, or hospice care covered under Medicare Part A but which are either not covered or are only partially covered by FEHBP plans.

Special Rules for Coordination of Payment for Physician and Part B Services

Physicians are paid under Part B of Medicare regardless of whether they see the patient in the office or in a hospital or other facility. Physicians who agree to "accept assignment" of Medicare payments accept Medicare's fee schedule amount as payment in full and may not bill beneficiaries (or secondary payers such as FEHBP insurance plans) for charges above Medicare's approved amount. Beneficiaries are responsible for a coinsurance payment of 20% of Medicare's approved amount and Medicare pays 80%. However, as second payer, an annuitant's FEHBP plan would pay the 20% coinsurance for annuitants with Medicare.

Physicians who do not accept assignment of Medicare's payment are restricted by Medicare law from billing their Medicare patients more than 115% of 95% of the Medicare approved amount. This formula works out to a cap of 109.25% of the Medicare approved amount and is known as the "limiting charge." For example, if a physician generally charged \$125 for a procedure, and if Medicare's approved amount for that procedure were \$100, a physician who did not accept assignment could not charge more than \$109.25 for a Medicare patient. Medicare would pay 80% of the approved amount (\$80 in this example), and the beneficiary would be responsible for \$29.25, which includes the \$20 coinsurance plus \$9.25 above the Medicare recognized payment amount.

Under an amendment to FEHBA enacted in 1993 (P.L. 103-66), physicians treating FEHBP enrollees who are 65 or over, who are retired from their federal job, and who have chosen not to participate in Medicare Part B, may not change the FEHBP plan more for a given services to those patients than Medicare would pay, and they may not bill the patient for any balance.[35] (Physicians and suppliers of physician services who accept Medicare assignment for their other patients must accept it for their FEHBP annuitants; those who do not accept assignment for their other patients may bill no more than the "limiting charge" for

[35] In addition to the amount paid to a physician for providing a service, the Medicare definition of the term "physician services" includes such things as outpatient physical and occupational therapy, certain cancer screening tests, X-ray and other diagnostic and preventive tests. Thus, payment for these services and tests are limited to Medicare's payment amount for annuitants age 65 or over without Medicare Part B.

FEHBP patients.) The limitation does *not* apply to other Part B services, including *facilities* in which a patient may receive medical care on an outpatient basis, such as hospital outpatient departments, certain outpatient clinics, and ambulatory surgical centers; it does not apply to suppliers of durable medical equipment and various devices.

A FEHBP plan would not pay all of an enrollee's Medicare cost sharing requirement if the plan's payment limit for the service were lower than the Medicare limit. FEHBP fee-for-service plans limit the amount of certain charges, such as physicians' charges, to the lesser of the provider's charge or the plan's "usual and customary limit." When FEHBP plan's usual and customary limit for a given procedure is less than the Medicare approved amount, or, for physicians not accepted assignment, less than the Medicare limiting charge, the FEHBP plan pays only the amount of the beneficiary coinsurance (or the limiting charge) that is below the plan's limit.

To continue with the above example, if a FEHBP plan's limit were $90 for a service for which Medicare's approved amount was $100, Medicare would pay $80 and the FEHBP plan would pay only $10 of the beneficiary's $20 coinsurance. Hence, the physician would receive a total payment of $90 after Medicare and the FEHBP plan had paid their shares, but the beneficiary would be responsible for $10 of coinsurance. If the physician did not accept assignment, he or she could bill the beneficiary for the balance up to limiting charge. In this example, a physician not accepting assignment could bill the beneficiary an additional $19.25, including the $10 of the beneficiary's coinsurance which was not paid by the FEHBP plan plus the $9.25 that would bring the physician's total payment up to the Medicare limiting charge of $109.25.

A special FEHBP rule applies to physicians who are part of a PPO network and who serve Medicare beneficiaries. PPO providers in FEHBP plans agree to accept discounted fees from the plan, and FEHBP enrollees cannot be charged more than the amount specified by the plan, for instance, $10 for a doctor visit. Nevertheless, Medicare would pay its share of the claim first, and, if that amount were the same as or more than the FEHBP plan's PPO rate, under regular PPO rules, the provider could not charge enrollee or the FEHBP plan for additional amounts. However, Medicare law does not permit providers to release either beneficiaries or secondary payers from Medicare's coinsurance requirement for Part B services (20% of the Medicare approved amount). Thus, an unusual situation arose in which PPO providers who had agreed to discounted fees from FEHBP nevertheless changed beneficiaries directly for the full Medicare coinsurance in order to comply with Medicare law. As a result, beneficiaries complained about unanticipated out-of- pocket costs for care from a physician in their FEHBP plan's PPO.

To remedy this situation, in an October 5, 1999, letter (No. 99-050) to participating FEHBP carriers, OPM instructed plans that:

> when a PPO network with which you [the FEHBP insurance plan] contract bills Medicare as the primary payer for Medicare allowable charges, we expect you to determine plan benefits on *the greater of* the negotiated PPO fee schedule or the Medicare allowable charge amount. This will ensure that providers do not bill your plan members for Medicare beneficiary cost sharing.

Thus, providers who participate in a FEHBP PPO are required to charge more than their discounted fee if the amount approved by Medicare is more, and they may charge the FEHBP plan for a beneficiary's coinsurance responsibility.

FEHBP as First Payer; Medicare as Second Payer

If a Medicare-eligible FEHBP policyholder is still working for the federal government, or a Medicare-eligible individual is covered as a family member on a working spouse's FEHBP policy, the FEHBP plan is first payer and Medicare pays second until the policyholder retires. If the FEHBP plan pays some, but not all, of the costs of a Medicare-covered service, Medicare credits the amount paid by the FEHBP plan toward the Medicare $812 inpatient deductible or $100 annual outpatient deductible and pays additional covered charges up to Medicare's approved amount. The formulas for determining how much Medicare pays for covered care differ depending on the type of payment system Medicare uses for that type of service. There is no assurance that the beneficiary will have no out-of-pocket costs after both the FEHBP and Medicare have paid their shares.

Issues Regarding Coordination of Benefits for Retirees with Employer-Sponsored Group Coverage

Private employers offering retiree health benefits often provide coverage that supplements Medicare coverage and/or pays beneficiary Medicare cost-sharing, although there are different methods used to coordinate what the plan pays in relation to what Medicare and the retiree pay. A small portion of private employers use a "full coordination of benefits" procedure under which retirees have no out-of-pocket cost sharing for services used, but most private plans apply their own payment formulas to costs not paid by Medicare, thereby requiring enrollee cost-sharing. (These are referred to as a "carve-out" integration plans.)[36] Most retirees in employer-sponsored plans pay at least part of the plan's premium, but the premiums for retirees are generally different from the premiums applicable to coverage for the employer's active workers because they are based on only those costs covered by the employer exclusive of Medicare.

Medicare beneficiaries who do not have supplemental coverage from a former employer or other source often purchase individual "medigap" policies from private insurance carriers (there are no family medigap policies). Medigap plans pay Medicare beneficiaries' deductibles, outpatient coinsurance requirements, and the cost of some services or care not covered by Medicare.

Coordination of FEHBP and Medicare is not like that used by private employers and is not the same as a medigap policy. Federal annuitants and workers age 65 and over choose among the same FEHBP plans, the same benefit packages, and pay the same premiums as workers, regardless of whether they are enrolled in Medicare Part A, Part B or both. Some argue that FEHBP is inefficient as Medicare supplemental coverage primarily because the price of the premium includes coverage of care that duplicates many Medicare benefits and for which Medicare, not the FEHBP plan, will pay. Federal annuitants must purchase a full FEHBP benefit package and pay the same full premium applicable to active workers without Medicare, including, for instance, coverage of inpatient hospital coverage, which annuitants with Medicare Part A already have. Some note that because the government pays a share of

[36] *The implications of Medicare Prescription Drug Proposals for Employer and Retirees,* prepared by Hewitt Associates LLC for the Henry J. Kaiser Family Foundation, July 2000.

FEHBP premiums, it, too, is paying FEHBP plans for services that will be covered by Medicare.

An important question is whether the government's total costs (including both Medicare and FEHBP) would be increased or decreased if FEHBP offered a supplemental plan for retirees with Medicare, that is, a plan which covered only Medicare's deductibles, coinsurance, and services not covered by Medicare. Medicare's costs would be largely unchanged because it is first payer. However, OPM reports that average claims for Medicare beneficiaries *even after Medicare has paid its first-payer amount* are slightly higher than average premiums for the universe of employees and annuitants in FEHBP. (Premiums directly reflect claims costs.) Thus, it appears that Medicare beneficiaries in FEHBP use so much more health care, and/or so much more costly health care than younger enrollees, that the premium cost of a supplemental policy that only paid Medicare's deductibles and coinsurance, and that covered prescription drugs, would be higher than premiums under the current arrangement in which younger and older enrollees are in the same risk pool.[37] As a result, the cost to the government for its share of a supplemental premium would be more than its share under the current program. If annuitants with Medicare were removed from the FEHBP risk pool on which premiums for all program participants are currently based, which includes young and old, workers and annuitants, then premiums for the younger, non-Medicare FEHBP population might be lower, and the government's share of premiums for them would be lower. Nevertheless, it would be important to consider how costs and premium shares for annuitants and others would change over time as the costs of the kinds of health care used by Medicare-covered retirees increases compared with the costs of care used by younger FEHBP participants.

Should FEHBP Enrollees Elect Medicare Part B?

Table 4 indicates that, of the 1.411 million federal annuitants age 65 or over enrolled in FEHBP in 2000, only 312,000, Or 22%, were *not enrolled* in Part B; thus, 78% of those 65 and over have Part B coverage. However, a frequently asked question is whether a retiree enrolled in FEHBP should elect Part B also, since most Part B benefits duplicate benefits covered by FEHBP.

In general, as illustrated by **Table 5,** an FEHBP enrollee who has Medicare Part A and elects Part B would have virtually no out-of-pocket costs for deductibles or coinsurance (except, perhaps, for separate deductibles and coinsurance for things not covered by Medicare, such as prescription drugs). However, an enrollee electing Part B has the additional out-of-pocket expense of the Part B premium ($54 monthly, or $648 annually, in 2002). Because all FEHBP fee-for-service plans have PPO networks for which enrollees pay minimal amounts out of pocket for outpatient services, it can be argued that an individual would have to use a lot of outpatient care *at PPO rates* to exceed $648 annually. Moreover, PPO providers and suppliers may not bill the patient for any balance of charges above the amount payable under their contract with the plan.

---

[37] Much of the higher costs incurred by FEHBP retirees are for prescription drugs, which older people are more likely to use than younger people, and which Medicare does not cover.

However, coinsurance and copayments for a person receiving ongoing costly treatments at a hospital outpatient department, or whose specialized care is not available from a PPO provider, might easily add up to $648 during a year. Also, a non-PPO provider facility (for example, outpatient care at a specialized hospital) may bill an FEHBP enrollee for the balance of charges above the FEHBP plan's limit, and such charges could be substantial. Since virtually all acute care hospitals and their outpatient facilities participate in Medicare, Part B enrollment would protect the beneficiary against any such balance billion charges. (As noted earlier, for enrollees without Medicare Part B, care defined as "physician services" may not be paid at rates above Medicare's allowed amount and the individual may not be billed for the balance of charges over Medicare's approved amount.)

Another consideration in answering this question is that all FEHBP plans have out-of-pocket annual limits on what enrollees can be required to pay ("catastrophic" limits). These annual limits are typically between $3,000 and $4,000, although amounts creditable toward reaching the limit differ among the plans. (Again, not all of an enrollee's out of-pocket expenses for prescription drugs are counted toward the limit.) In general, an annuitant electing Part B would be paying $648 out-of-pocket for the Part B premium (in 2002) to insure against the possibility of incurring up to $2,352 in certain additional out-of-pocket costs in the year if the catastrophic limit were $3,000. Some observe that if an individual expects that, for several years, he or she will not use outpatient care for which countable out-of-pocket expenses will exceed the annual amount of the part B premium, an amount equal to the premium could be saved in case expenses were very high in a future year. Nevertheless, FEHBP enrollees are protected from out-of-pocket expenses above the limit in their plan, assuming the catastrophic costs are for covered and covered charges and are included in the plan's countable expenses.

APPENDIX 1. THE POTENTIAL EFFECTS OF CHOICE IN FEHBP

Some say that offering FEHBP participants a choice among several plans and an opportunity to change plans annually restrains premium cost increases. They opine their most enrollees are price-sensitive and base their choice of plan primarily on their likely out-of-pocket costs, including premiums and coinsurance or copayment requirements. They note that enrollees change plans during an open season of they believe a plan with a lower [premium and/or lower out-of-pocket costs would provide the coverage they need; thus, plan switching virtually always is in the direction of enrollees' moving to lower-premium plans.

Others suggest that choice may have little effect on program costs or may actually increase costs *in the long term;* further, they note that choice among multiple plans may invite risk selection into the program.

Choice and Premium Costs

The argument that competition and choice among FEHBP plans restrains costs has initiative appeal. It can be demonstrated that, when participants switch to lower-cost plans during an open season, the program realizes savings in the first year after they switch. This cost reduction occurs because more enrollees are in lower-premium plans after an open season than before.

However, it is difficult to demonstrate that savings realized in the first year after an open season are maintained in subsequent years. The major cost of FEHBP is the sum of the premiums paid to all the plans in the program. We know how enrollees are distributed among the plans at the premiums in effect before an annual open season, and we know how enrollees are distributed among the plans at the premiums in effect in the year after an open season. The "savings" from enrollees' choosing new, generally lower-premium plans during an open season can be calculated by (a) adding up the cost of premiums for the distribution of enrollees in their new plan choices at the new premium rates after the open season, (b) adding up the cost of premiums using the distribution of enrollees *as it was before they charged plans,* but using the new, post-open season premiums, and (c) comparing, the two sums. Because, on balance, most participants who change plans move to lower-cost plans, this calculation indicates that choice of plans and the opportunity to change plans reduces costs *in that year*.

This calculation does not take into account premium increases that may occur in subsequent years as a result of enrollees changing to lower-premium plans 2, 3, or more years earlier. Given that, ultimately, the fee-for-service plan's premiums are equal to the cost of claims paid plus administrative costs and fees, consider the hypothetical case of Joe Enrollee and the effect on program costs of the plan choice he and others like him might make. Assume that Joe has a moderate amount of annual claims and uses about the same amount of health care regardless of what plan he is in. (Thus, he is not making a new plan choice based on an anticipated change in health status or utilization.) In year one, Joe, like most participants, is in a fee-for-service plan. He decides his usual annual claims do not warrant the premium level of the plan he is in, and during the open season at the end of the year, Joe switches to a lower-cost fee-for-service plan. In all probability, the lower-cost plan enrolls people who, on average, use less health care than Joe uses. Thus, because in year one, while in his original plan, Joe paid more in premiums than the value of the care he used, his premium payments subsidized the higher claims costs of others in the plan. Because that plan loses Joe's "subsidy," eventually it would have to raise its premium to cover claims. However, that increase would not occur until at least 2 or 3 years after the open season in which Joe opted for another plan.

When Joe joins a lower-premium plan he may be above that plan's average enrollee in claims costs. Thus, that plan's premiums would rise eventually (but not immediately) because it would have to cover Joe's higher claims. Therefore, 2 or 3 or more years after Joe changes plans, the premium of both the plan Joe left and the plan Joe joined would increase as a result of his having switched plans.

Other factors associated with plan-switching influence premiums in different directions. For instance, assume Joe were to switch from a fee-for-service plan to an HMO. Because the HMO's premium is pegged to the cost of enrollees of other employers in the community, its premiums might not be adjusted to reflect the changing utilization patterns of the federal enrollees who switch into or out of it.

Choice may cause premiums to rise if enrollees who anticipate the need for extensive or costly health care change to a high benefit/high cost plan, such as when a costly illness is diagnosed.

Overall, the annual churning that takes place in FEHBP as some participants seek lower-cost plans and others seek coverage for an anticipated high-cost need while plans are adjusting premiums to compensate for the claims effects of gaining and losing enrollees in previous years has unclear net cost effects over the long term. Nevertheless, less than 3% of all enrollees typically change plans during an open season.

Choice and Adverse Risk Selection

Adverse risk selection is another potential by-product of plan choice. If switching to lower-cost plans were to occur on a significant scale, higher-cost plans with richer benefit packages could be left with very high-cost enrollees, and the premiums would spiral upwards. This is what happened to the Aetna Life Insurance Company, which sponsored a governmentwide indemnity plan and which was originally authorized to participate in FEHBP in 1960 as an indemnity plan. Aetna withdrew from the program in 1990 because its viability was undermined as a result of an increasing concentration in its "high option" of largely older enrollees with high claims rates. Although the actuarial value of Aetna's high option plan was only slightly greater than that of its standard option at the time, the high claims of the enrolled group caused the premiums to increase significantly beyond the value of the benefit package.[38] Because the law required that the FEHBP plan filling the role of a government-wide indemnity plan offer two benefit options, Aetna withdraw from the program because its high option was not sustainable. To some extent, in recent year, the Blue Cross and Blue Shield high option plan was experiencing a concentration of costly users in its high option (although that option had comparatively few enrollees); thus, starting with 2002, it shifted its optional offerings to a standard plan, which will remain similar to its previous standard option, and a "basic," lower-cost option.

Certain employee unions at one time sponsored fee-for-service plans open to any government employee or retiree (e.g., the National Treasury Employees' Union, "NTEU," and the American Federation of Government Employees, "AFGE"). These plans tended to include generous benefits. The NTEU plan began to experience large enrollment gains, and in 1992 the underwriters indicated that their premiums, already high, would have to be raised significantly to cover utilization. Instead, the sponsoring organization decided to withdraw from the health insurance business. Some of these plans also encountered other administrative problems.

In the past decade, OPM has taken administrative steps to reduce risk segmentation in the program and has used its authority to negotiate each fee-for-service plan's benefit package to require some plans to drop certain benefits and require others to add benefits. These measures resulted in the plans becoming more similar over time. However, the GEHA standard option introduced in 2001 and the new Blue Cross and Blue Shield basic option illustrate a move to diversification among the plans.

It is important to bear in mind why Congress included plan choice under FEHBP. Choice is included to afford participants the opportunity to enroll in a plan that meets their health care needs and ability to pay. Thus, the law requires that high option plans be available to provide

[38] The actuarial value of a plan in the cost of the premiums for the benefit package if all FEHBP participants were in that one plan.

richer benefit packages to those needing such coverage. The legislative history does not indicate that Congress was concerned that adverse risk selection might be a drawback to inclusion of diverse types of plans. Although adverse selection does not appear to be a major problem in the program today, it warrants ongoing monitoring by OPM. As program managers annually review plan benefits and premiums they must balance the intent of Congress to provide enrollees a choice of plans against risk selection. Currently, the high option plans cover participants who use more care, and the price (premiums) for those plans may be somewhat greater than the actuarial value of the benefit package. However, the premiums of the high option plans appear to be fairly stable, and the grouping of higher-cost users in those plans may allow the premiums in the other plans to be lower than they would be if the risk pools were evenly mixed.

Chapter 7

HEALTH INSURANCE FOR DISPLACED WORKERS

Julie Stone, Hinda Ripps Chaikind, Jean Hearne and Heidi G. Yacker

INTRODUCTION

Largely in response to the events of September 11 and the economic downturn that followed, the House and Senate have considered a number of approaches to assist displaced workers with the cost of health insurance. Many of the proposals are in bills that include a wide array of provisions intended to stimulate the economy, addressing such areas as trade practices, tax policy, labor, state fiscal relief and health care. Part of this debate is whether, and how, to continue (or restore) health insurance for persons who have lost jobs as a result of the downturn in the economy, the terrorist activities of last fall, or the relocation of American-based factories abroad. Discussion concerning policy options for the uninsured is likely to continue into the 108th Congress, in part due to the U.S. Census Bureau's recent announcement that the number of uninsured increased by 1.4 million in 2001, totaling 41.2 million.[1]

The 107th Congress has considered several bills that would provide health care assistance to certain displaced workers and their families. The conference report (H.Rept. 107-624) for H.R. 3009 (the Andean Trade Preference Act) was passed by the House (July 27, 2002) and the Senate (August 1, 2002), and signed by the President (P.L. 107-210) on August 6, 2002. The law contains, among other things, authorization of presidential trade promotion authority (TPA) and includes provisions aimed at assisting workers, who have lost jobs and are receiving Trade Adjustment Assistance[2] (TAA), with the purchase of health insurance. It provides for a refundable and advanceable tax credit of up to 65% of a TAA recipient's health insurance premiums and will authorize funding for grant programs intended to encourage

[1] U.S. Census Bureau, September 30, 2002: Numbers of Americans With and Without Health Insurance Rise. Www.census.gov/Press-Release/www/2002/cb02-127.html

[2] Trade Adjustment Assistance (TAA) for workers offers extended unemployment benefits and job training to workers left jobless when imported goods have contributed importantly to their job loss. For more information see CRS Report: RS21078: Trade Adjustment Assistance for Workers: Legislation in the 107th Congress, by Paul J. Graney.

states to establish or expand programs for the uninsured. Many analysts expect that these provisions and the new programs they establish will provide a model for Congress to evaluate future proposals to provide assistance to other uninsured individuals.

Bills considered earlier in this Congress that failed to pass both houses, include H.R. 622, passed by the House on February 14, 2002, and H.R. 3529, passed by the House on January 20, 2002. Both bills would have provided a refundable, and, for certain individuals who had recently lost jobs and health care coverage, an advanceable tax credit equal to 60% of the amount paid during the taxable year for health insurance premiums. Under these proposals, individuals and their dependents would be eligible for a period not to exceed 12 months. Both bills would have provided a $4 billion increase to the National Emergency Grants program for subsidies for the purchase of insurance, among other purposes, and just under $4.6 billion to states through direct payments from the Secretary of Treasury for health care items and services. National Emergency Grants are currently administered by the Department of Labor and are available to states or localities affected by major economic dislocations. Unlike H.R. 3529, H.R. 622 also included a provision that would have provided a total of $100 million in grants to states to either create high risk pools or fund existing ones.[3]

H.R. 3090 was passed by the House on October 24, 2001. This bill would have provided health care assistance for the unemployed by increasing Social Service Block Grant funding by an additional $3 billion for FY2002. If enacted, states could have used these funds for several purposes, including paying for health insurance for certain unemployed individuals who are not eligible for other federal health insurance programs.

In the Senate, a variety of approaches were considered. On November 9, 2001 the Senate Finance Committee considered the House-passed H.R. 3090. The committee passed it with an amendment in the nature of a substitute. The Finance committee's version of H.R. 3090, The Economic Recovery and Assistance for American Workers Act of 2001, would have provided direct payments from the Department of Treasury to health plans to cover 75% of premiums on behalf of unemployed workers purchasing health insurance through their former employers under the continuation health benefits provisions of the Consolidated Omnibus Budget Reconciliation Act of 1986 (COBRA). The bill would also have allowed states to use Medicaid funds to subsidize the cost of the remaining 25% of COBRA continuation health benefits for certain low-income individuals unable to afford their share of the premium. States electing this option would have received federal matching dollars at the State Children's Health Insurance Program (SCHIP) enhanced match (described below). In addition, the bill would have provided states the option of extending Medicaid coverage temporarily to those displaced workers who do not qualify for COBRA continuation coverage.

---

[3] In general, high risk pools provide state subsidized health coverage to individuals who have been denied coverage through the private insurance market or charged premiums that they cannot afford due to their health states. Under high-risk programs, states typically cap premium rates at 125 to 200 percent of standard market rates. Most states use money from taxes levied on health insurers in the state and/or by allocating general revenue or special funds to subsidize the cost of care for these high-risk individuals (Achman, Lori and Chollet, Deborah. *Insuring the Uninsurable: An Overview of State High Risk Health Insurance Pools.* Mathematical Policy Research, Inc., August 2001). As of January 21, 2001, 29 states have set up high-risk pools (or similar comprehensive state programs) designed to provide insurance and risk-spreading for people who are medically uninsurable. (Comprehensive Health Insurance for High-Risk Individuals: A State-By-State Analysis Includes Operating Statistics, Model Bill, Current Premiums, Funding Mechanisms, State Contacts. Self-Employed Country, Inc., National Association of State Comprehensive Health Insurance Plans, Fourteenth Edition, 2000.)

On November 14, 2001, however, the Senate Finance Committee's version of H.R. 3090 failed to overcome two budget points of order. Finally, a proposal considered, but not introduced, would have provided refundable tax credit to help displaced workers pay up to 50% of the premiums for COBRA continuation health coverage. The proposal also included a $5 billion increase for National Emergency Grants to provide subsidies for the purchase of insurance, among other purposes.

This chapter will discuss enacted legislation as well as other proposed bills to show the scope of options considered by the 107th Congress. It will also discuss some of the issues raised by the legislation, including timeliness, affordability, populations impacted, gaps in coverage and state participation.

HEALTH INSURANCE COVERAGE FOR UNEMPLOYED WORKERS AND THEIR FAMILIES

Current Experience and Law

Figure 1 summarizes the insurance status, including COBRA participation, of non-elderly unemployed adults in 1999, the latest year for which such data are available. About one-third (31%) of unemployed non-elderly adults retained private health insurance coverage through their spouses' employers, by purchasing policies in the individual market for insurance, or through some combination of private and public coverage in 1999 (28% private, not COBRA, plus 3% public and private). The current law safety net for workers losing their jobs covered an additional 22% of unemployed non-elderly adults. The safety net consists of COBRA continuation coverage (6%) and public programs (16%), such as Medicaid, the State Children's Health Insurance Program (SCHIP) or other public programs. Among the unemployed, however, the largest group (46%) did not have health insurance coverage. Below is a description of the major options in current law that can be used to cover unemployed displaced workers.

Title X of COBRA

Title X of the Consolidated Omnibus Budget Reconciliation Act of 1986 (COBRA, P.L. 99-272) requires employers who have 20 or more employees and who offer health insurance to continue to offer coverage for their employees and their families under certain circumstances (termination or reduction in hours of employment, death, divorce or legal separation, enrollment in Medicare, or the end of a child's dependency under a parent's health plan). Individuals have a maximum 104-day window in which to purchase COBRA coverage.[4] The coverage generally lasts 18 months, but may be extended for a longer period depending on the nature of the event triggering coverage. Employers are not required to pay for this coverage; instead, they may charge the beneficiary up to 102% of the premium (100% of the premium plus a 2% administrative fee). Individuals who purchase COBRA continuation coverage are not eligible for as many tax advantages as those who purchase

[4] Employers must notify the health plan administrator of the "COBRA qualifying event' within 30 days. The plan administrator must notify the eligible individual within 14 days of receiving the employer's notice. The employee must choose whether or not to elect COBRA coverage within the election period of 60 days, bringing the total number of days to a maximum of 104.

health insurance through their employers (described below). Purchasers of COBRA continuation coverage may deduct the amount they pay on premiums, only if their total uncompensated medical expenses exceed 7.5% of adjusted income.

Figure 1. Increase Status of Non-Elderly Unemployed Adults, 1999

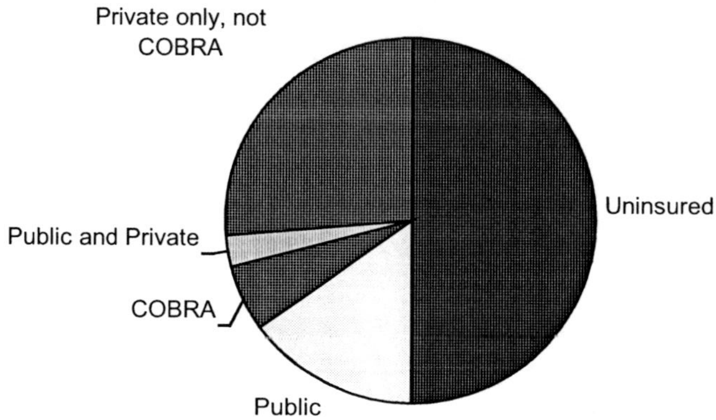

Source: CRS Analysis of Survey and Income and Program Participation data.

HIPAA Group to Individual Portability Protections

The health insurance reforms of the Health Insurance Portability and Accountability Act (HIPAA) of 1996 (HIPAA, P.L. 104-191) ensure that qualified individuals who are moving from one job to another or from employment to unemployment are not denied health insurance in the group or individual market because they have a preexisting medical condition (portability). HIPAA limits the amount of time a plan can postpone providing coverage to participants and beneficiaries in group health plans due to preexisting conditions and guarantees that qualified individuals and employers who choose to purchase coverage are able to find a plan (guaranteed offer). States have the choice of either enforcing the HIPAA individual market guarantees, referred to as the "federal fallback," or they may establish an "acceptable alternative state mechanism." Examples of potential alternative state mechanisms include health insurance coverage pools or programs, mandatory group conversion policies,[5] guaranteed issues of one or more plans of individual health insurance coverage, open enrollment by one or more health insurance issuers, or a combination of such mechanisms. Many states have elected to provide group-to-individual portability through high-risk pools, while others utilize a combination of high-risk pools, existing state insurance reform laws, and/or other mechanisms.

---

[5] Some states require health insurance issuers to allow a person to "covert" to an individual policy once he or she has lost group coverage. The individual maintains the policy generally with the same issuer, but it becomes an individual policy. The benefits offered by the conversion policy may not be the same as those under the group policy and the premiums are often more expensive.

Tax Advantages

Current law provides tax benefits, including federal income tax exclusions and deductions, for the purchase of employer-sponsored health insurance. Employers who choose to provide health insurance as part of an employee benefit package make a contribution toward the cost of the employees' monthly premium. These contributions cap be deducted as business expenses and are not counted toward employers' share of employment taxes. Employer-sponsored health insurance provides opportunities for workers to receive tax benefits as well. First, employer contributions are not counted toward the workers' taxable income. Second, the value of the insurance packages are excluded from employees' gross income. Further, premiums paid by employees, for either employer-sponsored or individual health insurance plans, can be deducted from their if they itemize and if premiums plus other unreimbursed medical expenses exceed 7.5% of adjusted gross income. Self-employed individuals can deduct up to 70% of the amount they pay in 2002 and 100% in 2003, from adjusted gross income.

Medicaid and SCHIP

Medicaid, Title XIX of the Social Security Act, and the State Children's Health Insurance Program (SCHIP), Title XXI of the Social Security Act, contribute to the health care safety net for uninsured children and for other specified groups of people with low income. Most healthy adults, however, do not qualify for Medicaid or SCHIP because enrollment is offered only to specific groups of parents and disabled individuals. Medical and SCHIP are more likely to be sources of coverage for the children of displaced workers.

Medicaid is a federal-state entitlement program providing medical assistance for low-income individuals who are aged, blind, disabled, members of families with dependent children, or who have one of a few specified conditions for which Medicaid coverage is conferred. Those conditions include pregnancy, tuberculosis, and breast or cervical cancer. SCHIP, also a federal-state program, builds upon Medicaid coverage for low- and modest-income children. States can choose to use SCHIP funding to cover certain children in families with income generally at or below 200% of the federal poverty level, but above the Medical income cutoff. The federal government shares in a state's Medicaid costs by means of a statutory formula designed to provide a higher federal matching rate, Federal Medical Assistance Percentage (FMAP), to states with lower per capita income. Matching payments are larger under SCHIP than they are under Medicaid and are called Enhanced Federal Medical Assistance Percentage (Enhanced FMAP). The Medicaid FMAP for FY2001 ranged from 50% to 76.8% while the SCHIP Enhanced FMAP ranged from 65% to 83.8%. Children whose health coverage is funded by SCHIP dollars can receive their health benefits through their state's Medicaid program, or states can establish separate health care programs. Coverage for adults under SCHIP is restricted to specific circumstances, either through subsidized employer-sponsored family coverage or special demonstration waivers.

GAPS IN CURRENT LAW COVERAGE

Provisions in the House and Senate bills reflect concerns among some Members of Congress that existing law may not provide a sufficient safety net for some displaced workers and their families. This concern is likely due to three contributing factors: health insurance is costly; COBRA has limited reach; and Medicaid and SCHIP are not available to all displaced workers.

The Cost of Health Insurance

For many, the cost of health insurance is burdensome. A recent survey of employers found that in 2001 employer-based health insurance policies cost on average $2,652 for single coverage. For family coverage, the average annual premium was estimated to be $7,056.[6] For a family of four, earning twice the poverty level ($35,300 in 2001), this is almost 20% of their annual income although employers often contribute to the cost. Often premiums are even higher for those purchasing comparable benefits in the individual market.

For several consecutive years, health insurance costs have risen rapidly, exceeding inflation, and large increases are projected to continue. For example, employer-based health insurance premiums are estimated to have risen by 11% in 2001, and some preliminary reports suggest that increases for 2002 are in the 13% to 16% range.[7]

COBRA's Limitations

About 4.7 million individuals were estimated to be enrolled in employer-based plans continued under COBRA's provisions at any one time in 1999. This represented only 6% of all unemployed workers. This low rate of COBRA coverage reflects COBRA's limited reach. Only certain employers are required to offer continuation health benefits - those firms that have 20 or more employees *and* that offer a group health plan. Firms are only requested under COBRA to offer continued coverage to individuals who were enrolled in the plan at the time their job was lost or their hours were reduced. A study released by the Kaiser Family Foundation estimated that in 1999 only 57% of workers and their adult dependents would have been eligible under COBRA's provisions of they had become unemployed.[8]

Low-wage workers are less likely to have access to COBRA's protections than other workers. This is largely for two reasons. First low-income workers are less likely to work for employers that offer coverage. An Urban Institute study estimates that about 32% of low-income (individuals with incomes under 200% FPL) workers and their adult dependents qualify for COBRA compared to 67% of high-income (individuals with incomes over 300% FPL) workers.[9] Second, when offered coverage, low-wage workers are less able to afford their required premium contributions. As described above, the beneficiary is responsible for up to 102% of the premium. The Kaiser study estimated that among those who are newly unemployed, fewer than 20% purchase it, and those with lower incomes are less likely to purchase it than their wealthier counterparts.[10]

---

[6] The Kaiser HRET Survey of Employer-Sponsored Health Benefits Estimates, 2001.

[7] Weber, Joseph, America, This is Really Gonna Hurt. *Business Week,* September 17, 2001.

[8] *COBRA Coverage for Low-Income Unemployed Workers.* The Kaiser Commission on Medicaid and the Uninsured. Washington, D.C., October 2001. (Hereafter cited as COBRA Coverage. The Kaiser Commission, 2001).

[9] Suckerman, Stephen, Jennifer Haley, and Matthew Fragale, *Could Subsidizing COBRA Health Insurance Coverage Help Most Low-Income Unemployed?* Urban Institute, Washington, DC, 2001.

[10] COBRA Coverage. The Kaiser Commission, 2001.

Medicaid/SCHIP Limitations

Under current law, Medicaid and SCHIP eligibility for non-disabled adults is allowed only under very limited circumstances. Through demonstration waivers, states can extend eligibility to non-traditional groups, such as childless adults. But those waivers are held to a budget neutrality requirement that prohibits new program spending. This means that states cannot expand coverage for some groups without reducing spending in some other part of the program. In most states, this is a barrier to large scale eligibility expansions, even in states that are prepared to devote additional state funds to expansion groups. SCHIP has another option for extending coverage to non-disabled adults who are parents of SCHIP eligible children. The "family variance" allows states to use SCHIP funds for a premium (presumably for employer-based coverage) for an entire family as long as the payment is not more than the agency would have paid for the SCHIP-eligible children in the household alone to be enrolled in traditional SCHIP coverage.

POLICY CONSIDERATIONS

Although a variety of measures have been proposed to assist displaced workers and their families in maintaining health insurance coverage or in acquiring new coverage, they diverge on who would be offered assistance, and what form of assistance should be provided.

Legislation in the 107th Congress

While all of the proposals target displaced workers, each defines the group of workers eligible for assistance differently. Table 1 describes the major legislation and populations they target.

Table 1. Health Provisions in Major Economic Stimulus Legislation

Proposal and status	Form of assistance	Method	Target group
P.L. 107-210, signed by the President on August 6, 2002	Tax credit	Up to 65% of health insurance premiums will be available as a refundable and advanceable tax credit payable to providers of qualified health insurance.	Persons who are receiving Trade Adjustment Assistance (TAA), who would be eligible to receive TAA but for the requirement to exhaust unemployment compensation, who are eligible for alternative TAA, under the Pension Benefit Guaranty Corporation.
	Grants to states	Authorizes grants to states of $510 million for 2002-2007.	Available to states for fiscal years 2002-2007 for enrollment assistance and for fiscal years 2002-2004 for health insurance and other support services.
	Grants to states	Establishes grants of $100 million for Qualified High Risk Pools.	Available to states for fiscal years 2003-2004 for establishing new qualified high risk pools and operation of existing pools. States with established high risk pools can receive a grant of up to 50% of the losses incurred by the state in connection with the operation of its pool.
H.R. 622 as amended and passed by the House on February 14, 2002	Tax credit	Up to 60% of health insurance premiums would be available either as a refundable tax credit or advanceable through direct payments from Treasury to health insurance plans.	Displaced workers who are receiving Unemployment Compensation (UC) or are certified by a state as eligible for UC benefits but are beyond their benefit year or have exhausted their maximum benefit levels. Qualifying plans would include individually-purchased plans as well as employer-based plans (such as COBRA continuation health benefits) for displaced workers responsible for more than 50% of the premiums. The credit would be available for no more than 12 months.
	Grants to states	Increases National Emergency Grants by $3.9 billion.	Distributed to states or localities affected by major economic dislocations for employment, training, and health insurance assistance.
	Grants to states	Establishes Temporary State Health Care Assistance grants of just below $4.6 billion.	Available for states through the end of 2002 to pay for health care items and services (not including Medicaid).
	Grants to states	Establishes $100 million in grants for Qualified High Risk Pools.	Same as P.L. 107-210.
H.R. 3529 as passed by the House on January 20, 2001	Tax credit	Up to 60% of health insurance premiums would be available either as a refundable tax credit or advanceable through direct payments from Treasury to health insurance plans.	Same as H.R. 622.
	Grants to states	Increases National Emergency Grants by $4 billion.	Same as H.R. 622.
	Grants to states	Establishes Temporary State Health Care Assistance grants of just below $4.6 billion.	Same as H.R. 622.

Proposal and status	Form of assistance	Method	Target group
H.R. 3090 as passed by the House on October 24, 2001	Grants to states	Increases Social Services Block Grant by $3 billion.	Unemployed individuals (and their families) who were employed at some point during 2001, are seeking and available to work and who are not eligible for any other federal health benefit program.
H.R. 3090 as reported by the Senate Finance Committee on November 9, 2001	Premium assistance for COBRA continuation health benefits	The Secretary of Treasury would make payments for up to 75% of the premium directly to group health plans, employers, and or state unemployment insurance offices.	Workers who lose their jobs at any time from September 11, 2001 through December 31, 2002, and who are eligible for and have elected COBRA continuation health benefits. The subsidies could last up to 12 months and would be paid by the Department of the Treasury directly to group health plans, employers, and/or state unemployment insurance offices.
	Medicaid payment of COBRA continuation health benefits	Provides states the option of extending Medicaid to low-income recipients of COBRA premium assistance to cover remaining 25% of premium at an enhanced matching rate.	Low-income individuals whose family income does not exceed 200% of the federal poverty level and who are receiving the proposed 75% subsidy.
	Temporary Medicaid expansion	Provides states the option of extending Medicaid to displaced workers who do not have access to COBRA continuation health benefits and to certain noncitizens. States would be required to terminate enrollment for this new group of beneficiaries once they become insured through another program or under employer-sponsored plans, States electing this option would receive federal matching dollars at the SCIP enhanced match.	Displaced workers who do not qualify for COBRA continuation coverage; are separated from employment at any time from September 11, 2001 through December 31, 2002; are uninsured; and whose income, asset and resource limitations do not exceed standards established by the state.
Senate Proposal Not Acted Upon	Tax credit for payment of COBRA continuation health benefits	Refundable credit that could be claimed in advance of filing one's tax return, covering up to 50% of COBRA premiums, not to exceed $140 per month for single coverage and $340 per month for family coverage.	Individuals who purchase COBRA coverage and file tax returns.
	Grants to states	Increases National Emergency Grants by $5 billion.	Distributed to states or localities affected by major economic dislocations, to be used for employment, training, and health insurance assistance.

For the time being, Congress has chosen to chosen to consider the health insurance needs of a very small group of uninsured individuals, namely those impacted by U.S. trade policies and those eligible for pensions through the Pension Benefit Guaranty Corporation. The number of individuals without insurance, however, is a much larger group. The different target groups in these bills reflect diverse opinions among Members of Congress about which group of uninsured individuals represents the highest priority for assistance. One year ago, the leading bills under consideration focused on those individuals impacted by the terrorist incidents of September 11, 2001. As time passed, the target population changed to individuals impacted by the economic recession. Still later, the leading bills' target group narrowed to extend benefits only to those recipients of Trade Adjustment Assistance. Little information is available to assist with prioritizing among groups of uninsured and determining the best form of assistance for the highest priority groups. It is unknown exactly how many individuals lost health insurance as a result of last year's terrorist incidents, the economic decline, and trade practices that impact U.S. workers. At a national level, there has been an increase in the number of persons experiencing unemployment. The unemployment rate rose to 5.7% in August 2002, among the highest levels since December 1996. Less is known, however, about how many of those recently unemployed individuals are uninsured. Further uncertainly exists about job losses that may yet occur as a result of the general economic downturn, U.S. policies reducing trade barriers, or even recent bankruptcies of several large corporations.

Proposed Forms of Assistance

Each of the options under consideration in the 107th Congress is described below and some of their varying aspects are raised. Each would provide assistance for either the purchase of health insurance or the provision of health care, but the approaches, as well as who would be eligible, differ.

Tax Credits for Health Insurance Premiums

A number of bills, including the recently passed Andean Trade Preference Act of 2002, contain health provisions that would provide tax credits for displaced workers. Although they differ in their details, their approaches share some common advantages and disadvantages.

Subsidies through the traditional tax system may not provide individuals with the money in time to pay health insurance premiums. Individuals file taxes annually and make claims based on the prior calendar year. Under this system, individuals would need to pay for health insurance premiums first and wait to receive the credit until the next consecutive tax calendar year. P.L. 107-210, the House-passed H.R. 622 and H.R. 3529 avoid this barrier by providing advanceable credits to eligible individuals through direct payments from the Secretary of Treasury to health insurance plans. Although advanceable payments could correct the timing problem for those who are qualified to receive them, their effectiveness would be determined by the speed in which the administrative processes are implemented to distribute them and by the eligible individual's ability to afford the reminder of the premium. Under some of these proposals, only individuals who file federal tax returns would be eligible for the tax credit. This might exclude some very low wage earners who do not file tax returns.

Block Grants

Block grants were proposed in a number of bills and included in P.L. 107-210. Grants to states to fund high risk pools can assist states in designing programs that provide health insurance coverage to persons who are high-risk and often otherwise uninsurable in the state. Under P.L. 107-210 and H.R. 622, funds could be used to either create high risk pools or fund existing ones. Under P.L. 107-210, funds will be directed toward pools in which the state restricts premiums charged to no more than 150% of the premium for applicable standard risk rates and that offers a choice of two or more coverage options. However, states would still be able to determine how much to charge enrollees in out-of-pocket costs, what benefits to include under the plans, the length of waiting periods for obtaining care for preexisting conditions, within federal standards, and whom among the otherwise uninsurable population they wanted to cover. H.R. 3090, as passed by the House, would have provided an additional $3 billion to the Social Services Block Grant (SSBG) program to allow states to assist the recently unemployed with the cost of health insurance.

Block grants offer predictability for both state and federal budgets, reducing the chance that costs will escalate uncontrollably. For states, on the other hand, the advantage predictability brings may be reduced if the funds are insufficient to cover the target population. If $3 billion is divided by the average cost of a private employer-based insurance plan (about $7,000 for a family policy in the group market in 2001, and $2,600 for an individual policy), then an estimate of how many average premiums could be paid with $3 billion can be calculated.[1] This calculation would suggest that just over 400,000 families or 1 million individuals could be covered with full subsidies for one full year.[2] If partial subsidies were provided, the number of people that could be reached would increase.

Two advantages of SSBG grants are simplicity and flexibility. Under H.R. 3090, funds would be distributed to states through an established program based on an established formula. The bill does not include specific requirements about who would be eligible for assistance under the grant program nor how such assistance would be provided. States would have the ability to design and administer the subsidy program that best fits their needs.

On the other hand, the block grant approach, states would be faced with difficult issues, such as how to reach the target population, how to administer funds quickly and efficiently, and what to do if the funds ran out without having covered all or most of the target population. Distributing funds for displaced workers and families through federal SSBG payments to states may create other inefficiencies as well. Social service programs are not likely to have staff experienced in purchasing health insurance on behalf of low-income people or administrations in place to do so. H.R. 3090 would prohibit states from using the funds to expand Medicaid or SCHIP, programs with experienced staff and existing administrations. Second, it is not clear that the current law formula used for distributing SSBG funds would be best for distributing health insurance assistance to people impacted by the recent recession. SSBG funds are distributed to states using a formula based on the population of the state, which may not correlate to the states with the greatest need created by the events of September 11, 2001 or another economic downturn.

[1] The Kaiser/HRET Survey of Employer-Sponsored Health Benefits Estimates, 2001.
[2] Such a program is likely to cover a mix of family and individual policies.

National Emergency Grants, like SSBG, can be used to quickly and efficiently move money to states.[3] An advantage of using the National Emergency Grant program is that funds can be targeted to areas that have been affected by major economic dislocations rather than through an allocation formula to all states. This could allow the Secretary the flexibility to target assistance. Health insurance advocates, on the other hand, opposed this approach because proposals would have allowed the authorization to pay for other employment and training assistance as well as for health insurance. It is thus possible that only some of the funds would be used to pay for health coverage for dislocated workers.

Subsidies for COBRA Continuation Coverage

Subsidies, like the Senate Finance Committee proposal, that pay all or part of premiums under COBRA's continuation health benefit provisions would have several advantages. Individuals who participate in these proposed subsidy programs would be able to remain in their current provider network and maintain continuous access to medical services. Further, the proposed programs could also reduce the number of uninsured. Subsidies could provide incentives to individuals and their families to purchase COBRA continuation health coverage when they might not otherwise do so.

The proposed legislation also has disadvantages. It would assist only those individuals who previously had insurance coverage (as described above). Subsidizing COBRA continuation health coverage may be relatively expensive because employees are guaranteed the same coverage as they had immediately before the qualifying event. Subsidies for more limited benefits packages may be more cost-effective both in terms of federal as well as for the enrollee who is required to pay the unsubsidized portion of the premium. In addition, subsidizing employer-based plans would result in larger subsidies for some individuals than for others since some employer plans are more expensive than other employer plans. Finally, subsidies might result in government payments for people who would have purchased insurance independently.

Although COBRA provides an established mechanism for continuing health insurance, COBRA subsidies would require the creation of a new administrative system. For example, to implement the 75% subsidy, the Senate Finance Committee proposed to make payments directly from the Department of Treasury to group health plans, employers, and/or state unemployment insurance offices. This activity is not currently conducted by any existing governmental administrative entity. Under the proposal, state Medicaid programs would have the option to pay the remaining 25% of premiums for individuals in families with income below 200% of FPL. To distribute these payments, state Medicaid offices would have to determine which individuals receive the 75% subsidy as well as their income levels possibly requiring coordination between state Medicaid offices and the Department of Treasury.

Temporary Medicaid Expansion Legislation

As a means-tested program, Medicaid is able to provide certain low-income individuals with health insurance coverage that they could not otherwise afford through the group or individual markets. Furthermore, Medicaid has an established administration designed to count applicants' income and resources to determine wealth status. Thus, the administrative

---

[3] National Emergency Grants were established by the Workforce Investment Act of 1998 and are administered by the Department of Labor. They are available to states or localities affected by major economic dislocations.

burden of providing coverage to this new eligibility group would be reduced. On the other hand, Medicaid is sometimes perceived negatively because of its association with welfare. This perception could deter some eligible individuals and families from enrolling in Medicaid.

An additional consideration is that Medicaid financing is shared by federal and state governments. Although the cost of this temporary eligibility expansion would be largely paid with federal dollars, the financial burden would be distributed across states and the federal government. The effectiveness of the proposal, therefore, depends on state decisions to elect to cover this new eligibility group, since they would not be required to do so. Many state budgets are already strained, with declining state revenue trends forcing many states to initiate funding cuts for their Medicaid programs.[4] The increase in unemployment rates will likely result in an increasing number of persons who will be eligible for Medicaid. States will therefore likely face a growth in enrollment, even without electing to cover this proposed new group. It is thus not clear how many states would participate.

The Senate Finance Committee proposal also included a provision that would have provided states with additional Medicaid funds to assist them in maintaining their current eligibility standards. It would have allowed states whose FMAP declined for 2002 to maintain their 2001 rates plus one percentage point. All other states would receive their 2002 FMAAP plus one percentage point. In addition, those states experiencing higher than average unemployment rates over 3 consecutive months (beginning on or after June 2001 and ending with the second month before the beginning of the calendar quarter), would receive an additional 1% percentage point increase in FMAP, raising their matching rate by a total of two percentage points.[5] The increased federal matching payments were intended to offset state budget shortfalls and increase the likelihood that states will maintain current eligibility levels. The Finance Committee proposal, as drafted, however, does not guarantee that states maintain current eligibility standards.

---

[4] State Budgets Under Stress: How are States Planing to Reduce the Growth in the Medicaid Costs. *Kaiser Commission on Medicaid and the Uninsured,* July 30, 2002. [http:www.kff.org/content/2002/20020730/statbudupdate73002.pdf]

[5] A similar provision was included in S. 812, as passed by the Senate on July 31, 2002. This provision would hold states with declining FY2003 FMAPs harmless, by allowing them to maintain their 2002 FMAPs and, in addition, would provide all states with an increase of 1.35 percentage points.

Chapter 8

HEALTH INSURANCE CONTINUATION COVERAGE UNDER COBRA

Heidi G. Yacker

BACKGROUND

Title X of the Consolidated Omnibus Budget Reconciliation Act of 1985 (COBRA, P.L. 99-272) requires employers who offer health insurance to continue coverage for their employees under certain circumstances. Congress enacted the legislation to expand access to coverage for at least those people who became uninsured as a result of changes in their employment or family status. Although the law allows employers to charge 102% of the group plan premium, this can be much less expensive than coverage available in the individual insurance market. The law affects private sector employer group health plans through amendments to the Employee Retirement Income Security Act (ERISA) and the Internal Revenue Code. COBRA continuation coverage for employees of state and local governments is required under amendments to the Public Health Service Act. Continuation coverage similar to COBRA is provided to federal employees through the law authorizing the Federal Employees Health Benefits program under Title V of the U. S. Code.

Before enactment of COBRA, if an employee's job was terminated (voluntarily or involuntarily), the insurance offered by the employer also ceased, usually within 30 to 60 days. Women were especially vulnerable to loss of insurance coverage if they became unemployed, widowed, or divorced. Although some employers offered the option of buying into the group plan, there was no certainty of that option. In 1985, 10 states had laws requiring insurance policies sold in their states to include a continuation of coverage option for laid-off workers. However, self-insured employers (employers that assume the risk of the health care costs of their employees rather than using private insurers) were not regulated by these state-mandated benefit laws; self-insured plans are regulated at the federal level under ERISA. Health insurance coverage for these affected workers and their families was not consistently available.

COBRA Coverage

General Requirements

Under COBRA, employers must offer the option of continued health insurance coverage at group rates to qualified employees and their families who are faced with loss of coverage due to certain events. Coverage generally lasts 18 months but, depending on the circumstances, can last for longer periods. COBRA requirements also apply to self-insured firms. An employer must comply with COBRA even if it does not contribute to the health plan; it need only maintain such a plan to come under the statute's continuation requirements.[1]

Covered Employers

COBRA covers all employers, with the following *exceptions:*

- Small employers. Employers with fewer than 20 employees are not covered under COBRA. An employer is considered to meet the small employer exception during a calendar year if on at least 50% of its typical business days during the preceding calendar year it had fewer than 20 employees.
- Church plans.
- Federal government. Although they are not covered under COBRA, since 1990, federal employees have been entitled to continued coverage under the Federal Employees Health Benefits Program.

Qualified Beneficiaries

In general, a qualified beneficiary is

- an employee covered under the group health plan who loses coverage due to termination of employment[2] or a reduction in hours;
- a retiree who loses retiree health insurance benefits due to the former employer's bankruptcy;

---

[1] On Feb. 3, 1999, the Internal Revenue Service (IRS) published final rules (64 *Federal Register* 5160-5188), effective on Jan. 1, 2000, defining COBRA coverage requirements. Final rules addressing COBRA issues applying to business reorganizations, bankruptcy, and COBRA's interaction with the Family and Medical Leave Act were issued on Jan. 10, 2001 (66 *Federal Register* 1843-1859).

[2] A termination of employment (for reasons other than the employee's gross misconduct) can be either voluntary or involuntary. Voluntary reasons include retirement, resignation, and failure to return to work after a leave of absence. Involuntary reasons include layoffs, firings and the employer's bankruptcy under Chapter 11 of Title XI of the U.S. Code. Strikes and walkouts might also trigger COBRA coverage if they result in a loss of health insurance coverage.

- a spouse or dependent child of the covered employee who, on the day before the "qualifying event" (see below), was covered under the employer's group health plan; or
- any child born to or placed for adoption with a covered employee during the period of COBRA coverage.

Qualifying Events

Circumstances that trigger COBRA coverage are known as "qualifying events." A qualifying event must cause an individual to lose health insurance coverage. Losing coverage means ceasing to be covered under the same terms and conditions as those available immediately before the event. For example, if an employee is laid off or experiences a reduction in hours that results in a loss of health insurance benefits, this is a qualifying event. Or, if an employer requires retiring individuals to pay a higher premium for the same coverage they received immediately before retiring, the retirement can be a qualifying event even though coverage is not lost or benefits reduced. Events that trigger COBRA continuation coverage include:

- termination or reduction in hours of employment (for reasons other than gross misconduct).

Spouses and dependent children can experience the following qualifying events leading to their loss of health insurance coverage:

- the death of the covered employee,
- divorce or legal separation from the employee,
- the employee's becoming eligible for Medicare, and
- the end of a child's dependency under a parent's health insurance policy.

In addition, retirees and their covered dependents who lose coverage under their former employer's retiree health plan as a result of the employer's declaring bankruptcy under Chapter 11 are qualified for COBRA continuation coverage.

Nature of COBRA Coverage

The continuation coverage must be identical to that provided to "similarly situated non-COBRA beneficiaries." The term "similarly situated" is intended to ensure that beneficiaries have access to the same options as those who have not experienced a qualifying event. For example, if the employer offers an open season for non-COBRA beneficiaries to change their health plan coverage, the COBRA beneficiary must also be able to take advantage of the open season. By the same token, COBRA continuation coverage can be terminated if an employer terminates health insurance coverage for all employees.

Duration of Coverage

The duration of COBRA coverage can vary, depending on the qualifying event.

- In general, when a covered employee experiences a termination or reduction in hours of employment, the continued coverage for the employee and the employee's spouse and dependent children must continue for 18 months.
- Retirees who lose retiree health insurance benefits due to the bankruptcy (a reorganization under Chapter 11) of their former employer may elect COBRA coverage that can continue until their death. The spouse and dependent children of the retiree may continue the coverage for an additional 36 months after the death of the retiree.
- For all the other qualifying events listed above (death of employee, divorce or legal separation from employee, employee's becoming eligible for Medicare, the end of a child's dependent status under the parents' health policy), the coverage for the qualified beneficiaries must be continued for 36 months.

Different provisions apply to disabled individuals. If the Social Security Administration (SSA) makes a determination that the date of an individual's onset of disability occurred during the first 60 days of COBRA coverage or earlier,[3] the employee and the employee's spouse and dependents are eligible for an additional 11 months of continuation coverage. This is a total of 29 months from the date of the qualifying event (which must have been a termination or reduction in hours of employment). This provision was designed to provide a source of coverage while individuals wait for Medicare coverage to begin. After a determination of disability, there is a 5-month waiting period for Social Security disability cash benefits and another 24-month waiting period for Medicare benefits. See "Paying for COBRA" section below regarding the premium for this additional 11 months.

Under some conditions, COBRA coverage can end earlier than the full term. Although coverage must begin on the date of the qualifying event, it can end on the earliest of the following:

- the first day for which timely payment of the premium is not made [Payment is timely if it is made within 30 days of the payment due date. Payment cannot be required before 45 days after the date of election (see below)];
- the date on which the employer ceases to maintain any group health plan;[4]

[3] In most cases, the SSA makes its disability determination later than within the first 60 days of COBRA coverage. However, the date of the disability onset can be set retroactively to a date within the first 60 days.

[4] A bankruptcy under Chapter 7 of Title XI of the U.S. Code would be such an instance. Chapter 7 bankruptcies (business liquidations) are distinct from Chapter 11 (reorganization) bankruptcies. Under Chapter 7, the employer goes out of existence. COBRA is provided through the employer; if there is no employer, there is no

- the first day after the qualified beneficiary becomes actually covered (and not just eligible to be covered) under another employer's group health plan, unless the new plan excludes coverage for a preexisting condition;[5] or

- the date the qualified beneficiary is entitled to Medicare benefits.

If a COBRA-covered beneficiary receiving coverage through a region-specific plan (such as a managed care organization) moves out of that area, the employer is required to provide coverage in the new area if this can be done under one of the employer's existing plans. For example, this might be possible if the employer maintains a self-insured plan, or if the employer's plan is through an insurer licensed in the new area to provide the same coverage available to the employer's similarlysituated non-COBRA employees. Further, if this same coverage would not be available in the new area, but the employer maintains another plan for employees who are *not* similarly-situated to the beneficiary (such as a plan offered to management or another group within the firm) that *would* be available in the new area, then that alternative coverage must be offered to the beneficiary. If, however, the only coverage offered by the employer is not available in the new area, the employer is not obliged to offer any other coverage to the relocating beneficiary.

Notice Requirements

Employers, employees, and the employer's health plan administrators all have to meet requirements for notifying each other regarding COBRA.

- At the time an employee first becomes covered under a health plan, the plan administrator must provide written notification to the employee and his or her spouse regarding COBRA rights if a qualifying event should occur.

If a qualifying event occurs, other notices are required.

- The employer must notify the plan administrator of the event within 30 days of the death of the employee, a termination or reduction in hours, the employee's becoming entitled to Medicare, or the beginning of bankruptcy proceedings.

- Within 14 days of receiving the employer's notice, the plan administrator must notify, in writing, each covered employee and his or her spouse of their right to elect continued coverage.

COBRA obligation. Under Chapter 11, the employer remains in business and must therefore honor his COBRA obligations.

[5] Under the Health Insurance Portability and Accountability Act (P.L. 104-191), the new health plan cannot impose a pre-existing condition limitation or exclusion longer than 12 months after the enrollment date. The new group plan must reduce the pre-existing condition limitation period by one month for every month the individual had creditable coverage under the previous plan or COBRA. If the individual has not had 12 months of such creditable coverage, the new plan can impose an appropriate limitation period. In this case, the individual may maintain COBRA coverage under the former employer's plan.

- The employee must notify the employer or plan administrator within 60 days of a divorce or legal separation of a covered employee or a dependent child's ceasing to be a dependent of the covered employee under the policy.

- COBRA beneficiaries who are determined by the SSA to have been disabled within the first 60 days of COBRA coverage must notify the plan administrator of this determination in order to be eligible for the additional 11 months of coverage. They must provide this notice within 60 days of receiving the SSA's decision.

Elections

A qualified individual must choose whether or not to elect COBRA coverage within an election period. This period is 60 days from the *later of* two dates: the date coverage would be lost due to the qualifying event, or the date that the beneficiary is sent notice of his right to elect COBRA coverage. The beneficiary must provide the employer or plan administrator with a formal notice of election. Coverage is retroactive to the date of the qualifying event. The employee or other affected person may also waive COBRA coverage. If that waiver is then revoked within the election period, COBRA coverage must still be provided. However, coverage begins on the date of the revocation rather than the date of the qualifying event.

Paying for COBRA

Employers are *not* required to pay for the cost of COBRA coverage. They are permitted to charge the covered beneficiary 100% of the premium (both the portion paid by the employee and the portion paid by the employer, if any), plus an additional 2% administrative fee. For disabled individuals who qualify for an additional 11 months of COBRA coverage, the employer may charge 150% of the premium for these months. The plan must allow a qualified beneficiary to pay for the coverage in monthly installments, although alternative intervals may also be offered.

Conversion Option

Many states require insurers to offer group health plan beneficiaries the option of converting their group coverage to individual coverage. Conversion enables individuals to buy health insurance from the employer's plan without being subject to medical screening. Under the Health Insurance Portability and Accountability Act (HIPAA, P.L. 104-191), a person moving from the group to individual insurance market is guaranteed access to health insurance coverage either under federal requirements or an acceptable alternative state mechanism. Although the policy must be issued, the premium might be less appealing than the premium under a group plan. The beneficiary must have exhausted all COBRA coverage before moving to the individual market. Although the premiums for an individual policy are higher, the conversion option may be attractive to a person who would otherwise have difficulty obtaining health insurance because of a major illness or disability.

Penalties for Noncompliance

Private group health plans are subject to an IRS excise tax for each violation involving a COBRA beneficiary. In general, the tax is $100 per day per beneficiary for each day of the period of noncompliance. ERISA also contains civil penalties of up to $100 per day for failure to provide the employee with the required COBRA notifications. State and local plans covered under the Public Health Service Act are not subject to the same financial penalties provided under the tax code or ERISA. However, state and local employees do have the right to bring an "action for appropriate equitable relief" if they are "aggrieved by the failure of a state, political subdivision, or agency or instrumentality thereof" to provide continuation health insurance coverage as required under the Act.

ISSUES

COBRA was enacted to provide access to group health insurance for people who lose their employer-sponsored coverage, and thus to help reduce the number of uninsured. However, the law has limitations in its effectiveness in covering persons leaving the workforce and, from the point of view of both employees and employers, has costs that can be burdensome.

Coverage Issues

In a report released in October 1999,[6] the Kaiser Family Foundation provided a picture of the COBRA population. Kaiser estimated that 4.7 million individuals were enrolled in COBRA plans at any one time, representing approximately 7% of unemployed workers and 3% of all insured workers. The numbers were fairly equally divided among regions of the country and according to firm size. There were, on average, 4.8 COBRA beneficiaries per firm, although this number varied widely by industry, ranging from 2.6 beneficiaries per firm in the mining/construction industry to 10.6 in the finance industry. The largest group of COBRA beneficiaries (approximately 35%) was in service industries, probably reflecting the high turnover rate in that industry. Estimates of the average length of time that beneficiaries keep their COBRA coverage range from 4.8 months to 10.5 months (for 18-month eligibles) or 22.0 months (for 36-month eligibles). Approximately 20% of COBRA eligible individuals actually elect coverage.

The universe of individuals covered by COBRA is limited in a number of ways. First, the small employer exception exempts employers with fewer than 20 employees from offering COBRA coverage. In addition, COBRA coverage is not extended to individuals who work for an employer, regardless of size, who does not offer group health insurance. Nor is it available to an employee who declines coverage under an employer's plan. Also, if the employer declares bankruptcy under Chapter 7 or simply discontinues operation, COBRA is not an option for employees. The Kaiser Family Foundation estimates that in 1999 only 57% of

[6] Kaiser Family Foundation and Health Research and Educational Trust, *Employer Health Benefits 1999 Annual Survey* (Washington: Kaiser Family Foundation, 1999).

workers and their adult dependents would have been eligible for COBRA if they had become unemployed.[7]

Employer Size

Currently, COBRA provides an exception for employers with fewer than 20 employees. Although 38 states require that continuation coverage be offered to employees in smaller firms, the coverage is not always as extensive as COBRA. According to figures from the Census Bureau's Statistics of U.S. Business, in 1998 approximately 20.3 million people, or 18.75% of employees covered in the survey, worked in firms with fewer than 20 employees.

One method proposed for increasing the number of those eligible for COBRA coverage would involve lowering the number of employees in the small employer exemption. According to the Census data, there were approximately 8 million people working in firms with 10 to 19 employees. If the definition of "small employer" was changed to "those having fewer than 10 employees," the employers of these 8 million workers would no longer be exempted from COBRA. However, such a proposal would likely be opposed by the small business community because it would result in potentially higher premium costs and added administrative burdens. Additionally, because the employee pool is small in these firms, the cost of covering COBRA individuals who use a lot of health care could result in raised premium costs for active employees in the long run.

Retirees

The Census Bureau estimates[8] that, in 2000, approximately 13.7% of people aged 55-64, many of whom are retirees, were uninsured. Many retirees obtain health insurance coverage through retiree plans offered by their former employers. However, the 2001 Kaiser annual employer survey reported that the percentage of employers who have 200 or more employees and who offer retiree health benefits had dropped from 66% in 1988 to 34% in 2001. Although 73% of those employers still offering coverage reported that they were very unlikely to eliminate retiree health benefits, 48% report that they were very or somewhat likely to increase the retiree share of contributions for premiums.

Under current law, an employee's act of retirement is a COBRA qualifying event. Although this might be an attractive option for those without access to a retiree health plan, the coverage is limited in its duration to the maximum applicable number of months (18, 29, or 36). Under the following circumstances, a covered employer must offer a retiring employee access to COBRA or to a retiree plan that satisfies COBRA's requirements for benefits, duration, and premium.

- If a covered employer offers no retiree health plan, the retiring employee must be offered COBRA coverage.
- If the employer does offer a retiree health plan but it is different from the coverage the employee had immediately before retirement (for example, if the plan is only offered for 6 months, or if the premium is higher than it was for the employee immediately before the retirement), the employer must offer the option of COBRA

[7] Kaiser Commission on Medicaid and the Uninsured, *COBRA Coverage for Low-Income Unemployed Workers* (Washington: Kaiser Commission, 2001).

[8] U.S. Bureau of the Census, *Health Insurance Coverage: 2000.* [http://www.census.gov/hhes/www/hlthin00.html]

coverage in addition to the offer of the alternative retiree plan. If the retiring employee opts for the alternative coverage and declines COBRA coverage, then she or he is no longer a qualified beneficiary under COBRA, and the employer is not required to offer COBRA coverage upon termination of the retiree plan.

- If the employer's retiree health plan satisfies COBRA's requirements for benefits, premium, and duration, the employer is not required to offer a COBRA option upon the employee's retiring (because coverage under the plan was not lost), and the coverage provided by the retiree plan can be counted against the maximum COBRA coverage period that applies to the retiree, spouse, and dependent children. If the employer terminates the plan before the retiree's or the retiree's spouse or dependent children's maximum coverage period has expired, COBRA coverage must be offered for the remainder of the period.

- The only other access a retiree has to COBRA coverage is in the event that a former employer terminates the retiree health plan under a bankruptcy reorganization under Chapter 11. In this case, the coverage can continue until the death of the retiree. The retiree's spouse and dependent children may purchase COBRA coverage from the former employer for 36 months after the retiree's death.

Cost Issues

Employees are concerned about the cost of COBRA coverage. A 2001 Kaiser study[9] provided figures for the average premiums for employer-sponsored health insurance coverage in 2001. The cost for single coverage was \$2,650 and for family coverage, \$7,053. On average, employers cover approximately 74% of the premium for a family plan, leaving the employee's share at about \$1830. Under COBRA, the employee must pay 102% of the premium, or almost \$7200. This can be a hardship for newly-unemployed individuals.

Employers also express concerns about costs. Charles D. Spencer & Associates, employee benefits analysts, produce an annual COBRA survey of employers who subscribe to their service.[10] In their 2000 survey, they found that the *claims costs* of COBRA continuation coverage for the plan year 1999 were on average 54% higher than the claims costs of insurance coverage for active employees. The average annual health insurance costs per active employee was \$3,936, the COBRA cost was \$6,051. The Spencer Associates analysts contend that this indicates that the COBRA population is sicker than active covered employees, and that the 2% administrative fee allowed in the law is insufficient to offset the difference in claims costs. However, because this survey does not represent a random sample of employers, it is not known whether its findings are representative of all employers in the United States.

---

[9] Kaiser Family Foundation and Health Research and Educational Trust, *Employer Health Benefits 2001 Annual Survey* (Washington: Kaiser Family Foundation, 2001).

[10] Charles D. Spencer & Associates, Inc., *2000 COBRA Survey* (Chicago: August, 2000).

Proposed Federal Subsidies for COBRA Premiums

Even before the terrorist attacks of September 11, 2001, the U.S. economy was undergoing a marked slowdown. The attacks led to a greater increase in the number of unemployed workers. The Bureau of Labor Statistics' October 2001 *Employment Situation* indicated that nonfarm payroll employment dropped by 415,000 between October 1 and October 31, resulting in an unemployment rate of 5.4%, which was the highest monthly rate since December 1996. Concern has risen for workers who will not only lose their jobs but will also lose their employer-sponsored health care insurance.

Some policymakers and analysts suggest providing federal subsidies for COBRA premiums as a possible means of lowering the number of uninsured. These subsidies could be in the form of direct payments to employees or employers, or as tax credits to either party.

In recent years, several studies have been conducted regarding the benefits and costs of proposed subsidies. A January 1998 report from the Congressional Budget Office (CBO)[11] constructed prototypes for 6-month subsidy programs that restricted eligibility to those who, among other criteria, were receiving unemployment compensation and whose income was below 240% of the poverty line. The subsidy would be 100% for those with incomes below the poverty line and would decrease linearly as the beneficiary's income rose, phasing out when income reached 240% of poverty. Assuming unemployment rates of 4.7% and 5.8%, CBO estimated that between 1.4 million and 1.7 million workers would take advantage of the program, at a cost of $1.7 billion to $2.1 billion to the federal government. The number of uninsured would have been reduced by about 350,000 to 425,000 (out of 40 million) in a typical month; slightly over 1 million people would get at least one month of coverage they would not otherwise have had. CBO determined that if there were no new federal subsidy program, about half of the individuals in the prototype would have had coverage either through a program subsidized by their former employer or through their own purchases of COBRA or individual health insurance. It concluded that although the prototype would provide continuity of coverage for some eligible individuals, the program would not make large changes in the numbers of uninsured and would not affect the chronically uninsured.

Other studies present varying options for federal subsidies for COBRA premiums. Thomas Rice of the University of California at Los Angeles School of Public Health[12] proposed a baseline policy for federal subsidies which would be made on behalf of COBRA-eligible employees (and their families) whose incomes did not exceed 300% of the poverty line and who had worked for their employer for at least the last 6 months. The maximum subsidy, available to people at or below 200% of poverty, would be 90% and would be reduced on a sliding scale, reaching 0% at 300% of poverty. The plan would target those who most need assistance with paying for COBRA coverage, but would add the administrative burden of determining income levels of COBRA-eligibles. Rice proposed alternative options which would eliminate income restrictions or limit coverage to employees receiving unemployment compensation.

[11] U.S. Congressional Budget Office, *Proposals to Subsidize Health Insurance for the Unemployed* (Washington: Congressional Budget Office, 1998). Two of the options are discussed here, but several additional variations are provided in the report.

[12] Thomas Rice, *Subsidizing COBRA: An Option for Expanding Health Insurance Coverage* (Washington: Kaiser Family Foundation, 1999).

Jonathan Gruber of the Massachusetts Institute of Technology[13] proposed the establishment of a "COBRA-LOAN" program, creating a new federal agency to provide loans for the full cost of the premium to any qualified COBRA-eligible individual. The employer would pay the COBRA premium on behalf of the employee and be reimbursed by the new government entity. The employer's payment would be in the form of a tax credit equal to the amount of the premium and the 2% administrative fee. Beneficiaries would repay the government entity beginning one year after their participation in COBRA ended. Loan forgiveness would be extended to low-income individuals.

Another suggested form of government subsidy has been a tax credit that could be applied to the cost of COBRA premiums. Under current law, for individuals whose uncompensated medical expenses exceed 7.5% of their adjusted gross income, COBRA premiums are a deductible medical expense. The *deduction* is taken when calculating taxable income—before determining what is owed in taxes. The deduction reduces the income level that is used to calculate the tax owed. However, this benefit is only available to those whose medical expenses are high and who itemize their tax returns, and the value of the deduction varies with an individual's tax rate. A tax *credit,* on the other hand, would be applied after the tax amount has been determined and it would reduce, by the full value of the credit, the amount of the tax that is owed. It would not be dependent upon whether the taxpayer itemizes their return, and it would not vary according to an individual's tax rate. A tax credit could be designed in various ways, depending on the target population. It could be a dollar amount (for example, a $1,000 tax credit for the purchase of health insurance) or a percentage (such as a credit equal to 50% or 75% of a premium). Or it could be a combination of both, such as a percentage with a dollar amount as a cap.

A tax credit is a method of encouraging those who might not otherwise buy health insurance to do so. However, this might not be attractive to individuals with small tax liabilities. For instance, if there was a $1,000 tax credit, but the taxpayer owed only $500 in tax, the taxpayer would not benefit from the full credit. Some proposals are designed to make the credit "refundable," that is, the taxpayer would receive a refund for the balance of the credit. In some instances, individuals do not have funds to pay their health insurance premiums on a monthly basis. They would not be helped by a tax credit that was not available until the end-of-the-year tax filing. Some tax analysts have suggested an "advanceable" tax credit, that is, one that would be available before a person files their tax return. Such a credit was enacted by the Trade Act of 2002 (see below under "Legislation").

Jeff Lemieux of the Progressive Policy Institute advocates refundable tax credit for COBRA coverage, which would be available to former employees who are receiving unemployment compensation.[14] The credit would be means-tested, that is, the full credit (either some determined dollar amount or a percentage of the premium) would be available to people at some established income level and would decrease as the income level rose. The credit would be available immediately, rather than later when employees pay their taxes. This would be accomplished by the employer's reducing the employee's COBRA premium payment by the applicable tax credit amount. The employer would then deduct that amount from its regular tax payments to the government.

---

[13] Jonathan Gruber, *Transitional Subsidies for Health Insurance Coverage* (New York: Commonwealth Fund, 2000).

[14] Jeff Lemieux, *Transitional Health Coverage: A Tax Credit for COBRA* (Washington: Progressive Policy Institute, 2001).

There are advantages to subsidizing COBRA benefits, especially with means-tested assistance such as mentioned above. For example, vulnerable populations would be provided with the means to purchase insurance coverage. Additionally, because more people would opt for COBRA coverage, the numbers of uninsured would be reduced. Further, people would be able to move more freely between jobs without losing health care coverage.

On the other hand, a relatively small part of the uninsured population is affected. Many work for small employers who are exempted from providing COBRA coverage. Others are offered insurance on the job, but cannot afford to purchase it. Further, subsidizing COBRA would likely be expensive. Because employees are guaranteed the same coverage they had immediately before the qualifying event, the policy might be a generous one with a high premium. In addition, government subsidies might be paid on behalf of people who would otherwise have purchased other insurance independently. Finally, subsidizing COBRA can provide disincentives to individuals seeking new employment, resulting in increased expenditures on unemployment compensation payments.

High-Deductible Plans

A different approach toward lowering premiums was included in S. 24, 107th Congress. It would have created two new high-deductible COBRA plans. These could have been selected by individuals who wanted coverage for catastrophic costs only. Beneficiaries would have been able to select among plans with either a $1,000 or $3,000 deductible or traditional COBRA coverage. The intent was to provide COBRA coverage options with lower premiums. Higher deductibles could have the effect of lowering the premium for the plan, thus encouraging more participation. This bill did not become law.

LEGISLATION IN THE 107TH CONGRESS

The Trade Act of 2002 (P.L. 107-210) included a provision establishing a refundable, advanceable tax credit (see discussion above) for the purchase of qualified health insurance, including COBRA coverage. The credit, equal to 65% of the amount paid in premiums, is available to workers (and their spouses and dependents) who have been certified as being adversely affected by foreign trade. To be covered, individuals must be eligible for a trade adjustment allowance (TAA) or be age 55 or over and receiving a pension through the Pension Benefit Guaranty Corporation (PBGC). The Act also provided for an additional election period for TAA-eligible individuals who did not elect COBRA initially at the time they lost coverage due to a TAA-related event. Such individuals may elect COBRA in a special 60-day period beginning on the first day of the month in which they become eligible for TAA, but only if the election is made within 6 months of the date of the original loss of coverage. Coverage itself begins on the first day of the special 60-day election period. In addition, the law states that the period between the date of the TAA-related loss of coverage and the first day of the special election period cannot be considered for purposes of preexisting conditions exclusions. (For a more complete discussion of this legislation, see CRS Issue Brief IB98037: *Tax Benefits for Health Insurance: Current Legislation,* by Bob Lyke.)

A number of bills were introduced in the 107th Congress to address some of the issues discussed above. Other legislation would have provided assistance with COBRA premiums for workers and their families who lost coverage due to events springing from the terrorist attacks of September 11, 2001. None of these bills was enacted before the end of the Congress.

Displaced Worker Legislation

- Title V of H.R. 3090, the Economic Security and Recovery Act of 2001, contained health care assistance for the unemployed through the Social Service Block Grant program (Title XX of the Social Security Act). It provided an additional $3 billion for FY2002 for states to assist unemployed individuals who were not eligible for any federal health insurance programs with the purchase of health insurance. Among other options open to them, states would have had the option to decide to use these funds to assist people with their COBRA premium payments. H.R. 3090 was passed by the House on October 24, 2001. The version of the bill that became public law (P.L. 107-147) did not contain the health care assistance provisions.
- The Senate's Economic Recovery and Assistance for American Workers Act of 2001, an amendment in the nature of a substitute to H.R. 3090, provided a 75% premium subsidy for COBRA-eligible people who lost their coverage due to the events of September 11. The subsidies could have lasted up to 12 months and would have been paid by the Department of the Treasury directly to group health plans, employers, or state unemployment insurance offices. The program would have expired December 31, 2002. The package was reported by the Senate Finance Committee on November 9, 2001, but was withdrawn from the Senate floor by unanimous consent on November 14.
- S. 1454, H.R. 2946, and H.R. 2955 would have required the Secretary of Labor to provide for government payment of COBRA premiums for those who had become totally or partially separated, as a result of the September 11 attacks, from employment with an air carrier, at a facility at an airport, with a provider of transportation to or from an airport, or with an "upstream producer or supplier for an air carrier."[15] H.R. 3045 would have provided the same payment of COBRA premiums, limited to the aircraft manufacturing industry.
- On October 4, 2001, President Bush unveiled his Back to Work Relief Package. Part of the package was directed at National Emergency Grants (NEGs), which are grants made by the Department of Labor to states experiencing plant closings or mass layoffs. An additional $3 billion would have been provided for these grants to assist dislocated workers. Under the President's plan, the governor of a state would certify that closures, layoffs, or dislocations in the state were closely linked to the terrorist attacks of September 11. States could use the grant money for, among other purposes, paying up to 75% of COBRA premiums for up to 10 months for these workers.

[15] The bill defines *upstream producer* as a firm that performs additional, value-added, production processes, including firms that perform final assembly, finishing, or packaging of articles for another firm.

- A bill unrelated to terrorism but aimed at displaced workers was S. 1209, which would have established a 50% tax credit for COBRA premiums paid by workers who lost their jobs due to the negative impact of foreign trade and were eligible for trade adjustment assistance.

Expanding COBRA Eligibility

Other bills would have expanded COBRA eligibility to include certain defined groups:

- A number of legislative proposals would have extended coverage to a small but potentially growing population—retirees whose former employer terminates or significantly reduces benefits provided under its retiree health insurance plan. H.R. 803, H.R. 1255, and S. 623 would have established a new qualifying event: loss of or a substantial reduction in coverage under a retiree health plan. "Substantial reduction" was defined as a 50% reduction in the total average actuarial value of the plan through a reduction or elimination of benefits or an increase in premiums. The new COBRA beneficiaries would have been offered the coverage option most commonly used by other COBRA beneficiaries in the group plan, or other coverage which might be offered and elected by the retiree. Employers would have been permitted to charge 125% of the premium. Coverage would have lasted until the retiree and his/her spouse became entitled to Medicare.
- H.R. 1078 contained similar provisions to those mentioned above, except they would have applied only when a retiree health plan was terminated. The bill would have allowed the employer to charge 110% of the cost of the coverage.

Other bills would have expanded the duration of COBRA coverage:

- H.R. 2005 would have allowed individuals aged 55-64 whose COBRA benefits would expire under current law to extend their COBRA coverage until they became entitled to Medicare.
- Two bills, H.R. 2005 and H.R. 1663, would have lengthened the duration of COBRA coverage from 18 or 36 months to 5 years. S. 24 would have lengthened the duration from 18 to 24 months. It would not have affected those situations where duration was 36 months.

Tax Provisions

Under the eligibility expansion bills discussed above, the administrative fee for retirees would have been raised to between 10% and 25%. The 2001 Kaiser study estimated that the average annual premium for active employees in employersponsored plans in 2001 was $2,650 (individual) and $7,053 (family). Assuming a 125% premium, these amounts would be $3,312 and $8,816, respectively. Such amounts could be prohibitively expensive for all but higher income retirees and those retirees for whom the coverage is critical because they have a preexisting medical condition.

Several bills would have provided tax breaks to address this problem. Under current law, for individuals whose uncompensated medical expenses exceed 7.5% of their adjusted gross income, COBRA premiums are a deductible medical expense. Although the deduction reduces the income that is used to calculate the tax owed, it is only available to those whose medical expenses are high and who itemize their tax returns. The bills listed below would have provided tax *credits* for COBRA premiums. A tax credit, not dependent upon itemization, is applied against the taxpayer's tax liability, reducing, dollar for dollar, the amount of tax owed.

- H.R. 803, H.R. 1255, and S. 623 would have allowed a tax credit of 50% on premiums paid for COBRA coverage by those retirees established as qualified beneficiaries under their provisions.
- H.R. 2005 would have allowed a 50% tax credit for all COBRA premiums.
- S. 590 would have allowed a tax credit for premiums paid for health insurance coverage, including COBRA coverage. It would have provided a $1,000 annual credit for a person with income up to $35,000 to purchase individual coverage and a $2,500 credit for a taxpayer with income up to $55,000 to purchase family coverage.

Chapter 9

HEALTH INSURANCE: FEDERAL DATA SOURCES FOR ANALYSES OF THE UNINSURED

Chris L. Peterson and Christine Devere

INTRODUCTION

The number of individuals without health insurance continues to be a key public policy concern. The majority of the U.S. population receives coverage through employment-based plans, and employers generally contribute to the cost of purchasing health insurance. Changes in employment often lead to a disruption or loss of health coverage, as individuals who lose an employer's health benefit contribution often consider the cost of purchasing health insurance on their own too high. Other working people do not have insurance because their employer does not offer health insurance coverage. For these individuals, policies to reduce the cost of health insurance (such as tax credits or other types of subsidies) may increase their enrollment in health coverage. Public programs such as Medicaid and the State Children's Health Insurance program (SCHIP) provide health insurance for certain groups of low-income families with children. But, these programs have eligibility requirements that may prevent other uninsured individuals from qualifying for coverage. At the same time, a number of individuals eligible for health insurance through these public programs are not enrolled and are therefore included in current estimates of the number of uninsured. For these groups, additional outreach activities could increase enrollment in these existing programs.

Given the various individuals lack health insurance coverage, analysis of the effectiveness of a proposal to reduce the number of uninsured (such as those discussed above) requires examining characteristics of individuals with and without health insurance coverage. Numerous sources of data have emerged over time that support estimates of the uninsured. However, each data source differs in how it collects information from individuals, as well as the amount of information it collects related to health insurance status. Therefore, the estimates of the number of uninsured produced by these data sources vary widely.[1] Because proposals to reduce the number of uninsured are informed by estimates of the number of individuals without health insurance as well as the characteristics of the uninsured population, determining the appropriate source of data to evaluate these proposals is important.

This chapter outlines the major advantages and limitations of four federally administered surveys[2] - the March Supplement to the Current Population Survey (CPS), the Survey of Income and Program Participation (SIPP), the National Health Interview Survey (NHIS), and the Medical Expenditure Panel Survey (MEPS) - in providing estimated of the uninsured population.[3] It begins by briefly describing the characteristics of each of these four surveys. Estimates of the uninsured from these datasets are then presented, followed by a discussion of possible reasons for the variation among the estimates. Finally, the report discusses potential areas in which each data source might be useful to respond to questions of interest to policymakers in outlining proposals to reduce the number of uninsured.

In brief, all four surveys support representative estimates of the uninsured U.S. civilian noninstitutionalized population, although the health insurance question asked among the surveys differ. The March CPS produces the most widely cited statistics on the number of uninsured, because the data provide the most recent full-year information and because the data may produce estimates that are representative for each of the 50 states and the District of Columbia. However, its focus is not health insurance but work, income and poverty statistics, and its does not delve deeply into issues of insurance coverage. Additionally, the March CPS provides estimates only of those who were without health insurance for the entire year as opposed to those without insurance for some portion of the year. The NHIS, SIPP, and MEPS can not provide state-level analysis similar to the March CPS, but these surveys do offer additional data to explore many questions about the uninsured. For example, the NHIS contains data to relate health insurance status to health risk factors and general health issues. Additionally, SIPP and MEPS collect data for every month that the individual is part of the survey and therefore, in addition to providing estimates of those without health insurance for an entire year, these surveys may also be used to examine changes in health insurance and other characteristics month-to-month or over a period of time, tasks that are not possible using the March CPS. MEPS also asks the most comprehensive questions about the type and source of people's health insurance. With data from these four surveys, it is possible to answer many questions about the uninsured. Because the estimates among the surveys differ

---

[1] A number of studies have attempted to explain why the data sources differ in their estimate of the uninsured. See, for example, U.S. Department of Health and Human Services (DHHS) Office of the Assistance Secretary for Planning and Evaluation. *Understanding Estimates of the Uninsured: Putting the Differences in Context.* [http://aspe.os.dhhs.gov/health/reports/hiestimates.htm]; Lewis, Kimball, Ellwood, Marilyn and Czajka, John L. Counting the Uninsured: A Review of the Literature. The Urban Institute, June 1998, [http://newfederalism.urban.org/html/occ8.htm]; and Fronstin, Paul *Counting the Uninsured: A Comparison of National Surveys* by Employee Benefit Research Institute, Issue Brief No. 225, September 2000.

[2] There are other federal sources for estimates of the uninsured, including the Behavioral Risk Factor Surveillance System (BRFSS) and the National Survey of Family Growth (NSFG).We did not include these particular surveys because they are not representative of the entire U.S. population. BRFSS collects information only on the adult who answers the phone, which excludes all of the children and the other adults household. The responding adult is not necessarily representative of the rest of the household, particularly the children. NSFG, a valuable survey of woman's health, limits its sample to woman aged 15 to 44. In addition, it does not occur annually; the latest survey was conducted in 1995. There are also non-federal sources for estimates of the uninsured. Analysis of these sources is beyond the scope of this report.

[3] We chose to discuss the surveys in this order simply for the benefit of our readers. It is not intended to represent any survey's importance or reliability.

by so much, however, the results should always interpreted with some caution until the differences can be reconciled.

OVERVIEW OF THE SURVEYS

Appendix A illustrates in a tabular format the characteristics of the four surveys discussed in this chapter. Each of these surveys is briefly described below.

March Supplement to the Current Population Survey (CPS)

The CPS, conducted by the U.S. Census Bureau, is the primary source of information on the labor force characteristics of the U.S. civilian noninstitutionalized population. The CPS is a cross-sectional survey, which means that it does not have the ability to track the same individuals from year to year. Although CPS interviews take place every month, the questions regarding health insurance status are asked only in March in the CPS's Annual Demographic Survey (often referred to as "the March supplement"), at which time individuals are asked to identify their sources of health insurance for the entire preceding year. Therefore, the March supplement to the CPS (herein referred to as the March CPS) supports estimates only of those who do not have health insurance for the *entire year* preceding their March interview. Of the four surveys reviewed in this chapter, the CPS has the largest sample size (approximately 50,000 households) and is the only one of the four surveys able to produce representative estimates for each of the 50 states and the District of Columbia. The formula that allocates funds to states for the SCHIP uses CPS state-level data.[4]

The Census Bureau releases data from the March CPS around September every year. The most recent data available are from the March 2001 CPS, and these data represent the *previous* calendar year (so the March 2001 CPS represents information for all of 2000). Of the four surveys reviewed in this chapter, the March CPS data provide the most recent full-year information on the uninsured. However, because the March CPS data is not designed to allow researchers to track individuals who may remain in the sample from year to year, it cannot pinpoint changes in an individual's health insurance status across time. Therefore, researchers using the March CPS can estimate the total number of uninsured for a given year and compare the total number of uninsured across a number of years (for example, 1997 through 1999), but can not examine individual changes in health insurance coverage throughout the year, or estimate the number of uninsured at a specific point in time during the year.

Survey of income and Program Participation (SIPP). In addition to the CPS, the Census Bureau also conducts the SIPP, a survey with detailed information on respondents' income as well as their participation in government programs. Unlike the CPS, the SIPP is a longitudinal survey, which means that individuals who are part of the sample are interviewed multiple

[4] For each state, the allocation is based on a 3-year average of the number of uninsured children under 19 years of age in families below 200% of the poverty thresholds. In some states, the number of children in these low-income families for whom the CPS obtains data may be small. This may cause the estimates to be less reliable and increase the variability in the estimates of the uninsured from year to year. The 3-year averages are used to counter these effects.

times over the life of the survey, referred to as a "panel," so that changes in various individual characteristics may be observed. Respondents in the SIPP sample are interviewed every four months, with these cycles referred to as "waves." Historically, the SIPP panels ranged in duration from 2 ½ years to 4 years. Although representative at the national level, SIPP does not support reliable state-by-state estimates. The sample size is approximately 37,000 households.

The most recent available data are from the 1996 SIPP panel, which followed a sample of individuals for 4 years, through March 2000.[5] Given the longitudinal design of the SIPP (as discussed above), these data may be used to estimate the total number of people uninsured for any month, for any part of the year, for an entire year, or over the life of the period. The next SIPP panel, which will be over a 3-year period, began earlier this year, with the first wave of results expected in the first quarter of 2002. However, there is no set schedule for SIPP data releases.

National Health Interview Survey (NHIS)

The National Center for Health Statistics (NCHS) oversees NHIS, a survey completed annually to gather information on Americans' health. Similar to the CPS, the NHIS is a cross-sectional survey and therefore does not allow analyses of the same people from year to year. NHIS is representative of the U.S. civilian noninstitutionalized population and has the ability to produce estimates for some large states; however, state-level estimates for all 50 states and the District of Columbia are not supported. The sample size is approximately 42,000 households.

The most recent available data from NHIS are for 2000. Although NHIS is similar to the CPS because it is a cross-sectional survey, the NHIS collects more detailed information on health insurance status among the survey sample than the March CPS. Therefore, NHIS can produce estimates of the total number of people who were ever uninsured during the year, for the entire year, or at the time of the survey. In addition to health insurance status, NHIS collects detailed health information on illness, chronic conditions, activity limitations and health risk behaviors. Another benefit of NHIS is that the survey serves as the sampling framework for a number of other smaller, federally administered surveys such as the Medical Expenditure Panel Survey (discussed below) and the National Survey of Family Growth (NSFG). Therefore, individuals in these smaller surveys have also been interviewed in NHIS. By linking these datasets, researchers may have a broader collection of health-related information for a subset of the population.

Medical Expenditure Panel Survey (MEPS). The Agency for Healthcare Research and Quality (AHRQ) administers MEPS in conjunction with NCHS. MEPS has been conducted annually since 1996. It is the most recent in a series of medical expenditure surveys that began in 1977 as the National Medical Care Expenditure Survey and later became the National Medical Expenditure Survey (NMES). The primary focus of MEPS is on the use of and expenditures for health care. MEPS is a longitudinal survey, like the SIPP, and interviews the same individuals five times over a period of 2 years. MEPS does not support state-level

[5] The core content of these files is available. The SIPP also includes additional survey questions that are included in selected waves on special topics. These questions are referred to as "topical models." Examples include topical modules on health care expenditures and utilization, disabilities and limitations, and home health care.

estimates of the uninsured, although (like the other three surveys discussed above) it does provide a nationally representative picture of the U.S. civilian noninstitutionalized population. MEPS has the smallest sample size of the surveys, with 12,000 eligible households interviewed each year.

Unique to MEPS are the "overlapping panels" - although individuals are followed for 2 years, each year a new sample is drawn from the previous year's NHIS, so the sample is replenished annually.[6] For example, the 1998 full-year MEPS data represents information from year 2 of households in the 1997 panel and year 1 of households in the 1998 panel. The implications of this are discussed in greater detail later in this chapter.

The most recent available full-year data for MEPS is 1998. However, MEPS also produces "point-in-time" files, which represent the first 6 months of a given year. Point-in-time information is available for 2000. Researchers using the full-year MEPS data can estimate the total number of uninsured for any month, for any part of the year, for an entire year, or over the life of the panel. In addition to health insurance status, MEPS supplies the most detailed information about Americans' health insurance benefits and premiums, as well as on health care use and spending.

COMPARING UNINSURED STATISTICS AMONG THE SURVEYS

Figure 1 illustrated statistics on the uninsured from 1998, them most recent year in which the full data from all four surveys are available. All four surveys provide a nationally representative picture of the U.S. population, however, the estimates of the uninsured vary widely among the surveys, as Figure 1 illustrates. These uninsured estimates are presented in a tabular format in Appendix B.

In 1998, using data from the March CPS, 43.6 million individuals (116.3% of the U.S. civilian noninstitutionalized population) were uninsured for the entire year. This compares to 31.3 million (11.8%) from MEPS. NHIS estimates that 25.8 million (9.7%) were uninsured for all of 1998. Using SIPP data, this number was 21.2 million (7.9%), which is less than half of the March CPS estimate - a difference of more than 22 million people.[7]

Examining the number uninsured at a point in time yields higher estimates than the full-year analysis as illustrated in Figure 1:39.2 million (14.6%) from SIPP, 39.5 million (14.7%) from NHIS, and 42.3 million (15.8%) from MEPS (the March CPS does not support these estimates).[8] Compared to the number uninsured for an entire year, the point-in-time estimates among these three surveys is higher because the number of people uninsured at a point in time would include those uninsured for the entire year plus those individuals who were uninsured at the time of the survey.

Finally, Figure 1 also illustrates estimates of those *ever* uninsured during the year from NHIS, MEPS, and SIPP (the March CPS does not support these estimates). As illustrated in Figure 1, these estimates are higher than the point-in-time estimates produced in each survey.

[6] As mentioned above, the NHIS serves as the sampling framework for MEPS, and therefore the MEPS survey sample is a subsample of the previous year's NHIS sample (which is considerably larger).

[7] For SIPP and MEPS, the percentage of uninsured for the full year excludes those who did not provide data for all 12 months.

[8] For the point-in-time, estimate, SIPP data are from March 1998, NHIS data are from interviews throughout the year, and MEPS data are from the first half of 1998.

This is expected, since the estimate of those who were ever uninsured during the year would include everyone uninsured at the time of the survey plus those individuals who were uninsured at any other time during the year. NHIS estimates that 50.0 million individuals (18.9%) were over uninsured in 1998. This compares to 52.2 million (20.7%) using SIPP and 60.3 million (22.7%) based on MEPS.[9]

Figure 1. Uninsured U.S. Civilian Noninstitutionaluized Population from Federally Administered Surveys, 1998
(in millions of individuals)

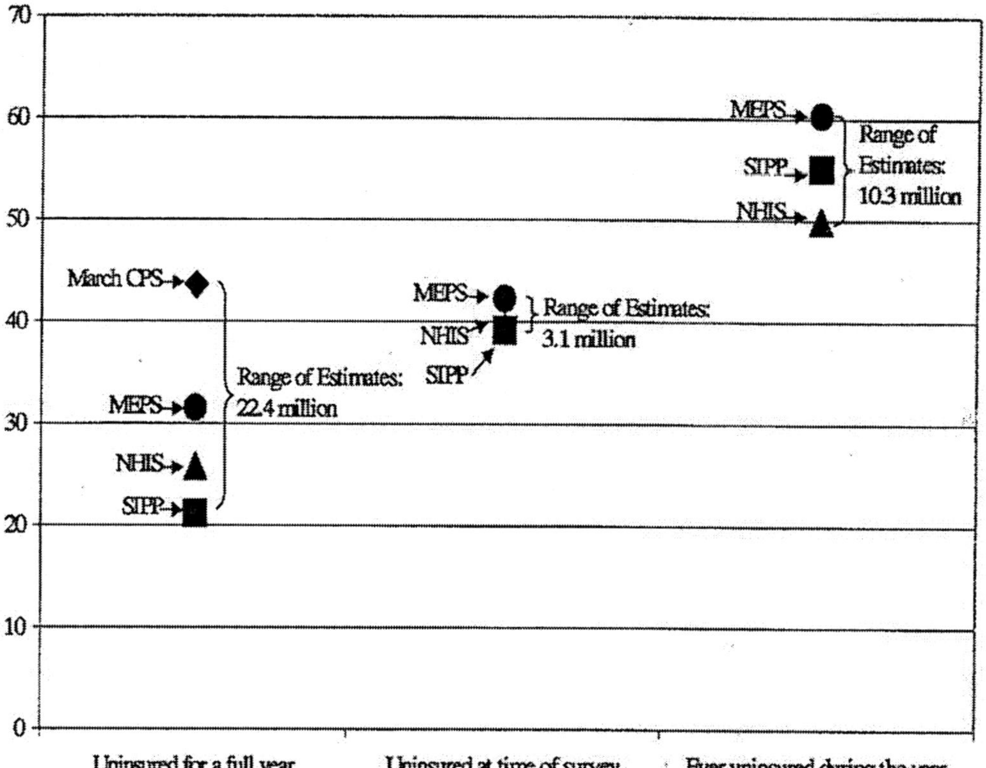

Source: Congressional Research Service (CRS) analysis of the March CPS, SIPP, NHIS, and MEPS.
Notes: As discussed in the memorandum, the March CPS does not support estimates of the number uninsured at the time of the survey or the number ever uninsured during the year, and therefore is not illustrated. Estimates for the number uninsured at the time of the survey (a profit-in-time estimate) using SIPP data are from March 1998, while NHIS data are from interviews throughout the year and MEPS data are from the first half of 1998. For SIPP and MEPS, the percentage of uninsured for the full year and at any time excludes those who did not provide data for all 12 months.

[9] For SIPP and MEPS, as with the full year estimates, the percentage of uninsured at any time excludes those who did not provide data for all 12 months.

POTENTIAL REASONS FOR VARIATION IN SURVEY ESTIMATES OF THE UNINSURED

As Figure 1 illustrates, the estimates of the uninsured among the surveys vary substantially. The march CPS produces the largest estimate of the number of uninsured for a full year and SIPP produces the lowest estimate. MEPS produces estimates of the uninsured that are higher than NHIS and SIPP in every time frame measured. The following discussion describes differences among the surveys that may account for some of the variation in the estimates.

Health Insurance Verification Question

One explanation for the differences in the uninsured estimates may be the variation in how the surveys determine who is uninsured. Unitl 2000, the March CPS asked respondents (generally an adult giving information on everyone in the household) whether anyone in the family was enrolled in a number of health insurance coverage categories, including private health insurance, Medicare and Medicaid at any time during the entire preceding year. If a respondent answered "yes" to any of the sources of coverage, the name(s) of those with that coverage was requested. Therefore, the March CPS products estimates of the number of individuals ever covered by Medicare, ever covered by Medicaid, etc., in the entire preceding year. The number who *do not* have health insurance is calculated by looking at the household roster (given by the respondent at the start of the interview) to determine if a source of health insurance coverage was mentioned for every individual. Those in the household whose names were not given for any source of coverage were then considered uninsured for the entire preceding year; however, this was not verified with the respondent, as there was no survey question on the March CPS to confirm that those individuals were indeed uninsured for the entire preceding year. It is possible that individuals often may not recognize their family member's coverage from the interviewer's list of health insurance types, or that the respondent may simply neglect to mention a family member's name. However, when asked directly to confirm that a family member was uninsured, respondents may be prompted to share that person's coverage.

To respond to this concern, a health insurance verification question was added in the March 2000 CPS to verify the uninsured status of individuals during 1999 (the entire preceding year). That is, beginning in March 2000, if an individual in the household was not mentioned as being covered by a health insurance category, the respondent was asked to verify that this individual was in fact uninsured in the entire preceding year. In an analysis of this new question conducted by the Census Bureau released in August 2001, about 8% of those previously calculated as uninsured because they did not indicate that they were covered by any source of health insurance coverage, when asked directly whether they were in fact uninsured, indicated that they did have coverage. Because this analysis was conducted *after* the March 2000 CPS data had been released, it was not included the original data source. However, the analysis completed by the Census Bureau indicates that, had these results been available and included when the data were first released, the Census Bureau would have reported that the number of uninsured was 39.3 million in 1999 - 3.3 million less than the

42.6 million previously published. Because of these results, the Census Bureau is making the verification question a permanent part of the survey and, beginning with the March 2001 CPS, their estimates of the uninsured will be based on the verification questions.[10] However, results without the verification question will also be available for those wanting to make historical comparisons.[11]

Figure 2 compares selected health insurance coverage estimates from the March CPS with and without the verification question to the SIPP, the only other survey that has released comparable full-year data for 1999. Although the verification question led to a significant decrease in the number of uninsured reported by the March CPS, to 39.3 million people (14.3%), it is still much higher than the SIPP estimate of 21.2 million uninsured individuals (7.7%) in 1999 - a difference of 18.1 million people (6.6 percentage points).

Figure 2. Source of Health Insurance Coverage for Any Part of 1999, March CPS and SIPP, Percent of U.S. Civilian Noninstitutionalized Population

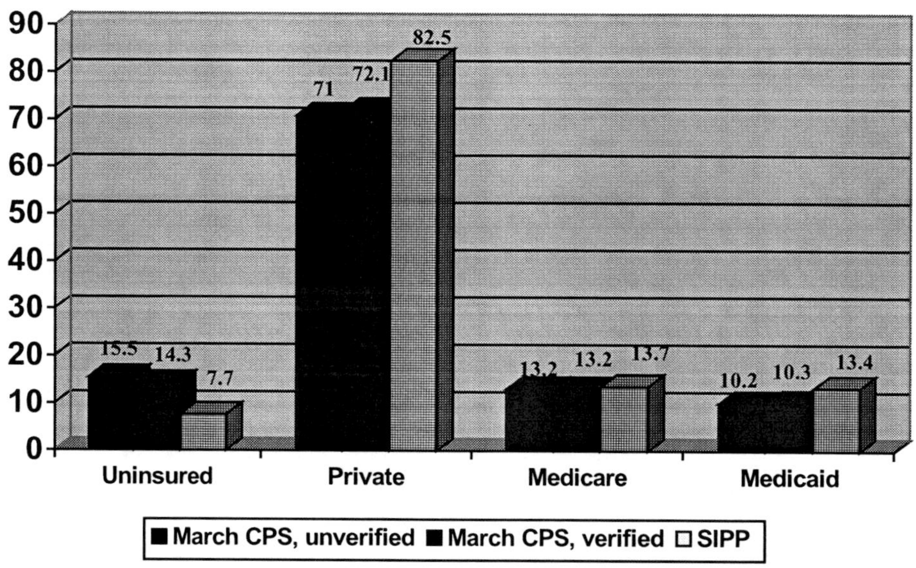

Source: Congressional Research Service (CRS) using census-reported percentages for the March CPS, and CRS analysis of SIPP.

Before the addition of the verification question, Census Bureau staff had analyzed differences between the March CPS and the SIPP.[12] They concluded that the differences were probably due largely to issues with the March CPS - in particular, underreporting of private coverage. The addition of the verification question to the March CPS addressed this in part by

[10] For information on the insured and uninsured population in 2000 based on the March 2001 CPS, see CRS Report 96-891, *Health Insurance Coverage: Characteristics of the Insured and Uninsured Populations in 2000,* by Chris L. Peterson.

[11] See Nelson, Charles T., and Robert J. Mills, *The March CPS Health Insurance Verification Question and its Effect on Estimates of the Uninsured.* August 2001, [http://www.census.gov/hhes/hlthins/verif.html].

[12] U.S. Bureau of the Census *A Comparative Analysis of Health Insurance Coverage Estimates: Data from CPS and SIPP,* by Robert L. Bennefield, 1996 (Hereafter cited as *Bennefield, A Comparative Analysis of Health Insurance Coverage Estimates).*

increasing the March CPS estimates of the percent ever covered by private health insurance during the year to 72.1%, compared to the previous estimate of 71.0%. While this narrowed the gap between the March CPS and the SIPP estimates ot the percent enrolled in private health insurance, a difference of 10.4 percentage points (28.1 million people) remains, as shown in Figure 2. The verification question also did little to substantially narrow the gaps between the surveys' estimates of those ever covered by Medicare or Medicaid during the year.

NHIS is the only other survey reviewed in this chapter that includes a direct health insurance verification question.[13] Unlike the March CPS data, however, the impact of the verification question on NHIS estimates of the uninsured has not been significant.[14] This may be because of the detailed followup questions asked of NHIS respondents when they do not indicate coverage - questions such as "About how long has it been since you last had health care coverage?" If a respondent had neglected to mention any source of coverage, these questions may make the respondent aware of the error and provide the opportunity to correct it. The March CPS is the only one of the four surveys reviewed in this chapter that does not ask such detailed followup questions about respondents' uninsured status. This could explain why the verification question yielded a significant difference in estimates of the uninsured in the March CPS but not NHIS. In fact, staff at AHRQ believe that the addition of a direct health insurance verification question in MEPS would be unnecessary because of the detailed followup questions asked in that survey.

While the March CPS now includes a question to verify that an individual is uninsured, it does not attempt to verify the coverage of those who indicate they are insured. In the 2000 NHIS, such a question was added that directly asks for a confirmation that the person was covered by comprehensive health insurance. According to a preliminary analysis by NCHS, most of the respondents who had originally claimed coverage but changed their answer did so because they were covered by less-than-comprehensive coverage, such as dental or workers' compensation insurance. The impact of the verification question was relatively small and approximately offset the effect of the uninsured-verification question on the NHIS.[15] Unfortunately, it is not possible to know what effect adding a verification question for those claiming insurance might have on the March CPS estimates.

Medicaid Under-reporting

Another commonly cited concern with the March CPS estimates of insurance status is the extent to which the number of people on Medicaid may be underestimated. In 1998, the Centers for Medicare and Medicaid Services (CMS, formerly known as the Health Care Financing Administration) reported that 38.6 million nonistitutionalized Americans (14.2%) were covered by Medicaid. Figure 3 compares CMS' s count of those covered by Medicaid to estimates from the March CPS, SIPP and MEPS in 1998 (NHIS cannot be used to estimate the number of people ever covered by Medicaid during the year).

---

[13] This direct health insurance verification question was added to NHIS in 1997.

[14] From conversations with Robin Cohen, statistician at the National Center for Health Statistics, Hyattsville, Maryland, who works with the health insurance variables in NHIS.

[15] *Ibid.*

Figure 3. Ever Covered by Medicaid During 1998, U.S. Civillan Noninstitutionalized Population
(in millions of individuals)

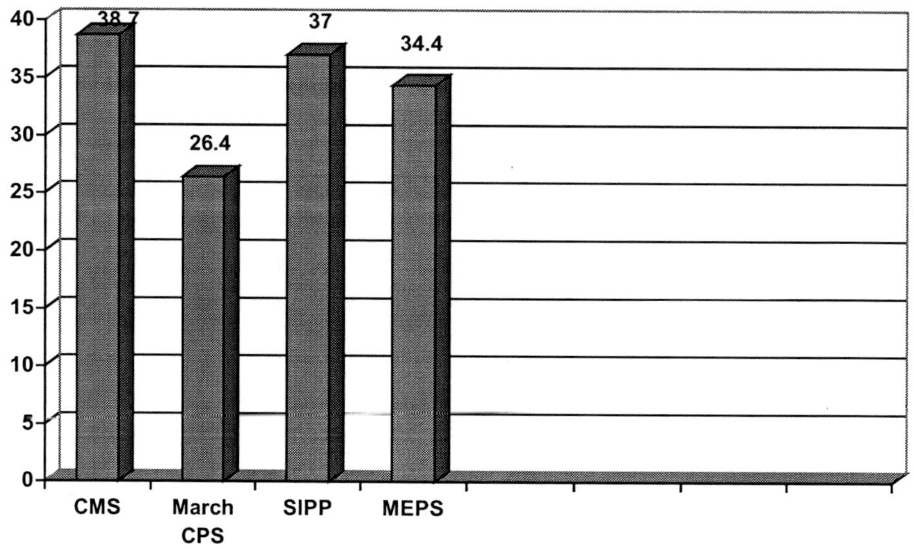

Source: Congressional Research Service (CRS) using data from the Centers for Medicare and Medicaid Services (CMS), the March CPS, SIPP, and MEPS. The CMS data cover the fiscal year 1998, while the other data are for the calendar year 1998. Efforts were made to increase the comparability of these estimates by adjusting the CMS data to reflect only the noninstitutionalized population. Three categories reflect services to the institutionalized Medicaid population: mental health facility services (NHF), nursing facility services (NFS), and intermediate care facility-mentally retarded services (ICF/MR). It is possible that individuals may receive more than one of these services, and therefore simply subtracting. All three categories of services may underestimate the total nonistitutionalized Medicaid population. Based on conversations with CMS officials, the CMS number was adjusted for Figure 3 by subtracting the number of recipients of NFPs and ICFs/MR. However, as it is possible that residents of MHF may also receive one of the other two previous services, these individuals remain in the estimate (accounting for approximately 125,000 of the 38.7 million reported by CMS).

The March CPS data yield the lowest estimate of the number ever covered by Medicaid in 1998 - 26.4 million people (9.7%), 12.2 million people less than the number using CMS data.[16] As seen in Figure 3, SIPP and MEPS data also produce estimates of Medicaid coverage that are lower than CMS' tabulations, though not as low as the March CPS. Survey respondents may under-report their coverage by Medicaid because they do not want to admit being covered by a public assistance program, and this may also contribute to the lower estimates of Medicaid coverage among the March CPS, SIPP and MEPS when compared to the CMS administrative data. In addition, if a survey's list of Medicaid programs does not include the particular state's name (or names) of its Medicaid program, respondents may not affirm that they are on Medicaid because the name of their state-specific program was not mentioned. For example, a paper from the Employee Benefit Research Institute includes an instance where a Medicaid managed care plan in Maryland was not listed in the March 1999 CPS and may have been responsible for undercounting Medicaid coverage in that state.[17]

---

[16] The CMS data are for fiscal year 1998; the survey data are for the calendar year 1998.

[17] See: Employee Benefit Research Institute. *Counting the Uninsured: A Comparison of National Surveys,* by Paul Fronstin.

While the March CPS, SIPP and MEPS report a lower number ever covered by Medicaid than reported by CMS, it is worth nothing that some analysts believe the data supplied by CMS may be of poor quality due to variations in state reporting styles, double counting of enrollees, and classification errors.[18]

The addition of the health insurance verification question beginning with the March 2000 CPS was expected to reduce the differences in the estimate of the number ever covered by Medicaid in a given year between the CMS and the March CPS. Although this chapter focuses on 1998 data in examining the underreporting of Medicaid, the addition of the health insurance verification question to the March 2000 CPS resulted in approximately 331,000 more people being classified as ever covered by Medicaid in 1999 (again, this was the first year this verification question was included as part of the survey). Therefore, while the addition of this question has led to more individuals reporting Medicaid coverage, it appears that the difference between estimates of Medicaid coverage between the March CPS and CMS remains sizable.

Recall Period

Another issue that may explain some of the variation in the uninsured estimates is the length of time respondents are asked to remember their health insurance status (the recall period). Individuals who are asked to report their status for a period of time might not accurately report changes in their health insurance status over that period of time. The March CPS requires respondents to recall their coverage over the longest time period (15 months), compared to the other surveys. For example, respondents were asked in the March 2001 CPS about their sources of health insurance coverage during the calendar year 2000. NHIS asks about health insurance coverage during the previous 12 months, SIPP during the previous 4 months, and MEPS during the previous 3 to 5 months. The longer the amount of time, the more likely that respondents may forget a source of coverage, particularly if the duration of that coverage was short.

Additionally, some respondents, when asked to report their health insurance status for the entire preceding year, may answer the health insurance questions based on their current coverage. If true, this could explain why the March CPS' full-year uninsured estimates are higher than those from the other surveys but are similar to their point-in-time estimates. However, aside from similar estimate values (as illustrated in Figure 1) there is little evidence to support this argument. In fact, according to the analysis by Census Bureau staff comparing the March CPS and SIPP, the respondents in the March CPS "do not report annual health insurance coverage information based on their current status rather than the previous year."[19] Instead, the analysis found that the key cause for the differences between the surveys is that March CPS respondents tended to underreport health insurance coverage from private sources when compared to SIPP respondents.[20]

---

[18] For a discussion of the reliability of Medicaid program data, see CRS Report RL30733, *Medicaid Expenditures and Enrollees, 1998,* by Evelyne Baumrucker and Jean Hearne.

[19] U.S. Bureau of Census. *A Comparative Analysis of Health Insurance Coverage Estimates: Data from CPA and SIPP,* by Robert L. Bennefield.

[20] The recent results from the Census Bureau's paper on the verification question may lend more credence to this statement. That paper stated that 89% of those who were initially classified as uninsured but who ultimately reported coverage because of the verification question revealed that they had private coverage.

Longitudinal Design

Unlike the CPS and NHIS, the SIPP and MEPS re-interview the same people over multiple years in order to track changes over time. With respect to health insurance, therefore, the SIPP and MEPS have the advantage of being able to analyze the duration of spells without insurance on a month-to month basis and over the entire duration of the panel. These longitudinal surveys do present unique issues, however. With each wave of interviews, fewer people respond, so the sample size and response rates shrink over the life of the panel. In the first wave of the 1996 SIPP panel, the response rate was 92%, but by the final wave 4 years later, the response rate was 65% of the original 1996 eligible sample. This may affect the estimates of the uninsured if those who are uninsured are either more or less likely to drop out of the survey than those who are insured. In other words, if over the life of the panel we see the percentage of uninsured individuals dropping, this may be because the number is truly dropping or because those who are uninsured are less likely to continue responding and therefore be counted in the survey.

The SIPP follows its respondents for 4 years, while MEPS follows its respondents for 2 years. Because the MEPS study period is shorter than the SIPP, MEPS does not experience a similar reduction in sample size. MEPS is also unique because its panels (i.e., survey samples) overlap. Each year, MEPS is administered to a new sample of individuals (who are drawn from the previous year's NHIS sample), and these individuals are followed for a period of 2 years. This allows a number of estimates to be produced. For example, the 1996 MEPS panel provides information on health care utilization and expenditures for calendar year 1996 and 1997, as the panels are followed for 2 years. In addition to the information provided in 1997 by the 1996 panel, a *new* panel of individuals is introduced in 1997 for whom information is also collected. Because information is available for both panels for 1997, they both contribute to a calendar year data file for 1997. By combining the two samples, the total combined sample size increases. Therefore, attrition will be a concern in analyzing data for the *same* panel of individuals (for example, looking at 2 years of information for the 1996 MEPS panel), as is the case with the 1996 SIPP. However, the calendar year data, which combine the overlapping MEPS panels, are valuable because the larger combined sample size enhances the reliability of estimates produced on the uninsured.

One advantage of longitudinal analyses is following the changing composition of households and families throughout the life of the panel. For example, suppose a single mother and her two children were uninsured at the time of her first interview for the 1996 SIPP. This mother would be interviewed 12 times the 4-year panel. In that time, it is possible that she would marry, at which point her husband would become part of her family. If her husband has health insurance, the mother and her two children may then be covered under his health insurance. Therefore, as a result of the change in family composition over the survey period (in this case, a marriage), the health insurance status of the woman and her children has changed. However, while panel surveys permit more types of analyses, they are also more complicated, and care must be taken when using these surveys' longitudinal capabilities. In order to follow changes in health insurance status over time within families or households, it is necessary to decide how the household and family changes will be handled.[21]

[21] This is not a major concern for analyses that are of individuals rather than families or households.

Full-year Analysis

The four surveys in this chapter can be used to count the uninsured using three different time periods: the number of people uninsured for a full year, at a point in time, and ever during the year. Each time period gives analysts a slightly different perspective on the uninsured. The full-year estimate looks at those who were chronically uninsured - those who were not enrolled in insurance at all during the year. However, many may move in and out of the ranks of the uninsured. Approximately twice as many people are ever uninsured during the year compared to the number uninsured for the entire year, according to SIPP, NHIS and MEPS estimates, as previously illustrated in Figure 1 and shown in Appendix B.[22]

Full-year analyses of the uninsured are also complicated by the presence of those who were not eligible for the survey over the entire year, particularly infants (defined here as those less than a year old). AHRQ economists exclude infants from their full-year analyses using MEPS, as they are interested in a person's unchanged uninsured status over a 12-month period. However, the Census Bureau includes infants in its estimate of the uninsured and in the formula to allocate funds to states for the SCHIP program. The March CPS questionnaire flows in such a way that infants who were uninsured for their entire lives, even if they were alive for only 1 month in the survey year, would be counted as uninsured for a full year.[23] Individual researchers need to decide what is best for their purposes.

Discussion

The four surveys reviewed in this chapter have unique strengths and limitations, resulting from differences in each survey's purpose, sample, and questions. One major concern about the March CPS has recently been addressed, with the decision to include a question that requires respondents to verify that one or more household members are uninsured. While the addition of this question has decreased the number reported without health insurance, the March CPS estimates remain much higher than those from the other surveys. Nevertheless, the March CPS continues to be the data source of choice by most for estimates of the uninsured because it provides the most recent full-year information and is representative of all 50 states and the District of Columbia. However, its focus is not health insurance but work, income and poverty statistics, and it does not delve deeply into issues of insurance coverage. In addition, the March CPS can not provide estimates of those uninsured at a point in time during the year or of those ever uninsured during the year; it permits estimates only of those individuals uninsured for the entire year. As a result, the other surveys provide additional useful related to people's enrollment in health insurance and their circumstances without it.

As policymakers develop proposals to reduce the number of uninsured, questions continue to be raised that relate to characteristics of the uninsured. Given the limitations of the March CPS, it becomes important to consider other sources for health insurance information, such as those available in NHIS, MEPS and SIPP. For analyses that relate health insurance status to health risk factors and general health issues, NHIS supplies the most

[22] The March CPS provides only full-year estimates.

[23] As a result, one might expect the full-year estimate for infants to be closer to the point-in-time estimate, compared to other age cohorts. Although our preliminary estimates bear this out, an in-dept discussion of this point is beyond the scope of this report.

complete data. In addition, NHIS is able to link to other surveys, such as MEPS and the National Survey of Family Growth (NSFG), which allows researchers to examine a broader range of issues. While NHIS collects more detailed information on health insurance coverage, the inability to produce reliable estimates for all 50 states and the District of Columbia limits its usefulness in evaluating proposals for the uninsured.

SIPP and MEPS both are useful in examining changes in health insurance and other characteristics over time because of their longitudinal designs. SIPP is most valuable in its capacity to relate people's insurance status to their income, poverty status, assets and liabilities, as well as their participation in government programs. MEPS, on the other hand, supplies the most detailed information to relate insurance status to people's use of and spending on health care. Of the surveys, MEPS also asks the most comprehensive questions about the type and source of people's health insurance. However, these panel surveys that delve deeper into issues face higher costs and longer interview periods with individuals, factors that often limit the size of the survey sample. Both MEPS and SIPP have smaller sample sizes than NHIS and CPS. Therefore, although these surveys may also produce representative estimates of the U.S. population, their inability to produce reliable estimates of the 50 states and the District of Columbia also hampers their usefulness in evaluating proposals for the uninsured.

With data from these four surveys, it is possible to answer many questions about the uninsured. As discussed in this chapter, the information collected among the four surveys varies, but by exploring the various aspects covered in each survey researchers are able to delve deeper into issues that affect the uninsured U.S. population. Because the estimates among the surveys differ by so much, however, the results should always be interpreted with some caution until the differences can be reconciled. In addition, given the variation among states in their policies and programs that affect the uninsured, the ability to calculate reliable estimates for each of the 50 states and the District of Columbia remains important. To this end, the March CPS remains the most widely cited estimate of the uninsured because of its ability to calculate reliable state-level estimates.

Appendix A. Comparison of Characteristics of Federally Administered Surveys

	March supplement to the CPS	SIPP	NHIS	MEPS
		Survey overview		
Primary Focus of Survey	To provide information on labor force characteristics	To provide information on income, program participation	To provide information on the health of the U.S. population	To provide information about the use of and expenditures for health care
Survey Design	Cross-sectional (i.e., not designed for analyses of the same person/household from year to year)	Longitudinal - For 1996 panel, followed each household in survey for 4 years. Subsequent panels to be 3 years in length	Cross-sectional	Longitudinal - follows each household for 2 years, with new households chosen annually (overlapping panels). Sample drawn from previous year's NHIS
Universe	U.S. civilian noninstitutionalized population and those members of the Armed Forces with a civilian adult in the household	U.S. civilian nonistitutionalized population and those members of the Armed Forces stationed locally and living in sample unit	U.S. civilian noninstitutionalized household population	Same as NHIS
Geographic Area	50 states and the District of Columbia.	Same	Same	Same
Most recent Data	2000 data from March 2001 supplement	November 1999 to February 2000 (Wave 12 of 1996 Panel)	2000 (provisional release)	2000 point-in-time data; 1998 full-year, month-to-month data
How often is data released?	Annually, typically in September	Periodically, with first wave of 2001 panel data to be released early 2002	Annually, though at no particular time of year	Periodically, with various data files released throughout the year
History	Health insurance questions added in March 1980 survey, though consistent data is only available beginning with 1988	Annual overlapping panel surveys ran from 1984 to 1993; in 1996, 4-year panel; new panels to be 3 years	Annually, beginning in 1957	Annually, beginning in 1996. Historically, two surveys (1977 NMCES and 1987 NMES) are considered predecessors
Administering Agency	Census Bureau and Bureau of Labor Statistics (BLS)	Census Bureau	National Center for Health Statistics (NCHS)	Agency for Healthcare Research and Quality (AHRQ), partnering with NCHS
		Survey details (Analytic Issues)		
Nationally representative estimates?	Yes	Yes	Yes	Yes
State-level estimates?	Yes	No	Largest states only	No

	March supplement to the CPS	SIPP	NHIS	MEPS
Respondent(s)	One person, usually the individual who owns or rents the housing unit, for everyone in the household. If that person is not knowledgeable regarding the other adults in the household, attempts are made to contract them.	All household members 15 years old and over, if possible; otherwise proxy response is permitted/ Adult(s) provides information on any children in the household.	All adult members of the household 17 years of age and over who are at home at the time of the interview are invited to participate and to respond for themselves. For children as well as adults not at home during the interview, information is provided by a responsible adult family member (18 years of age and over) residing in the household.	The one person in the household most knowledgeable about the household's medical situations provides information for everyone in the household. For information difficult for respondent to know, MEPS obtains permission to collect information from their employers, providers, and plans.
Information collected for everyone in household?	Yes	Yes	Yes	Yes
Definition of Household	All the persons who occupy a house, an apartment, or other group of rooms or a room, when occupied as separate living quarters.	All the persons for whom the sampled address is their usual place of residence (i.e., where a person normally lives and sleeps). Newcomers to the household during the panel are included. Those 15 and older who move from the household are contracted and that household is considered another household, with all residents interviewed.	An occupied dwelling unit with one or more civilian members.	Same as NHIS, except that college-aged students living away from home during the school year were interviewed at their place of residence for the NHIS but were identified by and linked to their parents' household for MEPS.
Sample Size	Approximately 50,000 eligible households (2001)	Approximately 37,000 eligible households (1996 panel).	Approximately 42,000 eligible households (1998).	Approximately 12,000 eligible households (2000 point-in-time file).
Units of Analysis	• Person • Family • Household	• Person • Family • Household • Program participants	• Person • Household • Condition • Doctor visit • Hospital stay	• Person • Family • Medical event • Condition • Job

	March supplement to the CPS	SIPP	NHIS	MEPS
Time Period Respondent Asked to Recall	15 months	4 months	Up to 12 months	3 to 5 months
Populations Oversampled	Hispanics	Low-income individuals	Blacks and Hispanics	Blacks and Hispanics Panel 2 (1997) also oversampled the functionally impaired, children with limited activity, individuals predicted to have high medical expenditures, and those predicted to have family income less than 200% of the poverty level.
Health Insurance Information				
Direct question to confirm uninsured status?	Yes (beginning in March 2000)	No (however, questions that restate respondents' insurance status may elicit a correction)	Yes (beginning in 1997)	No (however, questions that restate respondents' insurance status may elicit a correction)
Measurable Periods Without Insurance	• An entire year	• Any month • At time of survey (point in-time) • Ever during year • An entire year • For entire panel (e.g., 1996-1999)	• At time of survey • Any part of year • An entire year	• Any month • At time of survey (point-in-time) • Ever during year • An entire year • For entire panel (e.g., 1998-1999)
Able to follow an individual's changes in insurance status?	No	Yes (by month)	No	Yes (by month)

Source: Congressional Research Service (CRS).

Appendix B. Uninsured U.S. Civilian Noninstitutionalized Population, from Federally Administered Surveys, 1998

	March Supplement to CPS	SIPP	NHIS	MEPS
Uninsured for full year[a]	43.6 million (16.3%)	21.2 million (7.9%)	25.8 million (9.7%)	31.5 million (11.8%)
Uninsured at time of survey (point in time)	N/A	39.2 million (14.6%)	39.5 million (14.7%)	42.3 million (15.8%)
Ever uninsured during the year[a]	N/A	55.2 million (20.7%)	50.0 million (18.9%)	60.3 million (22.7%)

Source: Congressional Research Service (CRS) analysis of March CPS, SIPP, NHIS, and MEPAS.

Notes: The percentages represent the share of the U.S. civilian noninstitutionalized population without health insurance. As discussed in the memorandum, the March CPS does not support estimates of the number uninsured at the time of the survey or the number ever uninsured during the year. For the point-in-time estimate, SIPP data are from March 1998, NHIS data are from interviews throughout the year, and MEPS data are from the first half of 1998. For SIPP and MEPS, the percentage of uninsured for the full year and at any time excludes those who did not provide data for all 12 months.

[a] Excludes infants (i.e., those less than a year old). Although the commonly cited March CPS estimates of the full-year uninsured and CRS's own estimates include infants, infants are excluded from our full-year analysis here for purposes of comparability. Given differences among the surveys, it was not possible to calculate comparable estimates that include infants among the surveys. As a result, infants were dropped in all of the surveys' full-year analyses. For similar reasons, infants were also excluded from the any-time-in-year estimates. Similar concerns and complications do not exist for point-in-time estimates, so infants are included in those estimates.

Chapter 10

HEALTH INSURANCE: UNINSURED CHILDREN BY STATE, 1998-2000

Paulette C. Morgan

INTRODUCTION

An estimated 9.2 million children under age 19 were without health insurance in 2000, representing 12% of all children in the United States. The proportion of children without health insurance varies significantly from state to state. Data collected by the Bureau of the Census indicate that over the 3 years from 1998 through 2000, the average annual percentage of children without health insurance ranged from a low of 5.3% in Rhode Island to a high of 23.6% in Texas. The proportion of children without health insurance was lowest in the Midwest and New England, and highest in the South and West. In 17 states, less than 10% of children were uninsured on average from 1998 through 2000. Three states had an average annual rate of uninsured children that exceeded 20% during this period.

The proportion of children without health insurance varies among states both because of differences in states economies and in state policies with respect to the Medicaid program and other publicly funded health insurance plans. Both the economic climate in a state - its rate of unemployment and growth in household incomes, for example - and the industrial structure of its economy influence the prevalence of private health insurance among families and children. The differing mix of industries from region to region affects the extent of health insurance coverage because the prevalence of health insurance benefits differs by industry and occupation. States also differ with respect to the eligibility rules for their Medicaid programs and their State Children's Health Insurance (SCHIP) programs and in the degree to which they have established other public insurance programs for children who are not covered by private health insurance and are not eligible for Medicaid or SCHIP.

ESTIMATES OF UNINSURED CHILDREN BY STATE

The estimated average annual number and percentage of children in each state who were without health insurance[1] during the period from 1998 to 2000 are shown in Table 1 and Table 2.[2] States are listed alphabetically in Table 1 and are sorted from lowest to highest rate of uninsured children in Table 2. In 34 states, the 3-year average percentage of children without health insurance was lower than the 3-year national average annual rate of 13.5%, but not all of the differences from the national average rate of uninsured children are statistically significant. Twenty-four states had rates that were lower than the national average by a statistically significant amount; these are indicated in the tables by a single asterisk. In total, 16 states and the District of Columbia had average percentages of uninsured children that were higher than the national rate, but 11 states had differences that were statistically different and higher than the national average.

How can so many states have lower than national average 3-year rates? The answer is two-fold. First, the 47% of states with significantly lower than average rates of uninsured children included a disproportionately small share of all uninsured children in the nation (29%), while the 22% of states with higher than average rates of uninsured children included a disproportionately large share of all uninsured children in the nation (48%). Second, the difference from the national average rate of uninsured children was greater in states where the uninsured rate exceeded the national average than in states where it was less than the national average. The 11 states (22%) with greater than average rates of uninsured children had an average of 19.2% uninsured, a difference of 5.7 percentage points from the national average rate (13.5%). In contrast, the 24 states (47%) with lower than average rates of uninsured children had an average of 8.8% uninsured, a difference of 4.7 percentage points from the national rate.

REASONS FOR DIFFERENCES IN THE PERCENT OF CHILDREN UNINSURED

In the period from 1998 to 2000, the percentage of children without health insurance was lowest in the Midwest and New England, and highest in the South and West (Figure 1). The percentage of children without health insurance varies among the states for reasons related to differing economic and political climates. In the short run, rates of income growth and the rate of unemployment differ from state to state and region to region. The industrial structure of states varies as well, with some states having higher concentrations of industries in which health insurance has traditionally been part of a worker's compensation package (manufacturing, for example) and other states having economies more heavily concentrated in service industries or agriculture where employment based health insurance is less common.

[1] Health insurance as defined in the Current Population Survey (CPS) includes, but is not limited to: Medicare; Medicaid; S-CHIP; TRICARE or the Civilian Health and Medical Program of the Uniformed Services (CHAMPUS); the Civilian Health and Medical Program of the Department of Veteran's Affairs (CHAMPVA); Veteran's Administration health care; military health care, other government provided health care, employer/union-provided insurance, and privately purchased insurance.

[2] Due to changes in the health insurance portion of the CPS questionnaire, rates of uninsured in this report are not comparable to any previous version of this report.

States also differ with respect to the eligibility rules for their Medicaid programs and the degree to which they have expanded eligibility for children beyond the federal minimum requirements. These eligibility politics also have an impact on coverage that is available through the State Children's Health Insurance Program (SCHIP) established in 1997. Under SCHIP state build their eligibility criteria from the point where Medicaid rules end. States with more liberal eligibility policies under Medicaid end up covering children at higher levels of income than states with less liberal policies. The proportion of immigrants living in a state may also affect the proportion of uninsured children in the state to the extent that Medicaid and SCHIP are mistakenly perceived as not being available to legal immigrants. Finally, states differ by the amount of resources devoted to establishing other public health insurance programs for people with low incomes, or who are unable to purchase private health insurance policies for other reasons.

SOURCES AND LIMITATIONS OF DATA

The estimates presented in this chapter are based on data from the Current Population Survey (CPS), a survey of approximately 50,000 households selected to be demographically representative of the civilian noninstitutionalized population of the United States. The Census Bureau administers the CPS every month, primarily to collect data on labor force participation and to estimate the rate of unemployment. Each March, however, the survey also includes questions about health insurance coverage during the previous calendar year. People are classified as having been covered by health insurance if they had insurance *at any time* during the year. If the respondent does not report being covered by health insurance at any time during the year, he or she is classified as having been uninsured for the full year. Starting in 2000, an additional question was added to the CPS to verify the insurance status of respondents.[3] CPS estimates of the number of insured from previous years are not directly comparable with surveys containing the additional verification question.

Despite the large number of households surveyed in the CPS, estimates produced on the regional or state level should be interpreted with caution. The sample sizes available from the CPS for many states are small, especially when examining a subset of the sample such as children under the age of 19. Small sample sizes increase the likelihood that the characteristics of the survey participants differ systematically from the characteristics of the population they are meant represent. (This is known as sampling error). Therefore, two methods were used in this chapter to increase the reliability of state-level estimates of the number and percentage of children who were uninsured in each state: a range of possible values is provided and a multiple-year estimate was calculated.

Table 1 and Table 2 show the best point estimates of the number and percentage of children in each state who are uninsured. The point estimate is a 3-year average of the number and percentage of uninsured children in each state. The tables also present a low estimate and a high estimate for each state. These estimates represent a 90% confidence interval: We are 90% confident that the true number and percent of uninsured children in the state (the number

---

[3] Data from the Current Population Survey for 1999 through 2001 were used in this analysis. Only the CPS for 2000 and 2001 include the insurance verification question.

and percent we would get if we polled *every* household in the state) is between the high and low estimates.

Because fewer households are surveyed in any individual state in the nation as a whole, the likelihood of error in estimates based on *state-level* CPS data is significantly greater than the probable error associated with estimated based on *national* CPS data. For example, from 1998 to 2000 an annual average of 13.5% of children in the United States were without health insurance coverage. Given the sampling error associated with this estimate, there is approximately a 90% chance that the actual average percentage of children who were uninsured nationwide during this time was between 13.3% and 13.7%. Conversely, there is a 5% chance that the actual average percentage is less than 13.3% and a 5% chance that the actual average percentage is greater than 13.7%. The estimated 3-year average rate for Georgia (13.3%) was 0.2% less than the national rate of 13.5%. However, because only a fraction of the households surveyed were in Georgia, the possibility of sampling error in this number is greater, and the average percentage of children who were uninsured annually in Georgia from 1998 to 2000 may have been as low as 11.8% or as high as 14.7%. With repeated sampling in Georgia, we would expect that 9 times out of 10 (i.e., 90% of the time), the average percent uninsured would lie between 11.8% and 14.7%.

Because the sampling error associated with state-level estimated from the CPS is significantly greater than the sampling error accompanying national estimates, we averaged the number and percentage of uninsured children by state over a 3-year period. By averaging the estimates over 3 years, we reduce the size of the uncertainty that results from the potential for sampling error (i.e., the size of the difference between the low and high estimates).

Figure 1. Percent Uninsured Children by State, 1998-2000 Accounting for Statistical Variation in Estimates

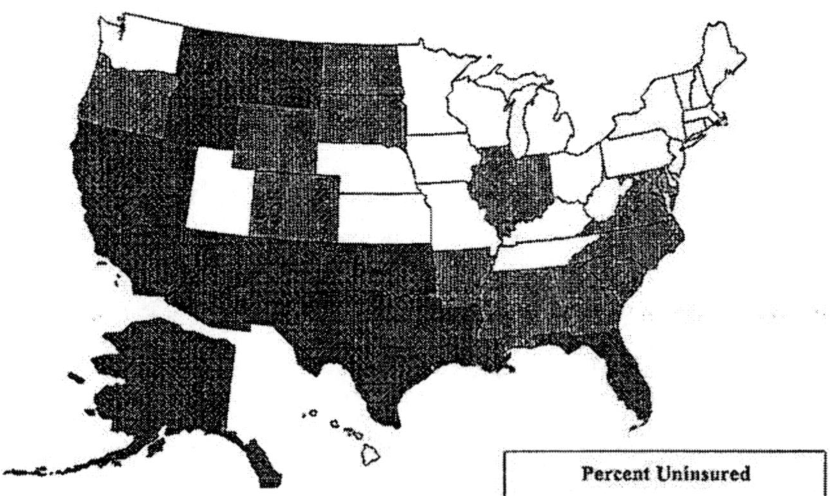

Table 1: Average Number and Percentage of Children Without Health Insurance, 1998 to 2000, Alphabetical by State

State	Number of Children Uninsured			Percentage of Children Uninsured			
	Point	Range of Estimate		Point		Range of Estimate	
	Estimate	Low	High	Estimate		Low	High
Alabama	141,000	120,000	161,000	12.4%		10.7%	14.0%
Alaska	35,000	31,000	39,000	16.%	**	14.4%	17.6%
Arizona	298,000	269,000	327,000	20.4%	**	18.6%	22.1%
Arkansas	103,000	90,000	117,000	14.3%	**	12.6%	16.0%
California	1,787,000	1,705,000	1,868,000	17.9%	*	17.2%	18.6%
Colorado	163,000	142,000	183,000	14.0%	*	12.3%	15.6%
Connecticut	68,000	54,000	83,000	7.6%	**	6.1%	9.1%
Delaware	24,000	20,000	28,000	10.7%	*	9.1%	12.3%
District of Columbia	16,000	13,000	18,000	14.2%	**	11.9%	16.5%
Florida	633,000	591,000	675,000	17.5%	*	16.5%	18.6%
Georgia	287,000	253,000	322,000	3.3%	*	11.8%	14.7%
Hawaii	32,000	26,000	38,000	9.8%	*	8.1%	11.5%
Idaho	67,000	59,000	74,000	17.3%	**	15.6%	19.0%
Illinois	451,000	415,000	488,000	12.3%	*	11.4%	13.3%
Indiana	195,000	167,000	223,000	12.3%	*	10.7%	14.0%
Iowa	55,000	45,000	66,000	7.1%	*	5.8%	8.4%
Kansas	75,000	63,000	87,000	10.4%	*	8.8%	11.9%
Kentucky	111,000	94,000	128,000	11.1%	*	9.5%	12.7%
Louisiana	231,000	206,000	256,000	19.6%	**	17.7%	21.5%
Maine	27,000	22,000	35,000	8.5%	*	6.9%	10.2%
Maryland	149,000	125,000	174,000	11.7%	**	9.9%	13.5%
Massachusetts	131,000	113,000	148,000	8.1%	*	7.0%	9.1%
Michigan	267,000	240,000	294,000	8.9%	*	8.0%	9.8%
Minnesota	120,000	100,000	140,000	8.4%	**	7.1%	9.7%
Mississippi	122,000	107,000	137,000	14.9%	*	13.2%	16.6%
Missouri	109,000	88,000	130,000	7.3%		5.9%	8.6%
Montana	48,000	43,000	54,000	19.3%	*	17.4%	21.2%
Nebraska	38,000	32,000	45,000	7.8%	**	6.5%	9.1%
Nevada	116,000	104,000	128,000	19.2%	*	17.3%	21.0%
New Hampshire	26,000	21,000	32,000	7.3%	**	5.8%	8.7%
New Jersey	229,000	205,000	252,000	10.5%		9.5%	11.5%
New Mexico	1223,000	111,000	135,000	21.7%	*	19.8%	23.5%
New York	606,000	566,000	646,000	12.0%	**	11.3%	12.7%
North Carolina	235,000	210,000	261,000	12.1%	*	10.9%	13.3%
North Dakota	23,000	19,000	26,000	12.9%	*	11.2%	14.7%
Ohio	294,000	264,000	323,000	9.1%	*	8.2%	9.9%
Oklahoma	163,000	144,000	181,000	19.0%	*	17.0%	20.9%

State	Number of Children Uninsured			Percentage of Children Uninsured			
	Point	Range of Estimate		Point		Range of Estimate	
	Estimate	Low	High	Estimate		Low	High
Oregon	116,000	99,000	133,000	12.7%	*	11.0%	14.5%
Pennsylvania	212,000	188,000	237,000	6.8%		6.1%	7.6%
Rhode Island	13,000	10,000	17,000	5.3%		4.0%	6.7%
South Carolina	138,000	118,000	158,000	14.0%		12.1%	15.9%
South Dakota	23,000	20,000	27,000	12.0%		10.3%	13.6%
Tennessee	125,000	103,000	147,000	8.4%		7.0%	9.8%
Texas	1,420,000	1,349,000	1,490,000	23.6%		22.6%	24.6%
Utah	80,000	70,000	90,000	10.7%		9.5%	12.0%
Vermont	12,000	10,000	15,000	7.3%		5.9%	8.7%
Virginia	229,000	198,000	260,000	12.7%		11.1%	14.3%
Washington	155,000	129,000	181.000	9.8%		8.3%	11.4%
West Virginia	43,000	36,000	49,000	11.0%		9.3%	12.7%
Wisconsin	117,000	96,000	137,000	7.7%		6.4%	9.0%
Wyoming	20,000	18,000	23,000	14.5%		12.8%	16.3%
United States	10,303,00	10,133,000	10,473,000	13.5%		13.3%	13.7%

Source: CRS analysis of the March supplement of the Current Population Survey (CPS), 1999-2001.

Note: * indicates percentage of children uninsured is statistically lower than the national rate;** indicates percentage uninsured is statistically higher than the national rate. Ranges represent low and high estimates given a 90% confidence interval.

Table 2: Average Number and percentage of children without Health Insurance, 1998 to 2000, states Sorted by Percentage Uninsured

State	Number of Children Uninsured			Percentage of Children Uninsured			
	Point	Range of Estimate		Point		Range of Estimate	
	Estimate	Low	High	Estimate		Low	High
Rhode Island	13,000	10,000	17,000	5.3%	*	4.0%	6.7%
Pennsylvania	212,000	188,000	237,000	6.8%	*	6.1%	7.6%
Iowa	55,000	45,000	66,000	7.1%	*	5.8%	8.4%
Missouri	109,000	88,000	130,000	7.3%	*	5.9%	8.6%
New Hampshire	26,000	21,000	32,000	7.3%	*	5.8%	8.7%
Vermont	12,000	10,000	15,000	7.3%	*	5.9%	8.7%
Connecticut	68,000	54,000	83,000	7.6%	*	6.1%	9.1%
Wisconsin	117,000	96,000	137,000	7.7%	*	6.4%	9.0%
Nebraska	38,000	32,000	45,000	7.8%	*	6.5%	9.1%
Massachusetts	131,000	113,000	148,000	8.1%	*	7.0%	9.1%
Tennessee	125,000	103,000	147,000	8.4%	*	7.0%	9.8%
Minnesota	120,000	100,000	140,000	8.4%	*	7.1%	9.7%
Maine	27,000	22,000	33,000	8.5%	*	6.9%	10.2%
Michigan	267,000	240,000	294,000	8.9%	*	8.0%	9.8%
Ohio	294,000	264,000	323,000	9.1%	*	8.2%	9.9%
Hawaii	32,000	26,000	38,000	9.8%	*	8.1%	11.5%
Washington	155,000	129,000	181,000	9.8%	*	8.3%	11.4%
Kansas	75,000	63,000	87,000	10.4%	*	8.8%	11.9%
New Jersey	229,000	205,000	252,000	10.5%	*	9.5%	11.5%
Delaware	24,000	20,000	28,000	10.7%	*	9.1%	12.3%
Utah	80,000	70,000	90,000	10.7%	*	9.5%	12.0%
West Virginia	43,000	36,000	49,000	11.0%	*	9.3%	12.7%
Kentucky	111,000	94,000	128,000	11.1%	*	9.5%	12.7%
Maryland	149,000	125,000	174,000	11.7%		9.9%	13.5%
South Dakota	23,000	20,000	27,000	12.0%	*	10.3%	13.6%
New York	606,000	566,000	646,000	12.0%		11.3%	12.7%
North Carolina	235,000	210,000	261,000	12.1%		10.9%	13.3%
Indiana	195,000	167,000	223,000	12.3%		10.7%	14.0%
Illinois	451,000	415,000	488,000	12.3%		11.4%	13.3%
Alabama	141,000	120,000	161,000	12.4%		10.7%	14.0%
Virginia	229,000	198,000	260,000	12.7%		11.1%	14.3%
Oregon	116,000	99,000	133,000	12.7%		11.0%	14.5%
North Dakota	23,000	19,000	26,000	12.9%	**	11.2%	14.7%
Georgia	287,000	253,000	322,000	13.3%	**	11.8%	14.7%
Colorado	163,000	142,000	183,000	14.0%	**	12.3%	15.6%
South Carolina	138,000	118,000	158,000	14.0%	**	12.1%	15.9%
District of Columbia	16,000	13,000	18,000	14.2%	**	11.9%	16.5%

State	Number of Children Uninsured			Percentage of Children Uninsured			
	Point Estimate	Range of Estimate Low	Range of Estimate High	Point Estimate		Range of Estimate Low	Range of Estimate High
Arkansas	103,000	90,000	117,000	14.3%	**	12.6%	16.0%
Wyoming	20,000	18,000	23,000	14.5%	**	12.8%	16.3%
Mississippi	122,000	107,000	137,000	14.9%	**	13.2%	16.6%
Alaska	35,000	31,000	39,000	16.0%	**	14.4%	17.6%
Idaho	67,000	59,000	74,000	17.3%	**	15.6%	19.0%
Florida	633,000	591,000	675,000	17.5%	**	16.5%	18.6%
California	1,787,000	1,705,000	1,868,000	17.9%		17.2%	18.6%
Oklahoma	163,000	144,000	181,000	19.0%		17.0%	20.9%
Nevada	116,000	104,000	128,000	19.2%		17.3%	21.0%
Montana	48,000	43,000	54,000	19.3%		17.4%	21.2%
Louisiana	231,000	206,000	256,000	19.6%		17.7%	21.5%
Arizona	298,000	269,000	327,000	20.4%		18.6%	22.1%
New Mexico	123,000	111,000	135,000	21.7%		19.8%	23.5%
Texas	1,420,000	1,349,000	1,490,000	23.6%		22.6%	24.6%
United States	10,303,000	10,133,000	10,473,000	13.5%		13.3%	13.7%

Source: CRS analysis of the March supplement of the Current Population Survey (CPS), 1999-2001.

Note: * indicates percentage of children uninsured is statistically lower than the national rate;** indicates percentage uninsured is statistically higher than the national rate. Ranges represent low and high estimates given a 90% confidence interval.

Chapter 11

HEALTH INSURANCE COVERAGE: CHARACTERISTICS OF THE INSURED AND UNINSURED POPULATIONS IN 2001

Chris L. Peterson

INTRODUCTION

The number of Americans without health insurance rose in 2001 to 41.2 million Americans (14.6%) — an increase of 1.4 million people from 2000. This reversed a two-year trend of falling numbers of uninsured. Approximately 1.3 million fewer Americans had employment-based health coverage, compared to 2000, according to the Census Bureau. From 1999 to 2000, this number had risen by 2.9 million. In spite of the decline, most Americans (64.1%) still received their health insurance through an employer. Yet full-time, full-year workers and their family members made up more than half of the uninsured. The percentage of individuals covered by Medicaid increased significantly in 2001. Among children in 2001, the percentage of uninsured did not change significantly. This chapter examines characteristics of both the insured and the uninsured populations in the United States. It will be updated in fall 2003.

HEALTH INSURANCE COVERAGE AND SELECTED POPULATION CHARACTERISTICS

Age

Table 1 provides a breakdown of health insurance coverage by type of insurance and age. In 2001, compared to other age groups, those under age 5 were most likely (29%) to have coverage through Medicaid, the State Children's Health Insurance Program (SCHIP), or some other program for low-income individuals. Young adults ages 19 to 24 were the most likely to have gone without health insurance for the entire year. While most in this age group (57%) were covered under an employment-based plan, 30% had no health insurance. Young adults are often too old to be covered as dependents on their parents' policies and, as entry-level workers, do not have strong ties to the work force. In addition, some may choose to remain uninsured and spend their money on other items. After age 25, the percentage of people without health insurance decreases. Of those age 65 and over, 96% were covered by Medicare, and less than 1% were uninsured for the entire year. The remainder of this chapter focuses on the population under age 65.

Table 1. Health Insurance Coverage by Type of Insurance and Age, 2001

		Type of insurance[a]					
Age	**Population (in millions)**	**Employment based[b]**	**Private nongroup**	**Medicare**	**Medicaid or other public[c]**	**Military/ veterans coverage**	**Uninsured**
Under 5	19.4	*60.8%*	*4.8%*	*0.7%*	*28.5%*	*3.5%*	*10.6%*
5-18	57.1	*66.3*	*5.1*	*0.6*	*20.2*	*3.2*	*12.6*
19-24	23.4	*57.3*	*6.0*	*0.7*	*9.6*	*2.7*	*29.7*
25-34	38.7	*66.2*	*5.3*	*1.3*	*6.7*	*2.1*	*23.4*
35-54	83.8	*74.4*	*6.8*	*2.6*	*5.5*	*2.7*	*14.7*
55-61	19.3	*70.4*	*9.9*	*7.1*	*7.0*	*4.3*	*12.8*
62-64	6.5	*61.9*	*12.9*	*14.2*	*6.9*	*5.9*	*14.1*
65+	33.8	*35.3*	*30.3*	*96.1*	*9.7*	*6.4*	*0.8*
Total	**282.1**	*64.1%*	*9.2%*	*13.5%*	*11.2%*	*3.4%*	*14.6%*

Source: CRS analysis of data from the March 2002 Current Population Survey (CPS).
[a] People may have had more than one source of health insurance over the course of the year.
[b] Group health insurance through employer or union.
[c] Nonmilitary. Includes State Children's Health Insurance Program (SCHIP) and other state programs for low-income individuals.

Other Demographic Characteristics

Table 2 shows the rate of health insurance coverage by type of insurance and selected demographic characteristics — race, family type, region, poverty level and citizenship — *for people under age 65*. In 2001, whites were least likely to be uninsured (12%), while Hispanics were most likely (35%). The rate of employment-based health coverage was highest among whites (76%), and the rate of public coverage[1] was highest among blacks (24%).

People in male-headed or two-parent families with children were less likely to be uninsured (13%) than those in female-headed families with children (21%) or in families with no children (19%). The sources of coverage were quite different for male-present (one or two parents) and female-headed (single parent) families with children: coverage was employment based for 74% of male-present families compared to 45% of female-headed families; 10% of male-present families had public coverage compared to 36% of female-headed families.

[1] Includes Medicare, Medicaid, the State Children's Health Insurance Program (SCHIP), or some other program for low-income individuals. Excludes military and veterans coverage.

Table 2. Health Insurance Coverage by Type of Insurance and Demographic Characteristics for People Under Age 65, 2001

	Population (in millions)	Type of insurance[a]			
		Employment based[b]	Public[c]	Other[d]	Uninsured
Race/ethnicity					
White	166.9	*75.6%*	*9.3%*	*10.3%*	*11.6%*
Black	31.9	*56.5*	*23.9*	*7.1*	*20.1*
Hispanic	35.5	*44.8*	*19.4*	*5.1*	*34.7*
Other	14.0	*62.1*	*13.0*	*10.8*	*20.5*
Family type					
Female-headed with children	29.6	*45.3*	*36.3*	*4.8*	*20.5*
Two parent or male-headed w/children	119.5	*73.9*	*10.3*	*9.0*	*13.1*
No children	99.2	*67.6*	*8.9*	*10.7*	*19.4*
Region					
Northeast	46.1	*71.8*	*13.6*	*6.5*	*13.8*
Midwest	55.9	*74.6*	*11.1*	*8.3*	*12.2*
South	88.5	*65.0*	*13.3*	*10.2*	*18.8*
West	57.8	*63.1*	*13.3*	*10.6*	*19.3*
Poverty level[e]					
Less than 100% of poverty	29.5	*20.6*	*44.0*	*6.7*	*33.9*
100%-149% of poverty	20.9	*37.8*	*29.9*	*8.7*	*30.6*
150%-199% of poverty	21.7	*52.8*	*19.0*	*9.8*	*25.8*
200%+ of poverty	176.6	*81.5*	*4.7*	*9.6*	*10.7*
Citizenship					
Native	219.2	*70.2*	*13.3*	*9.5*	*13.8*
Naturalized	9.6	*65.8*	*8.8*	*9.7*	*21.0*
Non-Citizens	19.5	*43.5*	*9.7*	*5.7*	*44.3*
Total	**248.3**	*68.0%*	*12.8%*	*9.2%*	*16.5%*

Source: CRS analysis of data from the March 2002 CPS.

[a] People may have more than one source of coverage; percentages may total to more than 100.

[b] Group health insurance through employer or union.

[c] Includes Medicare, Medicaid, the State Children's Health Insurance Program (SCHIP), and other state programs for low-income individuals. Excludes military and veterans coverage.

[d] Private nongroup health insurance, veterans coverage, or military health care.

[e] In 2001, the weighted average poverty threshold for a family of four was $18,104. Approximately 607,000 children are excluded from CPS-based poverty analyses because they are in unrelated subfamilies.

Table 3. Health Insurance Coverage by Employment Characteristics[a] for People Under Age 65, 2001

	Population (in millions)	Type of insurance[b]			
		From own job[c]	From other's job[c]	Other[d]	Uninsured
Firm size[e]					
Under 10	34.2	*20.5%*	*21.5%*	*30.5%*	*33.3%*
10-24	18.3	*31.0*	*28.1*	*20.3*	*27.3*
25-99	27.0	*37.9*	*36.2*	*16.4*	*18.0*
100-499	30.0	*40.8*	*42.9*	*14.0*	*11.6*
500-999	12.8	*42.9*	*43.2*	*12.4*	*10.2*
1,000 +	92.2	*42.5*	*45.5*	*14.4*	*8.2*
Industry[e]					
Agriculture	4.7	*16.9%*	*18.3%*	*32.0%*	*38.3%*
Personal services	5.5	*25.8*	*20.8*	*25.7*	*33.6*
Construction	17.0	*26.6*	*31.4*	*18.4*	*29.4*
Retail trade	28.6	*30.7*	*26.6*	*23.1*	*26.4*
Entertainment	3.3	*36.5*	*27.9*	*21.0*	*22.3*
Business services	14.7	*32.6*	*32.7*	*21.3*	*21.8*
Wholesale trade	8.8	*38.4*	*44.5*	*12.3*	*12.6*
Nondurable goods	14.2	*39.9*	*44.8*	*12.8*	*11.3*
Mining	1.2	*35.3*	*45.5*	*17.0*	*11.2*
Transportation	18.5	*39.7*	*45.6*	*12.6*	*11.2*
Professional services	49.6	*43.3*	*41.1*	*16.4*	*9.9*
Durable goods	22.0	*41.4*	*46.6*	*11.2*	*9.4*
Finance/insurance	13.4	*42.8*	*43.7*	*13.4*	*8.9*
Public administration	13.2	*39.9*	*47.0*	*25.5*	*3.4*
Labor force attachment of policyholder or, if no insurance, working family member[a]					
Workers					
Full time, full year	85.3	*78.2*	*6.6*	*10.6*	*16.0*
Full time, part year	15.1	*56.5*	*5.6*	*18.4*	*30.7*
Part time, full year	6.2	*46.9*	*6.6*	*24.0*	*33.3*
Part time, part year	5.1	*33.1*	*5.2*	*32.9*	*38.3*
Workers' Dependents					
Full time, full year	84.8	*0.0*	*77.5*	*18.2*	*10.4*
Full time, part year	11.0	*0.0*	*57.4*	*38.2*	*13.7*
Part time, full year	4.3	*0.0*	*53.1*	*35.4*	*16.5*
Part time, part year	2.8	*0.0*	*40.6*	*54.4*	*12.2*
Not working	26.3	*15.2[f]*	*9.8*	*54.3*	*27.7*
Coverage outside home	7.4	*8.0*	*100.0*	*16.5*	*0.0*
Total	**248.3**	*34.0%*	*37.3%*	*21.4%*	*16.5%*

Source: CRS analysis of data from the March 2002 CPS.

[a] The employment characteristics are those of the policyholder. In families without private coverage, "workers" are the family head or, if the head is not employed, the spouse. For "dependents," the employment characteristics are those of the person providing dependent coverage or, if the dependent has no private health insurance, to the head of household or spouse.

[b] People may have more than one source of health insurance during the year.

[c] Group health insurance through current or former employer or union.

[d] Medicare, Medicaid, the State Children's Health Insurance Program (SCHIP), nongroup health insurance, veterans coverage, and other government coverage.

[e] For persons who worked and their dependents.

[f] Nearly 90% of these policyholders (i.e., those who did not work during the year but had employment-based coverage in their name) were retirees, were ill or disabled, or were at home with the family and probably received coverage through their former employer.

People were less likely to be uninsured if they lived in the Midwest (12%) or the Northeast (14%), than if they lived in the South (19%) or West (19%). More than 70% of those living in the Northeast and Midwest had employment-based health insurance compared to 65% in the South and 63% in the West. Among individuals with incomes at least two times the poverty level, 11% went without health insurance compared to 34% of the poor (i.e., those with incomes below the poverty level). Only 21% of the poor received health coverage through employment, and 44% had public coverage. More than 80% of people with incomes at least two times the poverty level were covered through an employer, and only 5% had public coverage.

Non-citizens were more likely to be uninsured than people born with U.S. citizenship (i.e., "native") — 44% versus 14%, respectively. Non-citizens accounted for 8% of the population under 65, but were 21% of the uninsured. About 44% of non-citizens were covered through employment, compared to 70% of citizens.

Employment Characteristics

Following 2 years of significant increases in employment-based coverage, the prevalence of job-related health insurance fell in 2001 to 68%. **Table 3** shows the rate of health insurance coverage by employment characteristics for people under age 65 who were workers or their dependents. In 2001, only about 8% of workers and dependents of workers in large firms (1,000 or more employees) were uninsured compared to 33% in small firms (less than 10 employees). People who reported working in small firms and their dependents accounted for 14% of the under 65 population but 28% of the uninsured. Insurance coverage varied according to industry, as well. Agriculture and personal services had the highest proportion of uninsured workers and dependents — more than 30%; only 3% of those in public administration were uninsured. Among workers, 84% of those employed full time, full year had health insurance, most often through their own employment (78%). In 2001, nearly one-third of workers with less than full time, full year employment were uninsured.

CHARACTERISTICS OF THE UNINSURED POPULATION UNDER AGE 65

People who lack health insurance differ from the population as a whole: they are more likely to be young adults, poor, Hispanic, or employees in small firms. **Figure 1** illustrates selected characteristics of those under age 65 who were uninsured for 2001. Approximately 17% of the uninsured were 19 to 24 years old, even though this age group represents less than 9% of the under 65 population.

Our report for the year 2000 noted that for the first time since 1994, when CRS began this annual analysis, the percentage of the uninsured who were white fell below 50% — to 49%. In 2001, this percentage dropped again, to 47%, even though whites make up two-thirds (67%) of the under 65 population.

More than half (55%) of the uninsured were full time, full year workers or their dependents. Approximately 18% had no attachment to the labor force. Approximately three-quarters of the uninsured were above the poverty level. Even though the poor accounted for only 12% of the under 65 population, they represented 25% of the uninsured. For the first time since 1994, more than one-quarter of the uninsured were not native-born citizens (i.e., they were either not citizens or were naturalized citizens).

Figure 1. Characteristics of the Uninsured Population under Age 65, 2001

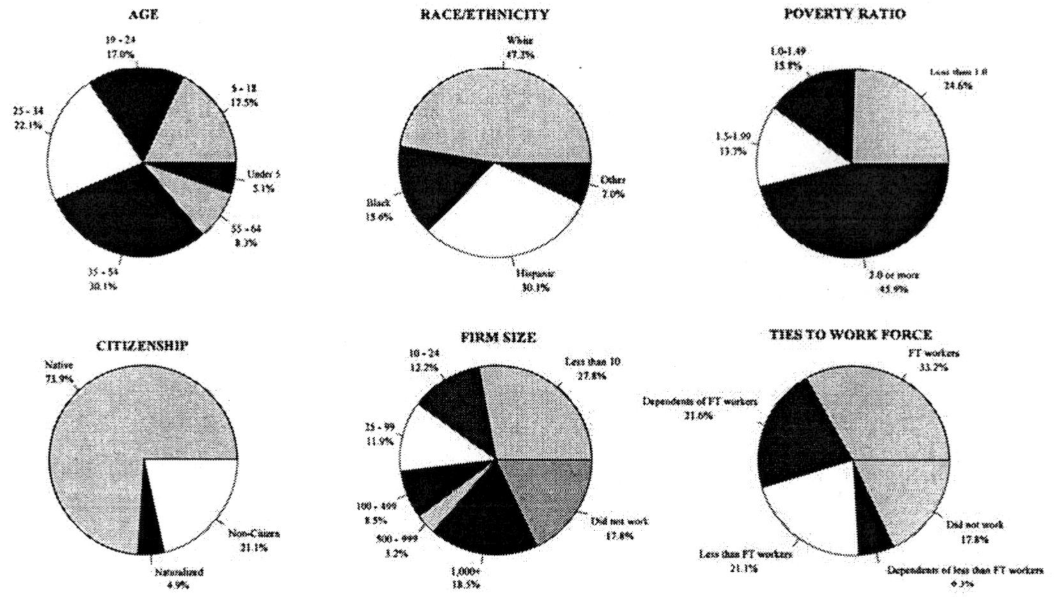

Source: Congressional Research Service (CRS) analysis of datat from the March 2002 Current Politics Survey (CPS).

Note: Totals may not sum to 100% due to rounding. "FT workers" represent full-time, full-year workers.

Chapter 12

HEALTH INSURANCE: UNINSURED BY STATE, 2001

Paulette C. Morgan

INTRODUCTION

An estimated 14.6% of the U.S. population lacked health insurance coverage in 2001, up from 14.2% in 2000. When examined by state, estimates of the percent uninsured ranged from a low of 7.5% in Iowa to a high of 23.5% in Texas. Generally, states in the Midwest and New England have lower rates of uninsured, while states in the Southwestern and Southern portions of the nation have higher shares of their populations without coverage.

These state-level estimates are based on the March 2002 Current Population Survey (CPS), and must be interpreted with caution because they are based on a survey sample. When sampling variation is taken into account, to allow one to say with 90% reliability that the percent uninsured in the state lies between specified low and high estimates, the uninsured rate in 3 states is not different statistically from the uninsured rate nationwide. The uninsured rate is statistically lower than the national rate in 31 states and the District of Columbia, and statistically higher in the remaining 16 states.

State-level analysis is only one way to examine data about health insurance coverage. Some factors related to the percent of a state's population that is uninsured may be affected by the state, such as eligibility criteria for the state's Medicaid and State Children's Health Insurance programs or other programs for those lacking health insurance. Other factors may be beyond the state's direct control, such as the willingness of employers to offer coverage and the financial resources of the state's population to purchase coverage.

ESTIMATES OF THE UNINSURED BY STATE

An estimated 14.6% of the U.S. population lack health insurance coverage in 2001, up from 14.2% in 2000.[1] **Table 1** shows that the estimated percent of each state's population that lacked health insurance[2] coverage in 2001 ranged from a low of 7.5% in Iowa to a high of 23.5% in Texas. Thirteen states[3] had estimated uninsured rates less than 10% and 2 states[4] had estimated rates greater than 20%. Generally, states with the lowest rates of uninsurance were located in the Midwest and Northeast; states with the highest rates were in the Southwest and South (**Figure 1**).

These estimates of the percent of the state population without health insurance coverage are based on data from the March 2002 Current Population Survey (CPS). The CPS is representative of the civilian, noninstitutionalized population, and is designed to produce reliable estimates at the national, regional and state level.

The small sample sizes available from the CPS for many states make it prudent to consider state-level estimates in terms of a range of values. This range is based on sampling theory, and takes into account the size of the sample. **Table 1** shows the best point estimates, or single values, for the numbers of people covered and not covered by health insurance, and the percent uninsured by state.[5] The table also reports a range in values for these numbers and percentages. The size of the range depends primarily upon the sample size. **Table 1** shows ranges based on a 90% confidence interval. A 90% confidence interval means that given repeated sampling of health insurance coverage in a state, 9 out of 10 times, the estimate of the percent uninsured (or number covered or not covered) will lie within the range set by the low and high estimates. For example, if one surveys people in Iowa about health insurance coverage, in 9 out of 10 sample surveys, on average, the percent uninsured in Iowa will be between 6.8% and 8.2%.[6]

Because of the uncertainty about state-level estimates of the percent uninsured, a more statistically conservative comparison across states takes ranges of values into account. This is done in **Figure 2**, which groups states according to differences from the nationwide percent uninsured, considering the estimated ranges in the percent uninsured by state. When statistical variation is taken into account, 3 states have percents uninsured that are *not statistically different* from the nationwide rate of 14.6%. (The nationwide percent uninsured has a range in estimates of between 14.4% and 14.8%.) These 3 states have percents uninsured ranging from a low point estimate of 13.6% in Montana (with a range in estimates between 12.6% and

---

[1] This report uses population estimates based on the 2000 Census instead of 1990 Census. The CPS for 2001 also includes an expanded sample of households. Due to these changes, rates of uninsured in this report are not comparable to any previous version of this report.

[2] Health insurance includes, but is not limited to: Medicare; Medicaid; S-CHIP; TRICARE or the Civilian Health and Medical Program of the Uniformed Services (CHAMPUS); the Civilian Health and Medical Program of the Department of Veteran's Affairs (CHAMPVA); Veteran's Administration health care; military health care; other government provided health care; employer/union-provided insurance; and privately purchased insurance.

[3] Iowa (7.5%), Rhode Island (7.7%), Wisconsin (7.7%), Minnesota (8.0%), Massachusetts (8.2%), Delaware (9.2%), Pennsylvania (9.2%), South Dakota (9.3%), New Hampshire (9.4%), Nebraska (9.5%), Hawaii (9.6%), North Dakota (9.6%), and Vermont (9.6%).

[4] New Mexico (20.7%), and Texas (23.5%).

[5] **Table 1** shows states sorted by the percent uninsured. **Table 2** reports the same data but sorts states alphabetically.

[6] Note that there is no way to determine if the results for Iowa in **Table 1** are the 1 time out of 10 that a different result is obtained, where the real percent uninsured is outside the confidence interval (i.e., less than 6.8% or greater than 8.2%).

14.6%) to a high point estimate of 14.8% in Utah (with a range in estimates between 14.0% and 15.6%.) Thirty-one states and the District of Columbia have percents uninsured that are statistically lower than the nationwide rate. These states include all states in New England and the Midwest, a few states in the eastern United States, as well as Washington, Oregon and Hawaii. The remaining 16 states, arrayed across the South and Southwest from Mississippi to California, as well as Florida, Georgia, Idaho, Wyoming, Alaska and New York, have uninsured rates that are statistically higher than the nationwide rate.

REASONS FOR DIFFERENCES IN THE PERCENT UNINSURED

Figures 1 and **2** indicate that residents of the Southern and Southwestern United States are more likely to lack health insurance and residents of the Midwest and New England are more likely to be covered. Various state characteristics may account for these differences. Nationwide, the percent uninsured is related to employment by industry, with workers in manufacturing of durable goods, professional services, finance/insurance, and public administration industries most often covered by health insurance and those employed in agriculture, and personal services least often covered. Employees who work for large firms, and their dependents, are more likely to be covered than those who work for small firms. Union members are more likely to be covered. The prevalence of particular industries, firm sizes, or unionization may account for some of the regional or state variation in percents uninsured.[7]

Some factors related to the percent of a state's population that is uninsured may be affected by state's policies, such as eligibility criteria for the state's Medicaid program or the State Children's Health Insurance Program. Other factors may be beyond the state's direct control, such as the willingness of employers to offer coverage and the financial resources of the state's population to purchase coverage. Only Hawaii has implemented state legislation mandating that an employer offer coverage, which is augmented with a health insurance program for the unemployed.[8]

[7] For additional information, see CRS Report 96-891, *Health Insurance Coverage: Characteristics of the Insured and Uninsured Populations in 2001*, by Chris Peterson.

[8] Hawaii received a congressional exemption from the Federal Employee Retirement and Income Security Act of 1974 (ERISA) to permit the employer mandate. No other state has received a similar exemption.

Table 1. Number of People Covered and Not Covered by Health Insurance, and Percent Not Covered, By State, 2001

Sorted by Percent Uninsured (numbers in thousands)

	Number covered			Number not covered			Percent not covered			
	Point	Range		Point	Range		Point		Range	
	estimate	Low	High	estimate	Low	High	estimate		Low	High
Iowa	2,645	2,581	2,709	216	198	234	7.5%	*	6.8%	8.2%
Rhode Island	963	942	984	80	73	87	7.7%	*	7.2%	8.2%
Wisconsin	4,927	4,817	5,037	409	378	440	7.7%	*	7.0%	8.4%
Minnesota	4,530	4,426	4,634	392	361	423	8.0%	*	7.3%	8.7%
Massachusetts	5,802	5,677	5,927	520	482	558	8.2%	*	7.7%	8.7%
Delaware	719	699	739	73	66	80	9.2%	*	8.5%	9.9%
Pennsylvania	10,983	10,805	11,161	1,119	1,061	1,177	9.2%	*	8.7%	9.7%
South Dakota	670	654	686	69	64	74	9.3%	*	8.6%	10.0%
New Hampshire	1,139	1,113	1,165	119	111	127	9.4%	*	8.7%	10.1%
Nebraska	1,523	1,484	1,562	160	147	173	9.5%	*	8.8%	10.2%
Hawaii	1,096	1,068	1,124	117	107	127	9.6%	*	8.9%	10.3%
North Dakota	561	546	576	60	55	65	9.6%	*	8.9%	10.3%
Vermont	549	536	562	58	53	63	9.6%	*	8.9%	10.3%
Connecticut	3,047	2,976	3,118	346	323	369	10.2%	*	9.5%	10.9%
Missouri	4,960	4,842	5,078	565	524	606	10.2%	*	9.5%	10.9%
Maine	1,147	1,121	1,173	132	124	140	10.3%	*	9.6%	11.0%
Michigan	8,864	8,703	9,025	1,028	972	1,084	10.4%	*	9.9%	10.9%
Virginia	6,331	6,176	6,486	774	720	828	10.9%	*	10.2%	11.6%
Ohio	9,943	9,767	10,119	1,248	1,184	1,312	11.2%	*	10.7%	11.7%
Tennessee	5,042	4,904	5,180	640	591	689	11.3%	*	10.5%	12.1%
Kansas	2,341	2,283	2,399	301	280	322	11.4%	*	10.6%	12.2%
Indiana	5,322	5,204	5,440	714	670	758	11.8%	*	11.1%	12.5%
Kentucky	3,505	3,413	3,597	492	457	527	12.3%	*	11.5%	13.1%
Maryland	4,673	4,561	4,785	653	610	696	12.3%	*	11.5%	13.1%
South Carolina	3,517	3,427	3,607	493	458	528	12.3%	*	11.5%	13.1%
D.C.	484	469	499	70	65	75	12.7%	*	11.7%	13.7%
Oregon	3,018	2,939	3,097	443	413	473	12.8%	*	12.0%	13.6%
Alabama	3,815	3,715	3,915	573	534	612	13.1%	*	12.3%	13.9%
New Jersey	7,361	7,221	7,501	1,109	1,055	1,163	13.1%	*	12.4%	13.8%
Washington	5,151	5,018	5,284	780	727	833	13.1%	*	12.3%	13.9%
West Virginia	1,539	1,501	1,577	234	219	249	13.2%	*	12.4%	14.0%
Illinois	10,655	10,471	10,839	1,676	1,602	1,750	13.6%	*	13.1%	14.1%
Montana	771	748	794	121	111	131	13.6%		12.6%	14.6%
North Carolina	6,932	6,782	7,082	1,167	1,104	1,230	14.4%		13.7%	15.1%
Utah	1,927	1,876	1,978	335	314	356	14.8%		14.0%	15.6%
New York	15,911	15,696	16,126	2,916	2,822	3,010	15.5%	**	15.0%	16.0%
Colorado	3,723	3,636	3,810	687	649	725	15.6%	**	14.8%	16.4%
Alaska	534	521	547	100	93	107	15.7%	**	14.9%	16.5%
Wyoming	411	399	423	78	73	83	15.9%	**	14.9%	16.9%
Idaho	1,105	1,074	1,136	210	197	223	16.0%	**	15.0%	17.0%
Arkansas	2,229	2,165	2,293	428	400	456	16.1%	**	15.1%	17.1%
Nevada	1,791	1,747	1,835	344	324	364	16.1%	**	15.3%	16.9%
Mississippi	2,341	2,270	2,412	459	428	490	16.4%	**	15.4%	17.4%
Georgia	6,912	6,729	7,095	1,376	1,294	1,458	16.6%	**	15.6%	17.6%
Florida	13,491	13,279	13,703	2,856	2,757	2,955	17.5%	**	17.0%	18.0%
Arizona	4,365	4,238	4,492	950	891	1,009	17.9%	**	16.9%	18.9%
Oklahoma	2,762	2,686	2,838	620	584	656	18.3%	**	17.3%	19.3%
Louisiana	3,544	3,440	3,648	845	794	896	19.3%	**	18.3%	20.3%
California	27,770	27,420	28,120	6,718	6,539	6,897	19.5%	**	19.0%	20.0%
New Mexico	1,431	1,383	1,479	373	348	398	20.7%	**	19.5%	21.9%
Texas	16,105	15,843	16,367	4,960	4,812	5,108	23.5%	**	22.8%	24.2%
U.S.	**240,875**	**n/a**	**n/a**	**41,207**	**40,881**	**41,533**	**14.6%**		**14.4%**	**14.8%**

Source: Bureau of the Census, based on the March 2002 Current Population Survey; ranges computed by the Congressional Research Service.

Notes: * indicates percent uninsured is statistically lower than the national rate; ** indicates percent uninsured is statistically higher than the national rate. Range represents low and high estimates given a 90% confidence interval. n/a indicates not applicable.

Table 2. Number of People Covered and Not Covered by Health Insurance, and Percent Not Covered, By State, 2001

Alphabetical by State (numbers in thousands)

	Number covered			Number not covered			Percent not covered			
	Point	Range		Point	Range		Point		Range	
	estimate	Low	High	estimate	Low	High	estimate		Low	High
Alabama	3,815	3,715	3,915	573	534	612	13.1%	*	12.3%	13.9%
Alaska	534	521	547	100	93	107	15.7%	**	14.9%	16.5%
Arizona	4,365	4,238	4,492	950	891	1,009	17.9%	**	16.9%	18.9%
Arkansas	2,229	2,165	2,293	428	400	456	16.1%	**	15.1%	17.1%
California	27,770	27,420	28,120	6,718	6,539	6,897	19.5%	**	19.0%	20.0%
Colorado	3,723	3,636	3,810	687	649	725	15.6%	**	14.8%	16.4%
Connecticut	3,047	2,976	3,118	346	323	369	10.2%	*	9.5%	10.9%
Delaware	719	699	739	73	66	80	9.2%	*	8.5%	9.9%
D.C.	484	469	499	70	65	75	12.7%	*	11.7%	13.7%
Florida	13,491	13,279	13,703	2,856	2,757	2,955	17.5%	**	17.0%	18.0%
Georgia	6,912	6,729	7,095	1,376	1,294	1,458	16.6%	**	15.6%	17.6%
Hawaii	1,096	1,068	1,124	117	107	127	9.6%	*	8.9%	10.3%
Idaho	1,105	1,074	1,136	210	197	223	16.0%	**	15.0%	17.0%
Illinois	10,655	10,471	10,839	1,676	1,602	1,750	13.6%	*	13.1%	14.1%
Indiana	5,322	5,204	5,440	714	670	758	11.8%	*	11.1%	12.5%
Iowa	2,645	2,581	2,709	216	198	234	7.5%	*	6.8%	8.2%
Kansas	2,341	2,283	2,399	301	280	322	11.4%	*	10.6%	12.2%
Kentucky	3,505	3,413	3,597	492	457	527	12.3%	*	11.5%	13.1%
Louisiana	3,544	3,440	3,648	845	794	896	19.3%	**	18.3%	20.3%
Maine	1,147	1,121	1,173	132	124	140	10.3%	*	9.6%	11.0%
Maryland	4,673	4,561	4,785	653	610	696	12.3%	*	11.5%	13.1%
Massachusetts	5,802	5,677	5,927	520	482	558	8.2%	*	7.7%	8.7%
Michigan	8,864	8,703	9,025	1,028	972	1,084	10.4%	*	9.9%	10.9%
Minnesota	4,530	4,426	4,634	392	361	423	8.0%	*	7.3%	8.7%
Mississippi	2,341	2,270	2,412	459	428	490	16.4%	**	15.4%	17.4%
Missouri	4,960	4,842	5,078	565	524	606	10.2%	*	9.5%	10.9%
Montana	771	748	794	121	111	131	13.6%		12.6%	14.6%
Nebraska	1,523	1,484	1,562	160	147	173	9.5%	*	8.8%	10.2%
Nevada	1,791	1,747	1,835	344	324	364	16.1%	**	15.3%	16.9%
New Hampshire	1,139	1,113	1,165	119	111	127	9.4%	*	8.7%	10.1%
New Jersey	7,361	7,221	7,501	1,109	1,055	1,163	13.1%	*	12.4%	13.8%
New Mexico	1,431	1,383	1,479	373	348	398	20.7%	**	19.5%	21.9%
New York	15,911	15,696	16,126	2,918	2,822	3,010	15.5%	**	15.0%	16.0%
North Carolina	6,932	6,782	7,082	1,167	1,104	1,230	14.4%		13.7%	15.1%
North Dakota	561	546	576	60	55	65	9.6%	*	8.9%	10.3%
Ohio	9,943	9,767	10,119	1,248	1,184	1,312	11.2%	*	10.7%	11.7%
Oklahoma	2,762	2,686	2,838	620	584	656	18.3%	**	17.3%	19.3%
Oregon	3,018	2,939	3,097	443	413	473	12.8%	*	12.0%	13.6%
Pennsylvania	10,983	10,805	11,161	1,119	1,061	1,177	9.2%	*	8.7%	9.7%
Rhode Island	963	942	984	80	73	87	7.7%	*	7.2%	8.2%
South Carolina	3,517	3,427	3,607	493	458	528	12.3%	*	11.5%	13.1%
South Dakota	670	654	686	69	64	74	9.3%	*	8.6%	10.0%
Tennessee	5,042	4,904	5,180	640	591	689	11.3%	*	10.5%	12.1%
Texas	16,105	15,843	16,367	4,960	4,812	5,108	23.5%	**	22.8%	24.2%
Utah	1,927	1,876	1,978	335	314	356	14.8%		14.0%	15.6%
Vermont	549	536	562	58	53	63	9.6%	*	8.9%	10.3%
Virginia	6,331	6,176	6,486	774	720	828	10.9%	*	10.2%	11.6%
Washington	5,151	5,018	5,284	780	727	833	13.1%	*	12.3%	13.9%
West Virginia	1,539	1,501	1,577	234	219	249	13.2%	*	12.4%	14.0%
Wisconsin	4,927	4,817	5,037	409	378	440	7.7%	*	7.0%	8.4%
Wyoming	411	399	423	78	73	83	15.9%	**	14.9%	16.9%
U.S.	**240,875**	**n/a**	**n/a**	**41,207**	**40,881**	**41,533**	**14.6%**		**14.4%**	**14.8%**

Source: Bureau of the Census, based on the March 2002 Current Population Survey; ranges computed by the Congressional Research Service.

Note: * indicates percent uninsured is statistically lower than the national rate; ** indicates percent uninsured is statistically higher than the national rate. Range represents low and high estimates given a 90% confidence interval. n/a indicates not applicable.

Figure 1. Percent Uninsured by State, 2001

US average is 14.6%

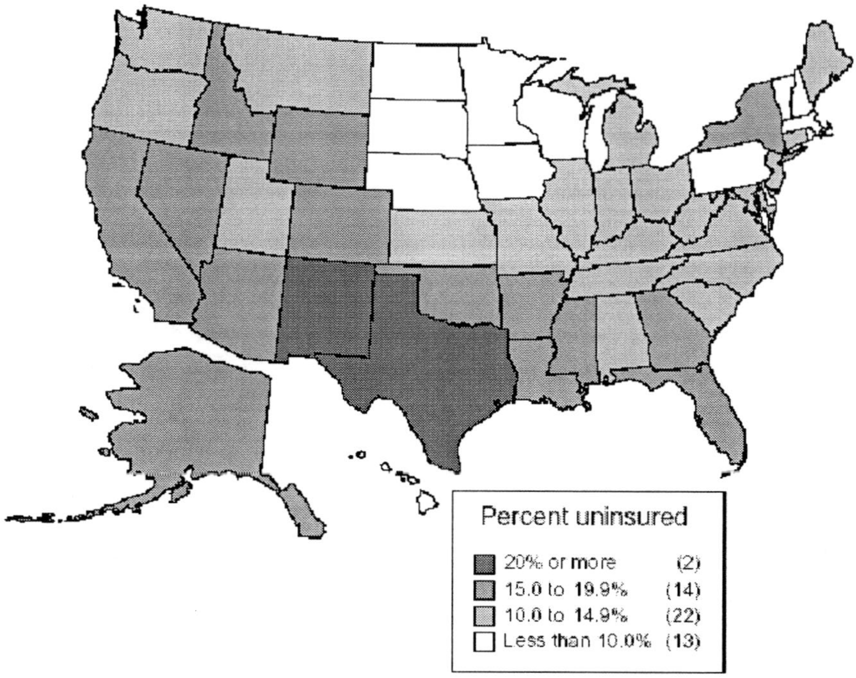

Figure 2. Percent Uninsured by State, 2001

Accounting for Statistical Variation in Estimates

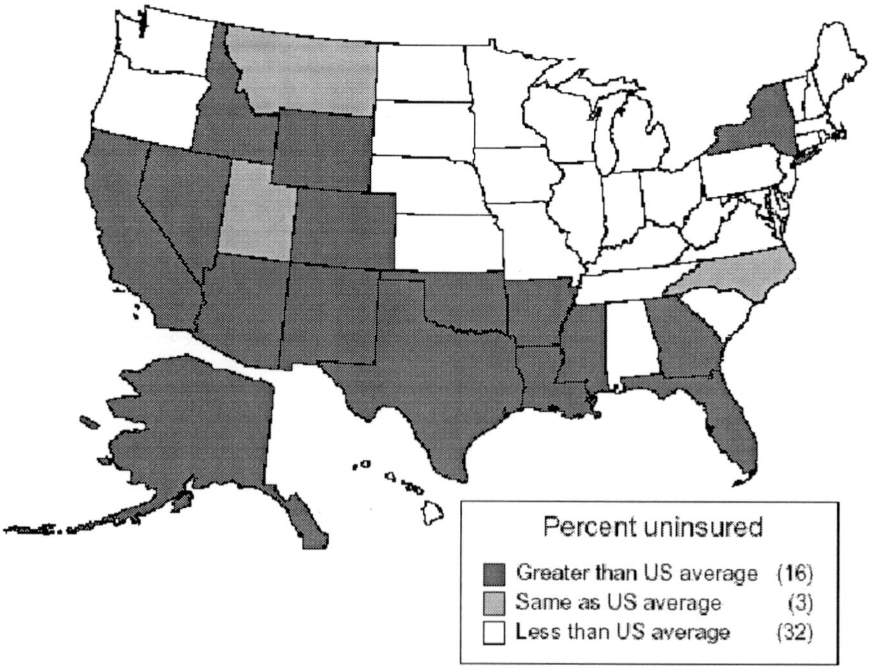

INDEX

A

B

C

D

E

F

G

H

I

J

K

L

M

N

O

P

W

Y